Between State and Market: Housing in the Post-Industrial Era

Editors:
Bengt Turner, Jim Kemeny, Lennart J Lundqvist
The National Swedish Institute for Building Research

Almqvist & Wiksell International

©1987 The individual authors
ISBN 91-22-00896-9
Printed in Sweden by Graphic Systems AB, Göteborg 1987

Preface

The International Research Conference on Housing Policy was held in Gävle, Sweden, in June 1986. Hosted by the National Swedish Institute for Building Research, the conference was convened to assess the present state of the art of housing research in the social sciences. In the call for papers, it was noted that over the postwar period the state has become increasingly involved in intervening in the housing market. A wide range of policy measures have been developed and used. Now, after 40 years of policy development and elaboration, a major political reassessment of the role of government in housing is under way in many countries.

The conference provided an opportunity for stocktaking and reassessment after a long period of proliferation of, and experimentation with, different approaches to state intervention in the housing market. The conference was designed to bring together social science scholars from a wide range of industrialized countries to assess the housing research and to consider its further development in relation to housing policy and its changes.

The conference was framed by a number of thematic papers, intended to provide a framework for working groups at the conference to examine different aspects of housing theory and housing policy.

As these thematic papers turned out to have significance far beyond the working groups and the conference, they are now revised and published in this volume. In all they give an impression of both the present situation in developed countries, and the state of the art in housing research. It is our hope that published in this form, they will provide inspiration for many researchers and projects in this important field.

Bengt Turner, Jim Kemeny, Lennart J. Lundqvist

Gävle, February 1987

Contents

Housing and Economic Research

Introduction

Bengt Turner, The National Swedish Institute
for Building Research

There has been a rapid development of economic research over the last
decades. I would like to point out three features in this development, all
of which are reflected in the economic/geographical contributions in this
volume.

First of all, there has been considerable progress made in the development of refined micro-economic models. These have typically been multi-
sectoral and multi-attributive models, sometimes of a high statistical
complexity. The aim is to improve understanding of the housing market
and to build more "relevant" or "accurate" models.

Secondly, there have been a considerable number of attempts to link
microeconomic models to the macro context. This reflects a growing
awareness among economists of the political, social and institutional
framework within which the micro-economic models work.

Thirdly, there has been a growing concern among economists about
the distributional aspects of housing consumption. The foci of interest
are both empirical observations of the distribution of housing consumption, and the development of models to guide public authorities intervening in the market.

However, there remains a gap between housing market researchers and
policy-makers. An overwhelming proportion of economic research will
never be implemented – directly or indirectly – in actual policy-making. The
contributions in this section shows however that a change is coming closer.

William A.V. Clark is concerned with a number of general problems within
economic and geographical research. He is first of all addressing the
dichotomy between micro oriented research and "the broader brush discussions of housing policy at the macro level". Discussing micro economic
modelling he argues; "What I think has happened is that we have been
seduced by the elegance of our models derived from good theroretical ideas.

The models have in fact outstripped both the data and our ability to create formal tests. Moreover, there has been insufficient attention to real world applications."

He argues that social and political housing problems should be solved with the help of micro models, which are both relevant and transparent. This does however not mean that he argues for less theory. The development of a theory-based social science has been critical to the improvement of his modeling strategies. In his contribution he demonstrates examples of "robust" models, which fit into this vision. He presents a statistical analysis of propensity to move for different socio/economic groups on a housing market that is split up into different submarkets. The statistical procedure can best be characterised as a simplified logit analysis — as opposed to the nested multinominal logit models which now are widely used by model makers.

Duncan Maclennan observes that the ". . .issue of housing market structure can be reasonably dichotomised into 'theoretical' views, where the market is viewed as operating as a unitary and equilibrating device, and 'policy' approaches, where crude administrative boundaries are drawn around particular areas or sectors."

This leads Maclennan to stress the importance of developing a more rigorous economic theory for the housing market. One ingredient of this development is to recognize the importance of submarkets on the housing market. He goes even further and argues that the recognition of submarkets is a prerequisite for applying a view of permanent disequilibrium as a "central feature of the housing market." This means that price differences are important and likely to persist.

The theoretical starting point for a disequilibrium definition of submarkets and thus observations of price differences is in Maclennan's context threefold; a hedonic/lancastrian approach, a search theory and market situation of imperfect "monopolistic" competition.

In an empirical section Maclennan uses standard hedonic technique to define submarkets. He then applies a time series approach to prove that price differences between submarkets tend to persist.

John Quigley also stresses the importance of recognizing the "multi-attributive" character of the housing market. Unlike Maclennan he is not using a hedonic approach to define submarkets and clarifying the function of the housing market. Quigley's main focus is on the welfare economies of housing demand. He notes that some attributes of housing "are essentially private goods, publicly supplied (e.g., refuse collection). Some are public goods subject to congestion (e.g., local parks), and some are pure public goods (e.g., noise levels, and the aesthetics of neighbourhoods)."

The main point is that these collective attributes in housing are ". . .supplied consciously by the public sector or arise as the result of regulation or regulatory oversight (or the neglect of regulatory oversight) by public authorities."

Quigley's point is that the optimal amount of collective attributes may be calculated on market price information, through a hedonic approach. The result will be separate hedonic price estimates of these public attributes, which could be used by public authorities in a benefit/cost-analysis, aimed at increasing or decreasing the amount of these collective goods.

After an extensive overview of relevant empirical studies Quigley finally discusses the implications for policy makers of his approach. He concludes that policy makers are seldom willing to base policy decisions on (elaborate) hedonic estimations. But Quigley has a very strong point when he argues that the technique gives an opportunity to measure the market valuation of intangible (collective) benefits. And as these goods, according to empirical demand analysis, have an income elastic demand, then public authorities may well increase the amount, and finance it by progressive taxes. And it would be a pareto improvement.

The contributions so far have all dealt with different aspects of housing markets, how to increase our understanding of housing markets, and how to make housing market theory more "relevant" to housing policy. *Raymond Struyk's* contribution takes a quite different view. His main interest is the position and behavior of a specific subgroup on the housing market; the elderly. This represents an example of a new tradition among economists: to study a social/demographic submarket — as opposed to other research lines: studies of general housing market behaviour, specific physical submarkets, effects of specific economic measures etc.

Struyk's contribution consists of three sections. In the first section he presents an empirical investigation of the housing situation for the elderly: physical deficiency, overcrowding, underutilization, rent/income-ratio, dwelling specific needs compared to dwelling equipment etc. In the second section he presents an analysis of the behavior of the elderly: mobility rates and in-place adjustments as a consequence of occurred changes in economic conditions, asset wealth etc. In a final section he discusses the consequences for policy-makers who want to improve the situation for the elderly in the most efficient manner possible.

What is interesting about Struyk's contribution is that it gives a new insight into the distributional pattern of the housing market. It also presents an analysis of the behavioral conditions and policy implications for a specific subgroup. This is an analysis that may well be utilized for studies of other subgroups on the housing market. It also stands as a symbol for growing social and political awareness among economists and geographers in the field of housing research.

Theory and Practice in Housing Market Research

11-25

U.S.
9320

William A. V. Clark, Department of
Geography, UCLA, USA

In the past half dozen years, there has been an increasing differentiation in in the research reported in housing journals and at housing conferences - - a differentiation between detailed theoretical and empirical micro level discussions on the one hand and macro commentary on housing policy on the other. A casual perusal of the literature suggests that this difference in approach is paralleled by differences in the methods of analysis. At the micro level, there is an emphasis on detailed empirical modeling, but at the macro level the discussions have many fewer testable propositions. An examination of this dichotomy is at the heart of the remarks I want to make in this paper - - remarks which are designed to explore its basis and develop the ramifications for modeling and policy analysis in housing market contexts.

To begin, I will address some issues of the context of research in housing, notably the changing philosophies of research and the varying disciplinary approaches to analyzing housing and housing markets. Second, I will develop a specific discussion of the micro-macro distinction, and embedded within it, the issues of choice versus constraint. Third, and not unrelated, is how the issue of policy outcomes and decision making by policy makers can be strengthened with research on what I will call robust models. The conclusion will include observations on housing and housing policy from a demographic perspective.

THE CONTEXT OF RESEARCH IN HOUSING

If we have learned one thing from the burgeoning literature on housing choice and the analysis of housing markets, it is that there is no single approach to understanding the complex behavior of individuals on the one hand, and the aggregation of these decisions as housing market behavior on the other. Even so, the myriad approaches can be reduced to those that have taken a micro perspective and focused on individual choice behavior of households, with respect to search behavior, search patterns, and relocation behavior (see Maclennan and Woods 1982, for example), and those studies that have focused on the provision of housing and the institutional actors in the production, distribution, and consumption of housing at the macro scale (see, for example, Dickens, et al. 1985). But this distinction reflects the changing philosophies of research in the social sciences and a brief comment is appropriate.

MICRO-MACRO ALTERNATIVES

The micro-macro, or the individual action-social constraint, debate reflects changing philosophies of research. In geography, sociology, and economics, the concern with economic man, with rational decision making, focused attention on individual actions and on micro behavioral (choice) issues. The behaviorists borrowed from psychology and the borrowed concepts formed a basis for a broadened social science of behavior which was concerned with the way in which choices are made and the way in which knowledge influences those choices, in sum, the decision process in its spatial context. The failure of these approaches to reflect the complex events of an increasingly structured society led to a vigorous debate about the role of individual action and social structure. Whether these debates are imbedded in discussions of structuration or the social reproduction of classes and labor, they have forced the focus away from individual action towards a wider concern with institutional forces and their role in influencing, even controlling, societal processes (Duncan, 1985, Sayer, 1985). As housing is one of the critical components of societal organization, it is necessarily involved in these debates.

The micro-macro split is nowhere more evident than in studies of mobility and migration. To a large extent, outcomes in the housing market are the results or effects of individual decisions on where to search for housing and on a household's ultimate housing choices - - their mobility behavior. Thus, migration and mobility are inextricably linked with housing market decisions by individual households. The decision to choose a house and to relocate is made at the level of the individual or household, but the consequences are felt at the level of the society. The problem arises because the individual behaviors may produce unpredicted societal consequences, sometimes resulting in attempts by government to influence the population distribution in order to attain certain goals. It is this conflict between individual action and social intervention that is at the heart of many of the interesting problems which have arisen in trying to understand choice in the housing markets, housing market behavior, and societal impacts. Further, the simple discussion of individual choice and social constraint does not necessarily reflect the fact that the decisions are themselves embedded in larger societal processes. The larger societal processes, especially the demographic ones, may, in the last analysis, even overwhelm the best intended interventions.

But, to turn specifically to the micro-macro debate, we might begin by noting that a commonly agreed upon approach to studying housing market choice is one that involves micro-level theory and micro-level empirical investigation. Housing choice at the individual level is often viewed as a result of a rational decision making process, in which the individual evaluates perceived costs and benefits of one location versus another, and the costs of moving versus not moving. The decision to choose a particular house and to move is made when the benefits are deemed to outweigh the costs. The shorthand that is used in these discussions is that of housing disequilibrium. In such models, households choose new housing in response to a difference between their current housing and their optimal housing (Quigley and Hanushek 1978; Clark, 1981). Because the decision to choose a particular house is concerned with an individual's perceptions of origin and destination characteristics, it is necessarily a micro level or an individual approach.

But at the same time, housing choice can be seen as the outcome of changes in social systems, and those with a macro perspective argue for a focus on institutions and their actors. Thus, housing choice in and of itself is not of specific interest; rather the focus is on the social systems that generate patterns of housing choice in response to their own needs. Population exchange in those situations exists as an outcome of changes in social systems rather than vice versa. The macro perspective is summed up by Boddy and Gray:

> access to housing resources of households of differing financial status and other characteristics and their mobility within the housing system is structured by a set of financial and government institutions situated within the broader economic, political, and ideological structures of society (Boddy and Gray, 1979, p. 51).

Macro level approaches have sometimes been couched in terms of aggregating subgroups that are supposedly homogeneous with respect to demographic, social, and economic characteristics, and then examining these contrasting subgroups with respect to their differential propensities to choose houses, to move, and to form neighborhoods. However, some theorists, faced with perhaps the possibility of an infinite heterogeneity in the factors that go into the behavioral decisions, have questioned whether we can use individual level theory at all for the explanation of housing choice dynamics at the macro level.

The issue of the relationship between micro and macro analyses turns up repeatedly, both in "pure" scientific work and in empirical applications. The essence of the question that is being raised here is how can we expand micro models to understand macro structures, structures that are essential when one wants to use the results of an individualistic choice analysis to predict development patterns for the entire society, or to study multilevel spatial systems. While those who have used the micro level approach have argued for a close connection between micro and macro analyses, they provide little in the way of a methodology of how such a connection can be established. One suggestion is that the sum of the individuals moving or choosing houses has an equilibrating or disequilibrating effect on origins and destinations. In fact, there are two contrasting views. Migration and housing choice as an equilibrating mechanism, based on individual actions, versus a conceptualization of housing choice and migration as an adaptive response to organizational change.

More recently, it has been argued that these differences in macro and micro approaches to the understanding of behavior in the housing market can be subsumed within a broader Marxist perspective which suggests that the provision of housing, its production, distribution, and consumption, is merely one part of everyday life and its social organization, and that the understanding of housing behavior is outside the focus of micro-macro perspectives. Such an approach argues for:

> the rejection of the neo-Classical paradigm for its economism and generally grossly inadequate representations of the relations between individual, economy, and society. . . (Dickens, et al., 1985 p. 197).

While the attempt to step out of the micro-macro debate and to utilize a Marxist perspective has forced individuals doing research in the housing area to at least consider a broader social context for housing, *how* the political, the economic, the social, and the spatial are interlinked is unspecified. Moreover, the idea that a Marxist perspective provides the only alternative to understanding these interrelationships must be viewed with caution.

Within the micro-macro debate, an issue which is critical for geographers is that neither the macro nor the micro approaches have paid sufficient attention to the spatial and demographic perspective - - especially the spatial context within which the housing system operates, and which is part of the system itself. The focus has often been on the economic relationships or the social systems and not on the spatial context. Yet without specific attention to the locations within which the micro-macro debate is situated, it is more than possible, indeed probable, that the nature of the relationships will remain opaque. In fact, housing market choices and decisions are made in a complex spatial-demographic web that may well provide us with the links between micro and macro models. I will explore this theme later in the paper.

MICRO AND MACRO MODELS AND PLANNING OUTCOMES

Although the research literature is clear about the distinctions between the micro and macro approaches, there has been less emphasis on the application of either micro or macro models. The question is how might either micro-macro research foci be best developed so that they have a more relevant and applied outcome than has been true in the past. This political, or policy impact of modeling, is perhaps the most frequently discussed but least practiced of all of the issues related to housing market research. In making these comments on modeling relevance, I draw heavily on a a similar position advocated recently by Openshaw (1986), who argues that our research is insufficiently concerned with real world problems (p. 143). But this is not an advocacy for abandoning models, rather, as Openshaw notes,

> planners, administrators, and entrepreneurs belonging to all manner of public and private concerns, could probably find many uses, for the models already in existence, if only they knew what was an offer. The problem is that academic modelers. . . do not provide a good shop window (Openshaw 1986, p. 143).

Users (planners and administrators) require models that can be made operational, that can be empirically tested, and that are relevant. Of course, such comments are true of all standard model building recipes but. . .

> the problem is that few modelers complete the model building process from purpose through to evaluation. Far too many never get past the theoretical stage, partly one suspects because it involves less effort and it offers far more publication possibilites in journals. . . The demand for ever more complex and comprehensive theories of regional phenomena has already passed the stage where testing is possible. In many areas it is no longer possible to obtain data to operationalize models based on the latest theories. This does not stop numerical experimentation, but there are limits to the usefulness of models that have no prospect whatsoever of ever being applied to real world situations" (Openshaw 1986, p. 144–45).

There is a different but not unrelated situation where we already have both data and theory, but in which we have failed to adequately present our explanations. In the often quoted Supreme Court case, *Milliken v. Bradley* (U.S. Supreme Court 1974), a supreme court justice suggested that the forces which account for the concentration of blacks in certain schools were unknown and perhaps unknowable. Clearly, the social scientists charged with enlightening the court on housing patterns did not convince the judge. Yet, we have a very good idea of the forces which have led to social separation in cities, even if we disagree on their relative weighting (see Clark 1982 for a more extended discussion). To characterize this situation as "unknowable" suggests that further clarifications are not possible.

This situation, the established but unaccepted and unused (or underused) models emphasize the need for more sensitive modeling strategies. There is a distinct need for pragmatic models that use existing data to make the best possible predictions and forecasts for the behavior of urban and regional systems, something that is especially true in housing market research and analysis (Openshaw, p. 145). In trying to meet this goal, we should try and keep an "appropriate balance between the development of theory for the sake of developing theory and the development of theory that can usefully inform practical model applications" (Openshaw, p. 145).

This is not an argument for less theory. The development of a theory-based social science has been critical to the improvement of our modeling strategies. What I think has happened is that we have been seduced by the elegance of our models derived from good theoretical ideas. The models have in fact outstripped both the data and our ability to create formal tests. Moreover, there has been insufficient attention to real world applications. An excellent example is the increasing interest in nested multinomial logit models of housing choices. The data requirements of such models and the difficulty of testing are clear (Lerman 1976; Wrigley 1985). Although it is possible to provide creative conceptualizations with the nested logit structures (Clark and Onaka 1985), alternative models of choice suggest that useful and interpretable results of choice processes can be based on simple notions of house type and simple triggers, such as the birth of a child (Clark, Deurloo, and Dieleman, 1984). This is an argument not to abandon our theoretical approaches, but rather that we parallel them with alternative model structures — one of which informs and extends the theory, the other, applicable in decision-making contexts. Let me illustrate at least two such approaches at the micro level and discuss a strategy at the macro level, as ways in which we might provide agendas for applied modeling in housing market contexts.

ROBUST MODELS OF MICRO PROCESSES

It is to repeat the obvious to note that there has been an explosion of interest in logit and log-linear models in the last half-dozen years. This is not surprising, because many situations and issues in the social sciences deal with categorical data, and previously, much of the analysis was in the form of simple contingency table investigations, with little assessment of either the main effects or the interaction effects of the variables. Moreover, the linking of discrete choice theory to log-linear and logit models provided a theoretical basis for choices between alternatives, and so gave greater impetus to the concern with models of categorical data. The problem with the logit model is illustrated by numerous reports in which the levels of fit are low and in which the parameters are difficult to interpret. Even in the situation where they are interpretable, analyses of main effects only limits the contribution of such models. In addition, if one has a large data set, many explanatory factors will be significant. In such circumstances, it makes more sense to focus attention on the strength of the relationships and on the simple structure of the relationships, rather than on significance testing itself.

A solution is contained in a large set of techniques which are designed to examine categorical relationships in a manner analogous to logit and loglinear approaches, but in a simpler form. Recent research in collaboration with two Dutch colleagues has demonstrated the value of these techniques which are designed to provide a more parsimonious selection of variables for the models, and simplify the categorical structure of such variables (Clark, Deurloo, and Dieleman 1986; Deurloo, Dieleman and Clark 1987). I will illustrate the proportional reduction in uncertainty, (PRU), which is well suited for simplifying variables, and the analysis of tables technique (ANOTA), which is designed as a simplified logit analysis where there is a dependent variable with multiple categories.

PRU Models

The PRU technique is a stepwise pre-processing procedure in which at each step, the most effective variable is added to the tabulation of the binary dependent variable, and the previous selected explanatory factors. This newly added dimension is examined for its effect on the association between the dependent variable and the set of independent variables in the tabulation as the categories in the new variable are aggregated. The technique is stepwise in terms of the selection of variables, and simplifying in terms of the number of categories for each variable. The explanatory power of the independent variables at each step as well as the loss from uniting some categories, is measured by the PRU. The PRU methodology is based on the entropy statistic as a measure of the variation in a nominal discrete variable. More extensive discussion of the technique is contained in Clark, Deurloo, and Dieleman (1986).

A straightforward illustration of the simplification process is given in Table 1, where we note that the independent variable with the highest

Table 1. Variable Choice and Category Combination for the Decision to Move by Owner Occupiers.

Step 1A. Independent Variables	Number Categories	Dependent Variable Move/No Move	
		PRU	G
Age	7	0.023058	334.52
Size of Household	6	0.000761	11.04
Income	9	0.003438	49.88
Number of Rooms	8	0.004614	66.94
Price of House	9	0.004484	65.05
Type of House	2	0.004046	58.70
Region	4	0.001146	16.62
Rooms/Size of Household	6	0.002384	34.59
Price of House/Income	6	0.009820	142.48
Step IB.			
Age Category Simplification			
1, 2, 3, 4, 5, 6 + 7		0.023003	333.74
1, 2, 3. 4 + 5, 6 + 7		0.022932	332.70
1 + 2, 3, 4 + 5, 6 + 7		0.022794	330.69
1 + 2, 3, 4 + 5 + 6 + 7		0.022271	323.11
1 + 2 + 3, 4 + 5 + 6 + 7		0.018158	263.44

Source: Clark, Deurloo, and Dieleman (1986).

PRU is selected and the loss in the PRU for several combinations of categories is evaluated. The combination with the lowest decrease in the PRU is selected and this process is continued for additional variables and categorizations. Variables are selected and combined in the same manner as the initial variable, and finally added to the model. Thus, it is a method for variable selection-category combination. The selected subsets of variables may not be the only ones of interst, but they are a representative set of reasonable classifications and they provide a substantial amount of explanation. In addition, they minimize empty cells or cells with few observations. While it is only one of a number of other possibilities including those by Higgins and Koch (1977) and Conant (1980), there are advantages to the PRU technique. In any event, the important thing here is to emphasize the contribution of such approaches to simplifying procedures for developing robust models in the housing context.

ANOTA Models

ANOTA, or the analysis of tables (Keller and Verbeek 1984) is a "preprocessing" and simpler alternative to logit and probit models for the multivariate analysis of qualitative data. There are a variety of debates about the difficulty of interpreting logit and probit transformations, but more to the point, ANOTA is easy to apply (it may be run on personal computers). There is of course a price for the ease of computation - - the proportions are not guaranteed to be within the 0−1 range. Even accepting that problem, the overall value of such approaches seems to outweigh the limitations.

The rows of coefficients in the ANOTA table can be interpreted in a similar way to the regression coefficients from the multiple regression equation. The coefficients measure the effect of the categories of the explanatory variables on the categories of the dependent variable. The coefficients are corrected for the interdependencies between the predictor variables as in regression analysis. In Table 2, the effect of income on choice is the effect of income holding region and age constant (Deurloo, Clark and Dieleman 1987). In fact, we can read Table 2 in one of two ways. If we read it in terms of rows, a row gives the coefficients which give the contribution of that variable to the explanation of the dependent variable. The

Table 2. Coefficients for Choices from Anota Analysis of Private Renters (significant parameters underlined).

Choice category	average	coefficients for income					coefficients for variable region			coefficients for variable age		
		1	2	3	4	9	1	2+3	4	1	2	3
multifamily private rent	15.1	8.1	3.4	-3.0	-2.2	-1.4	-7.0	-8.1	11.0	1.3	-1.3	-1.3
multifamily public rent	20.9	13.0	12.9	-3.4	-9.5	-.3.4	-9.7	-4.8	8.5	-2.0	-4.0	6.1
single family rent <f. 350	10.0	11.9	5.0	-2.0	-6.9	-1.3	10.2	2.0	-5.9	-.6	-1.5	2.0
single family rent ≥f. 350	19.4	-8.7	.3	6.4	-4.8	1.8	0	5.2	-5.4	-2.6	-3.2	6.4
owner price <f. 150,000	21.0	-12.9	-11.4	3.7	12.3	.9	6.9	3.2	5.9	6.0	3.1	-11.8
owner price ≥f. 150,000	13.6	-11.4	-10.2	-1.7	11.2	3.5	-1.0	2.4	-2.3	-2.2	6.9	-1.5

Source: Deurloo, Dieleman, and Clark (1986).
Categories income (1 low. . . 4 high, 9 unknown), region (4 Randstad 1 rural 2 +3 else) age (1 <35 yrs 2 35-44 yrs 3 45 yrs >).

columns, on the other hand, are the standardized distribution expressed as deviations from the average. To take a specific example, the probability of private renter households with income categories over 42,000 Dutch florins, who were between 35−44 years of age, and who do not live in the Randstad, and who are choosing category 6, expensive owner occupied dwellings, is 13.6 (the average), plus 11.2 the income effect, plus 2.4 the region effect, plus 6.9 the age effect, for a total of 34 percent (this discussion is derived from Deurloo, Dieleman, and Clark 1987). Thus, we can characterize a household in a private rental unit as being estimated to have a one-third chance of making an upgrading move to large, expensive, ownership housing. It follows that the chances of making a particular choice, given the categories of the independent variables is a relatively straightforward interpretation of the table.

It is also possible to elaborate these tables to measure the fit of the ANOTA model, and to yield an answer to the overall influence of a predictor variable on a particular choice. Detailed information and applications are provided in Deurloo, Dieleman, and Clark (1987). It is sufficient here just to note that the PRU value can be calculated for the ANOTA table and can be interpreted as the proportional explanation of the variation in the dependent variable.

MACRO APPROACHES AND ROBUST MODELS

It is at the macro level that it is somewhat harder to illustrate the value of building robust models. But, a mobility application, while somewhat peripheral to major housing market concerns, is still illustrative of the issues that we need to face if we are to provide robust models.

An oft reiterated observation about the structure of modern Western society is the level of separation between minority and majority populations in large urban areas. It is clear that the separation is a reflection of larger societal processes, including the role of economics, choice, the inertia in the urban structure, and of the forces of discrimination.

Given the structural separation and its social implications, it was not surprising that eventually there would be an attempt to redress this situation. The 1954 *Brown v. Board of Education* and the later *Swann* (1971), and *Keyes* (1974) cases, were designed to desegregate school systems such that neighborhood structures would no longer generate segregated school systems. Now, the position that schools must actively pursue desegregation by busing children from one school to another to establish integrated schools has depended on the argument that racially identifiable schools contribute to the maintenance of segregated neighborhoods. Thus, housing patterns and housing choices are seen as inextricably linked to social processes. Attempts to understand and model this interconnection have been discursive rather than analytic, but it is just such a situation which could be addressed with macro modeling, specifically, simulation techniques.

Interventions in school systems have occurred without an understanding of individual preferences and political choices. Yet had the results of simple stress models been aggregated (Phipps and Holden 1985, Phipps and Clark 1987), they would have yielded better predictions of the likely outcomes of such intervention. The intervention in the Los Angeles urban system accelerated the movement of white households to the suburbs, the shift to private schools, and avoidance of central city schools. It has been observed quite often in the emotional debate over the nature of white enrollment loss and white flight that the outmigration of white households is not a new phenomenon, and the white suburbanization has been a significant part of readjustment in the metropolitan areas in the U.S., at least since the second World War. However, it is just this issue that is central in understanding the larger link of mobility, social processes, and the housing market. There is a complex set of forces that influence the decision making of individual households and these forces both influence the decision to move and the decision of where to move. Since mandatory or assigned busing is perceived as undesirable by a large segment of the population, it is not surprising that households choose not to relocate in areas in which these policies are implemented. This lack of understanding of the mobility process *in its spatial context* has thus exacerbated the division between black central cities and white suburbs. Thus, not only has there been a negative impact, in this case on the school structure, with significant white enrollment loss for the central city school systems, such actions have the aggregate effect of structuring minority central cities and white suburbs - - at least for large metropolitan areas. Clearly, there is an ongoing demographic process in which mobility, migration, and housing choices are embedded. The ways of linking demographic processes, urban structure, and individual behavior are amongst the most exciting and difficult problems in research on residential mobility, migration, and housing choice. This discussion of demographic impacts is a natural introduction to the last section of the paper.

HOUSING DEMOGRAPHICS AND HOUSING POLICY

There is increasing awareness of the fact that demographic trends, independent of simple income effects, have important impacts on housing markets (Struyk and Marshall, 1975; Sternlieb and Hughes, 1982). There have been significant social changes in household compositions, not the least of which are the baby boom and now the aging of the population. Because economists have been at the forefront of much of the housing research there has been much less interest in the demographic impacts on housing demand. The economic approach has usually involved introducing controls for demographic events rather than embedding them in the model structure. There has been a vigorous debate about the role of demographic events. On the one hand, for example, Sternlieb and Hughes (1982) argue that the availability of affordable homes may not merely reflect trends in household formation, but may also help to shape these trends. To them, social trends (the caboose of demographic changes) follow the engine of housing (Sternlieb and Hughes 1984, p. 22). On the other, considering the role of two-income earners and the impact of wives' earnings on home-ownership, Myers (1985) suggests that there is a much more complicated interaction between housing and demography. Myers make a convincing case that it is not simply a housing locomotive and a demographic caboose, or alternatively a demographic locomotive and a housing caboose, but rather a circular model, in which the caboose carries the fuel to make the locomotive run. In a circular series of never-ending linkages the locomotive and caboose chase each other, but with the difference that one cohort's demographic change fuels the housing locomitive that drives the next cohort's demographic change (Myers, 1982).

The point to be made here is to emphasize the context within which housing is set, and that, at least as much attention needs to be applied to the macro demographic processes as to housing markets. Indeed, in studies of the aging of the population (the reduction phase), and entrances into the housing market ("starters"), it is clear that the low turnover in the submarkets with households whose children who have already left can be expected to block the opportunities to upward filtering in the existing housing stock. As additions to the housing stock decrease because of the expected stabilization of the number of households, there will be a lower primary supply and lower mobility and fewer chances for households to achieve equilibrium in the housing market (Hooimeijer, Clark, and Dieleman, 1986). The implications both politically and socially have yet to be explored.

Because housing is so intimately connected, on the one hand, with the shelter of society, and on the other, with saving and equity (especially for the middle classes), it will continue to be both a political and a social issue. But, unlike some policy arenas where the argument is that the difficulty is in obtaining good useful numbers, that is not the problem in housing market research. Indeed, just the opposite is true. We have a great deal of data and we have a situation in which we have accumulated enough cases to make studying them worthwhile from a policy standpoint. Our problem, rather, is characterized by the application of increasingly powerful and sophisticated quantitative techniques. This power, however, is coming at a price. The price is that it is more and more difficult to comprehend the relationship between the data we begin with, and the results that flow from our statistical analysis (Sechrest, 1985). At one time, we had only simple t-test and analysis of variance. Now, we have gone from factor analysis to logit, probit, and discrete choice analyses. It is worthwhile discussing a return to statistics that are "transparent" in the sense that one can look at the original data and the outcome and have an intuitive feel for what we meant (Sechrest 1985). It is not clear, even that the robust models suggested here will do that, although I believe that they are a step in the right direction.

Finally, the constraint (macro) versus choice (micro) debate leads us to ask a different set of questions. Not who chooses which housing, but rather how does the larger social system mediate the adjustments of different groups to needs and opportunities? Or, how does the social system direct the housing choices that are occurring? To what extent does the social structure itself create the housing choice processes by its creating of differences in the needs for housing adjustment? This, of course, raises the central issue which I have skirted, but which is central to the social science agenda, that is, the problem of developing an understanding of individual behavior which is compatible with theories of social change. Clearly, it is a research agenda worth pursuing.

REFERENCES

Boddy, M.J. (1976) "The Structure of Mortgage Finance: Building Societies and the British Social Formation", *Transactions of the Institute for British Geographers* pp. 58–71.

Boddy, M.J., and F. Gray (1979) "Filtering Theory, Housing Policy, and the Legitimation of Inequality", *Policy in Politics* 7:39–54.

Clark, W.A.V. (1981) "On Modeling Search Behavior", pp. 102–131 in D.A. Griffith and R.D. MacKinnon, *Dynamic Spatial Models*. Alpen aan den Rijn: Sijthoff and Noordhoff.

Clark, W.A.V. (1982) "Judicial Intervention as Policy: Impacts on Population Distribution and Redistribution in Urban Areas of the U.S.", *Population Research and Policy Review* 1:79–100.

Clark, W.A.V., M.C. Deurloo, and F.M. Dieleman (1984) "Housing Consumption and Residential Mobility", *Annals of the Association of American Geographers* 74:29–43.

Clark, W.A.V., M.C, Deurloo, and F.M. Dieleman (1986) "Residential Mobility in Dutch Housing Markets", *Environment and Planning A* (forthcoming).

Clark, W.A.V., and J. Onaka (1985) "An Empirical Test of a Joint Model of Residential Mobility and Housing Choice", *Environment and Planning A* 17:915–930.

Cook, T.D. (1985) "Post-positivist Critical Multiplism", pp. 21–62 in R.L. Shotland and M.M. Mark (eds.), *Social Science and Social Policy*. Beverly Hills: Sage Publications.

Conant, R.C. (1980) "Structural Modelling Using a Simple Information Measure", *International Journal of Systems Science* 11:721–730.

Deurloo, M.C., F.M. Dieleman, and W.A.V, Clark (1987) "Tenure Choice in the Dutch Housing Market", *Environment and Planning A* (forthcoming).

Dickens, P., S. Duncan, M. Goodwin, and F. Gray (1985) *Housing, States, and Localities*. London: Methuen.

Dieleman, F.M. (1983) "Tenure and Housing Allocation Policy in the Tilburg Housing Market", *Tijdschrift voor Economische en Sociale Geografie* 24:162–174.

Duncan, J.S. (1985) "Individual Action and Political Power: A Structuration Perspective", pp. 174–189 in R.J. Johnston (ed.), *The Future of Geography*. London: Methuen.

Hanushek, E. and J. Quigley (1978) "Housing Disequilibrium and Residential Mobility", pp. 51–98 in W.A.V. Clark and E.G. Moore (eds.) *Popula-*

tion Mobility and Residential Change. Evanston, IL: Northwestern University Studies in Geography #25.

Higgins, J.E. and G.G. Koch (1977) "Variable Selection and Generalized Chisquare Analysis of Categorical Data Applied to a Large Cross Sectional Occupational Health Survey", *International Statistical Review* 45:51–62.

Keller, W.J. and A. Verbeek (1984) "ANOTA: Analysis of Tables", *Kwantitaieve Methoden* 1–16.

Lerman, S.R. (1976) "Location, Housing, Automobile Ownership, and Mode to Work: A Joint Choice Model", *Transportation Research Record* 610:6–11.

Maclennan, D. and G. Woods (1982) "Information Acquisition: Patterns and Strategies", pp. 134–159 in W.A.V. Clark (ed.) *Modelling Housing Market Search.* London: Croom Helm.

Myers, D. (1982) "A Cohort Based Indicator of Housing Progress", *Population Research and Policy Review* 1:109–136.

Myers, D. (1985) "Reliance upon Wives' Earnings for Home Ownership Attainment: Caught Between the Locomotive and the Caboose", *Journal of Planning, Education, and Research* 4:167–176.

Openshaw, S. (1986) "Editorial: Modeling Relevance", *Environment and Planning A* 18:143–147.

Phipps, A.G. and W.J. Holden (1985) "Intended Mobility Responses to Inner-City School Closure", *Environment and Planning A* 17:1169–1183.

Phipps, A.G. and W.A.V. Clark (1987) "Interactive Recovery and Validation of Households' Residential Utility Functions", forthcoming in R.G. Golledge and H. Timmermans (eds.), *Behavioral Modelling Approaches in Geography and Planning,* London: Croom Helm.

Sayer, A. (1985) "Realism and Geography", pp. 159–173 in R.J. Johnston (ed.), *The Future of Geography.* London: Methuen.

Serchrest, L. (1985) "Social Science and Social Policy: Will Our Numbers Ever Be Good Enough?", pp. 63–95 in R.L. Shotland and M.M. Mark (eds.), *Social Science and Social Policy.* Beverly Hills: Sage Publications.

Sternlieb, G., and J.W. Hughes (1984) "The Housing Locomotive and the Demographic Caboose", *American Demographics* 6:22–27.

Struyk, R.J., and S.A. Marshall (1975) "Income and Urban Home Ownership", *Review of Economics and Statistics* 57:19–25.

Willekens, F. (1985) "Migration and Development: A Micro Perspective". Working Papers of the Netherlands Interuniversity Demographic Institute #62.

Wrigley, N. (1985) *Categorical Data Analysis for Geographers and Environmental Scientists.* London: Longman.

Housing Choices and the Structure of Housing Markets

26-52

U.K. (Scotland)
9320

Duncan Maclennan, with Moira Munro and
Gavin Wood, Centre for Housing Research,
University of Glasgow, Scotland.

INTRODUCTION

This paper focuses upon the operational structure of large urban or metropolitan housing markets and the spatial structure of these systems is the
main concern. It is commonly recognised that economic forces acting
through the housing market have a particularly criticial influence upon the
development of urban structure. The nature of the urban housing market
could then be anticipated to have a key and carefully considered role in a
range of urban analyses. Theoretical models of spatial structure and "inner-
city" policy formulation, for instance, both contain explicit and implicit
assumptions about housing system structure. However, housing and urban
analysts have often been quite cavalier in their approaches to the modelling
of the housing market. For instance, approaches to the issue of housing
market structure can be reasonably dichotomised into "theoretical" views,
where the market is viewed as operating as a unitary and equilibrating
device, and "policy" approaches, where crude administrative boundaries
are drawn around particular areas or sectors. This paper maintains that a
more rigorous and disaggregated approach may be required to develop insights for urban theory and policy.

The proposition that the urban housing market can be viewed as being
constituted of a series of linked sub-markets is not a novel one. During the
last two decades there has been continuing discussion regarding the appropriate ways in which to describe and conceptualise urban housing market
structures in applied economic research. At one extreme the abstract,
theoretical view alluded to above is often carried over into more applied
studies (e.g. Muth, 1977). At the other, "commonsense" and "intuition"
are used as the rationale on which to identify disaggregated areas for
applied housing market research. More recently, and particularly in the
United States, neoclassical economic conceptions of submarkets and

associated econometric criteria for establishing their existence have produced a literature which is diverse in applied methodology and findings. Applied econometric studies have themselves been inconclusive (some are examined in more detail below) though the only systematic British study (Kirwan and Ball, 1977) rejected the hypothesis that submarkets existed (in a particular place and time).

This paper examines why the issue of the existence of submarkets is important and explores in some detail the notion of market and submarket in relation to housing. Then, using cross-section and time related data from the City of Glasgow a series of econometric tests are conducted to establish the extent to which variation in housing attribute prices systematically exists and persists. Finally, with reference to the conceptual framework explored in the paper, a number of hypothesis regarding the causes of submarkets are advanced.

The Importance of Submarkets

The existence of submarkets and market segments is important in housing market research for at least two reasons. First, when a general competitive market model is the framework used for research then the existence of subdivisions may raise some important problems (especially aggregation bias) in the estimation of market parameters and thus adaptations of technique may be required. Second, the existence of submarkets, if sustained for some time, can be construed as being a case for the abandonment of a simple competitive equilibrium model and its replacement by some alternative investigative logic with recurrent or permanent disequilibrium recognised as a central feature of the housing market. In such a view (see Maclennan, 1982) the issue of submarket existence and origins is central and not peripheral to the development of applied housing economics.

Parameters in the Competitive Model. The standard neoclassical equilibrium approach for housing research, based either upon Marshallian or Walrasian frameworks, puts considerable emphasis upon the estimation of summary criteria such as the price and income elasticities of demand for housing. This approach, with the estimation of hedonic prices an essential prior step, dominates urban economic housing research. A number of authors, for instance Straszheim (Straszheim, 1975) have noted that if price observations are drawn from different submarkets, with observed variations in price per unit of attribute, then an aggregative approach not only lowers overall levels of statistical "explanation" but may also generate biases in coefficients estimated. Thus, even within the framework of competitive market analysis there is a problem of applying the theoretical model.

In the conventional access-space model, of which the theoretical models of Straszheim and subsequent authors are extensions, the system is assumed to achieve long run equilibrium instrantaneously. Therein the market and the price system are merely logical devices to translate causes (changes in supply and demand conditions) into effects (changes in rents, densities, etc.). However, as noted by J.M. Clark (Clark, 1912) more than sixty years ago, differences in the price of a commodity are the mechanisms by which markets actually adjust or equilibrate. Thus in an essentially competitive framework for applied analysis, price differences will exist and econometric tests must recognise their existence. Of course, this also implies that the identification of submarkets requires more than cross section analysis — the persistence of differences in prices is critical. But as is elaborated below, in the neoclassical model there is an assumption that such price disparities are ephemeral and that market forces will *soon* remove them. The critical concern here is what time period constitutes "soon" in the real time of applied work. Any more sustained divergence will be assumed to be exceptional and attributed to some unusual or exogenous barrier to market adjustment. This approach is generally similar to the way in which labour economics had dealt with submarkets — they have long been deemed to exist (see Kerr, 1953), they are thought to have policy significance (see Cain, 1977) but are handled and identified in a generally pragmatic fashion (see Lowell, 1979).

A Different Perspective. A number of authors have raised the possibility that housing markets are not best conceived as being unitary, competitive and equilibrium systems (Whitehead and Odling-Smee, 1975; Maclennan, 1982). Indeed, the latter has argued that if submarkets exist and persist then an alternative meta-theory or investigative logic may be required for housing economics which asks questions and uses research methods additional to or different from the hedonic-elasticity approach outlined above.

But why should an aggregate unitary approach yield such different insights from a model based on submarkets? Why should this dichotomy be important? In a recent volume Coddington (Coddington, 1982) argued that broad dichotomies in economic analysis can often be reconciled by sensible "second-round" development of a basic model. In this instance, could the competitive-unitary approach offer useful general insights which can be modified to take account of local conditions and circumstances? At the same time, can locally oriented or sub-system models be re-integrated to allow some wider system overview? In many instances debates between rival analysts can be reduced and the real points of difference made clear.

There are, however, two reasons why the reconciliation of the theoretical dichotomy posed above is more difficult in the area of applied analysis under discussion. First, the initial stage or first step model is more difficult to revise in applied than theoretical study. That is, whilst theoretical speculation and experiment to link system-subsystem models may be useful, applied revisions are difficult. Second, and more important, the debate about submarkets is not merely a discussion about levels of aggregation. Roy Weintraub's discussion of the difficulties of linking microeconomics and macroeconomics is informative in this context (Weintraub, 1980). He argues that microeconomic (neoclassical) models are concerned with the operation and consequences of "coherent" markets, whereas macroeconomics have been concerned with "discordance" or "dysfunction" in the economic system (inflation, unemployment, etc.). Although the system scales are reversed, this view is important in the present context — here the "coherent" outcomes are associated with the "unitary" neoclassical approach whilst the existence of "submarkets" will tend to be associated, indeed caused by and contribute to, coordination failure in the market. Thus, Weintraub argues that economists mistakenly cut phenomena (in terms of conventional models) into "micro and macro" (in our case "unitary market and submarket") when the informative split is into markets or systems with coordination success or failure.

Thus, in the present discussion the importance of the existence of submarkets is that for some spatial scales, locations and time periods, a "nonor partly coordinated" view of the housing market is more appropriate than a "unitary" equlibrium" view. Such an approach requires different research methods and asks some different questions — at present the dichotomy is a real and important one in housing economics.

In the following section a number of ideas are presented to indicate how the concept of submarket has been progressively abstracted from economic models and in turn how the abstractions of the standard competitive model need to be relaxed in order to cope adequately with characteristics of the housing market.

THE MARKET AS AN APPLIED ECONOMIC PHENOMENON

Whilst the operation and role of markets is central to most discussions of economic phenomena, the actual nature, definition and identification of market systems has, until the last decade, been given negligible attention. The "market" in most urban and housing analysis is, as noted above, a simple theoretical construct with a specific form and often it has no explicit qualitative, temporal or spatial dimensions. However, in the search to expand competitive and other neoclassical equilibrium models, theorists have tended to disregard two important concerns for applied researchers. Firstly, the operational nature of the market, and hence the coherence or otherwise of the overall outcome, depends (in part) on the nature of the commodity. Secondly, when markets have real dimensions then various criteria have to be devised from which "markets" and "submarkets" can be identified. Reiterating Weintraub's point there have to be criteria for identifying disaggregated systems in non-coherent markets. The same observations apply to the identification of labour markets, "regions" or groups of goods.

The Abstraction of Submarkets from Market Models

Since it was suggested above urban economic models based on Walrasian or Marshallian theories of markets may act as a straightjacket for housing economic research, it is appropriate to consider how such restrictions came to be imposed upon the analytical framework and how they might be removed. Walras, for instance, argued that markets were most conveniently viewed as being a single point in space and that they contained perfectly informed traders with the market clearing in the market period. This view of the world naturally precludes the possibility of submarkets existing — price differences per unit of commodity are arbitraged with no or minimal consequences of false trading. The Marshallian view is initially more eclectic. Marshall noted "a market is not any particular market place... but the whole region in which buyers and sellers are in such free intercourse with one another that the prices of the same goods tend to equality easily and quickly". (Marshall, 1892, p. 205.) Of course this provides us with obvious clues to the identification of submarkets based upon price dispersion (of a non-random nature) which was equalised over time. Marshall also recognised that "free intercourse" implied not only flows of information but of traders and resources and he added that "in practice it is often difficult to ascertain how far the movements of supply and demand in any one place are influenced by those in another" (Marshall, op.cit. p. 205), and he noted that increased information flow increases interaction. However whilst recognising that many factors influence or widen markets, he argued that almost all commodities in 'universal demand' were capable of being "easily and exactly described" and that only transport costs (for which he uses bricks as an example) remain as a problem. Marshall therefore chose to ignore, in developing his temporally oriented analysis, commodities which were not "in general demand, cognisable and portable".

The implications of Marshall's emphasis were that not only were temporal considerations placed ahead of spatial factors but also that the spatial factors which could be accommodated in the paradigm were restricted to transport cost frictions. Spatial rigidities and information gaps which make for submarket formation and market discoordination were ruled out of consideration. Such judgements were common to most writers of that period. For instance (somewhat earlier) Jevons argued that "A great city may contain as many markets as there are branches of trade, and these markets may or may not be localised... the traders may be spread over a whole town... and yet make a market if they are in close communication with each other". He believed that these conditions to be "more or less completely carried out in practice" (Jevons, 1879, p. 91).

Space and submarkets are, apparently, inadvertent victims of early neo-classical formalisation. An analysis of earlier contributions indicates that "disequilibrium" and spatial phenomena, even spatial submarkets, had previously been regarded as being important. For instance, in Smith's "Wealth of Nations", not only is system dysfunction (described in terms of the divergence between the natural and the market price) admitted as a logical possibility but it is also explicitly stated to be important. And, of couse, Smith was centrally concerned with the "divisions" and "extent" of markets. Further, these divisions were recognised to be, on occasion, spatial in nature, viz., "The whole of the advantages of the different employments of labour and stock must, *in the same neighbourhood,* be either perfectly equal or *tending to equality* (our emphasis). (Skinner, 1974, p. 157). Smith notes that the market price in a neighbourhood may not always be equal to "natural price". He continues that the natural price is "the central price to which the prices of all commodities are continually gravitating" but also that "Different accidents may sometimes keep them (market prices) suspended above it, and sometimes force them down even somewhat below it. *But whatever may be the obstacles* which hinder them from settling in this centre of repose and continuance they are constantly tending to it". (our parenthesis and emphasis), (Skinner, op.cit. p. 157). This may seem, prima facia, to be virtually identical to the Marshallian tradition but whereas Marshall assumes disequilibrium to be removed quickly Smith argues that "sometimes particular accidents, sometimes 'natural' causes and sometimes regulations of policy, may in many commidities, keep up the market price for a long time together, a good deal above the natural price". (Skinner, op.cit., p. 157).

Indeed, Smith argues that where there is spatial separation and lack of information flow and where production requires specific and fixed (inelastic) supply inputs that "such commodities may continue *for whole centuries* to be set at this high price" (where the market exceeds the natural price). And, of particular relevance to the context of fixed stocks of housing and land already developed within the city, notes that "the rent of the land which affords such singular and esteemed proportions bears no regular proportion to the rent of other equally fertile and well cultivated land in its neighbourhood". (Skinner op.cit., p. 165.) Finally, and most telling of all, Smith argues that "Such enchancements of the market price are evidently *the effect of natural causes* which may hinder the effectual demand from ever being fully supplied and which may continue, therefore, to operate for ever". (Skinner, op.cit., p. 164.)

This digression into the history of economic thought illustrates the submarket issue in a number of ways. Contemporary microeconomics largely denies their existence and either abstracts the issue or implies that submarkets are separate markets. They imply that submarkets will only exist ephemerally for most major commodities. The Smithian analysis is markedly different — the Invisible Hand may struggle, price differences are generally important, they may be expressed spatially and arise naturally and they are likely to persist. These submarkets or segments, although never explicitly defined, are viewed as being pervasive and "natural" phenomena, that is, they are not exclusively temporary restrictions on system equilibration. It is our contention that the operational characteristics of the housing market are such that persistent disequilibrium can be observed.

A Way Forward

In developing a framework for defining and identifying housing submarkets three major strands of microeconomic analysis can be drawn together. First, we draw upon the theoretical investigations of Lancaster which describe and analyse the economics of complex commodities — in this instance, housing. A number of housing demand studies use Lancaster's theory (Lancaster, 1979) as a point of departure but by retaining the traditional assumption of simple competitive markets fail to face the logical consequences of commodity complexity and variety. Second, attention is drawn to the growing literature on the informational and trading characteristics of non-Walrasian markets (see Hey, 1982), and to the nature of information flows and search processes within the housing market. Third, and arising from the nature of housing as a commodity and related feasible systems of exchange, we consider the sale of housing in a model of extensive seller price discrimination, (see Phlips, 1983). That is, to define and identify the origins of submarkets for housing we reject a simple competitive equilibrium view of the market (which is still possible as a special rather than general case) and instead lean towards a model of more or less imperfect "monopolistic" competition. In such a model the origins, persistence and significance of systematic price variation within a market (i.e. the existence of submarkets) can be convincingly examined. These are, of course, strong assertions but they essentially flow from the maxim noted above that *"the nature of the market can be a function of the nature of the commodity"*. At this juncture it is relevant then to consider some propositions about the broad nature of housing and housing markets.

Housing as a Commodity

Housing is both a varied and complex commodity. It is complex insofar as each dwelling comprises a series of internal structures, has a number of external characteristics and embraces locational and neighbourhood attributes. It is varied insofar as, in a given neighbourhood, house size and style may vary or, across neighbourhoods, locational and neighbourhood attributes may differ. The variety of the housing stock arises from a number of different kinds of factors. There is inherent dimensional variety in that some housing is old and some new, or housing may be more or less accessible to employment centres. Further variety exists because producers differentiate housing production at the date of construction and such variation may be enhanced by differential obsolescence, customising (by either sellers or buyers), improvement, conversion, etc.

Adopting Lancaster's perspective, housing should not be viewed as being desired as a good per se (a point which immediately casts doubt upon the validity of studies, which estimate elasticities of "housing" demand). Rather, housing can be viewed as a collection of attributes (or characteristics) which in conjunction with the household's consumption technology, are used to satisfy more basic consumption objectives such as shelter, comfort, aesthetics, accessibility, etc. That is, goods are only intermediaries in the consumption process.

This view of goods, which has been used in a fairly simplistic fashion by housing economists, is quite consistent with neoclassical models and with the view that some basic consumption objective may be achieved by a use of different observable characteristics. This implies that observed characteristic choices may vary markedly for identical income households and it may also imply that observable submarkets may only exist on the main house characteristics for which there are no substitution possibilities. Characteristics may contribute to more than one basic consumption objective or that objectives are satisfied by some interaction of housing characteristics. A further complication, which we largely ignore in Section III below, is that the housing characteristics are combined with non housing goods to provide basic services. For instance, locational characteristics should not be examined independently of transport choices by the household. We also note, in Lancaster's terminology, that houses contain a mix of divisible and indivisible attributes. For instance, location in a high status neighbourhood or even shelter from the elements is indivisible but more room space or housing comfort can be added in situ. Also, for most purposes housing must be classed as non-combinable, that is, housing objectives must be satisfied via a single dwelling and not by using more than one dwelling.

If houses are examined on the basis of the characteristics that they contain (at least the identifiable characteristics) then a considerable variety exists. Product variety may be classed as whether the product contains more or less of the same attributes (vertical differentiation) or whether they contain a different essential mix of characteristics (horizontal differentiation). Of course the set of houses within an urban area is both vertically and horizontally differentiated. If the price of given housing attributes is constant throughout a given market then the range of house prices reflects variation in the quantity and mix of attributes. A number of analysts and ad hoc policy analyses often class such qualitatively different groups as constituting submarkets. This terminology is misleading and in such instances price variety merely reflects product variety. The term "housing product groups" is used below to indicate such variation with the term "submarket" restricted to instances where persistent, significant disparities in attribute prices are observed across product groups.

Using Lancaster's method (which is a substantial extension of the Hotelling model in "characteristics space") products may be grouped according to the amounts and proportions of characteristics they contain. In applied work this is formally equivalent to a factor analysis grouping of houses by characteristics. Thus, as in the empirical section below, analysis of housing market structure should not be conducted in relation to ad hoc aggregations of dwelling units but should start from a grouping of dwelling units based upon their observable characteristics. The full model of product differentiation advanced by Lancaster includes an analysis of the production as well as the consumption of variety. The analysis presented here is short run in the sense that the supply characteristics of housing stock are taken to be fixed. That is consumers are choosing from the existing housing stock.

The basis of applying Lancaster's model to housing choice of this kind can be illustrated as follows. Individuals will choose housing bundles both in relation to the way in which characteristics satisfy preferences represented in figure 1 by indifference curves $I_1 ... I_n$, and by the consumption possibilities. The latter is determined by household income, the prices of characteristics and the mix of characteristics embodied in goods. In a world of continuous product variety the consumption possibilities for a given household will be represented by a schedule such as $C_1 -_C 1$, with equilibrium product choice E^1. Another household with different preferences $(J^1 ... J^n)$ may select a different mix E^2, (at the same income level). Variations in income level shift the consumption possibilities frontier.

The above comments on commodity complexity are now commonplace in the literature of housing economics. Variety is then examined in the context of perfectly informed, competitive markets assumed to be at or near equilibrium. With such assumptions, submarkets can arise only as a result of short period inelasticity in attribute supply, a likely occurence with product variety. However such an approach may fail to capture all the important consequences of spatially variable commodity variety. Product variety affects the behaviour of consumers through search and information processes, and sellers in relation to their ability to gain from desired varieties. Therefore quality variation has implications for the processes as well as the objects of market behaviour and such processes could contribute to submarket formation.

The Microeconomics of Seller and Buyer Behaviour

Buyer behaviour in the housing market is critically influenced by characteristics of the commodity and the auction/trading system used to exchange housing assets. In particular, and as is now widely discussed elsewhere (Maclennan, 1982, Clark, 1982), housing searchers are likely to have less than full information and to incur search costs – both of which influence trading behaviour. The information imperfection arises from a number of aspects of housing. First, at least in the owned sector, the high level of exchange costs, means that housing market trades by an individual are relatively infrequent (between 7 to 10 years for the average UK owner occupier). Clearly information on specific vacancies perishes rapidly and, indeed, historically stored information may be irrelevant as moves are usually to a different housing product group. Other items of information may become obsolescent as housing and neighbourhood characteristics may alter. Thus each buying phase requires renewed search.

Consumer search, of a fairly intensive kind, is also necessitated by the fact that the range and quality of housing characteristics contained in a dwelling may not be apparent from adverts, casual visits and even professional evaluation. Consumers of a particular income and preference class, at the initial stages of search, may have their search activity shaped into particular neighbourhoods or broader geographic areas by information and financing agents, see Maclennan and Jones (1985). Even where prior structuring does not occur exogenously the need to search specific housing units, spread as they are over space, may begin to tie potential buyers into "familiar" segments of the consumption possibility schedule. Further, when costs of professional valuations and of securing loan finance permissions are concerned, then consumers become "tied" or "locked-in" to forming a bid on particular properties. This point, as explained below, is important in relation to seller behaviour. There are also expectational elements in buyer behaviour – for instance, the actual quality of particular characheristics may only be assessed after purchase, such as the noisiness of plumbing or the sociability of neighbours, and this is especially important in relation to future capital values of the stock. Thus the existence of imperfect information generates search costs, which can partition households across the range of consumption possibilities, and even within a selected product group may lead to different price bids if expectations differ.

Seller Behaviour. The informational problems of buyers are exacerbated by the widely used system of selling dwellings, at least in Scotland. The housing "market", at any point in time, is not a single auction involving multiple buyers and sellers. Rather, the market is fragmented into a series of individual auctions where sellers extract bids from a relatively small number of potential buyers who have intensively searched particular purchase options. In the Scottish selling system, sellers commonly state a reservation price and then receive a series of sealed and legally binding bids which are opened at an agreed time with subsequent sale to the highest bidder (assuming the true reservation level is satisfied). The bid made by an individual will reflect not only the past search experience but will also be related to intensity of preference for that particular dwelling or neighbourhood. The preference of sellers for this form of auction largely stems from the fact that it is otherwise difficult for sellers to identify the "best bid customer" and because bids, from apparently similar buyers, may vary markedly. For not only will potential buyers of a given income class have different search experience, but the dwelling may yield quite different levels of services to them. Such variation arises particularly in relation to accessibility and neighbourhood characteristics. For instance, at any given location, a two earner family working near the site will bid more (ceteris paribus) than a one earner family working some distance away. The bidding system used allows sellers to discriminate between buyers and to extract consumer surplus. This is, emphatically, not perfect competition. Rather, the seller recognises that either because of preference intensity or search costs or imperfect information, that his dwelling has distinctiveness (at least temporarily) for the bidders and that there is some elasticity in the demand curve for the individual dwelling (ex post). This seller price descrimination capability depends upon the subsequent non transferability of the product (due to high recontracting costs) and the relative fixity, by information and preference, of purchasers into a narrow range of the set of consumption possibilitites as well as fairly complete information on buyers price bids (see Phlips, 1983, p. 16).

These observations mean that the housing market should not be viewed as being perfectly and atomistically competitive but that a framework of analysis based upon "imperfect" monopolistic competition (see Lancaster, 1979, Ch. 8) may be more appropriate. Within this framework a range of influences, other than short run supply inelasticities, which arises from the nature of housing system may cause submarkets. However, the arguments above (except in relation to spatially structured information deficiencies or financial lending rules) primarily cause variation in the relationship between observed prices and dwelling characteristics. That is, they may generate price dispersion within a market. But to sustain the contention that they create housing submarkets it is necessary to establish that they contribute to price differences per unit of characteristic which exist and persist over different submarkets. In the penultimate section we indicate that factors such as expectational influences and price discriminating power can vary systematically across submarkets. However, it is first important to establish whether persistent price differences do persist in local housing markets.

IDENTIFYING SUBMARKETS

Existing Methodologies

Submarkets are deemed to exist when systematic differences exist in housing attribute prices over areas or sectors and where variations show some persistence. Of course, this begs the question as to what constitutes "significant" and "persistent", and whether the price variations relate to all or some housing characteristics. We make the explicit judgement here that "submarkets" exist if at the 0.10 significant level attribute prices are significantly different and if such differences persist for more than a year. We are also primarily concerned with the major housing characteristics (size, style, etc.). In a number of studies, for instance see Schnare and Struyk (1976) and Kirwan and Ball (1977) the common methodology is to estimate hedonic housing prices for a number of areas based on census data and to attempt to establish price differences. Naturally, neither of these studies, because they draw negative conclusions regarding the existence of cross section differences in attribute prices, attempts to examine longer periods of persistence or emergence of differentials. More recently, Goodman (Goodman, 1981) extended the time horizon over a three year period and the results reported below relate to a similar time period.

The methodology employed here involves a number of steps. First, dwelling unit level data on housing characteristics and prices is aggregated, by factor analysis, into statially defined product groups. Second, for each product group zone (PGZ), a hedonic regression model is specified and estimated. Third, within a metropolitan area the regression results for each PGZ are systematically compared for similarities and differences. Finally, there is an attempt to establish whether such price differences persist over a three year period.

Time Series on Small Area Housing Prices

Since this procedure was extensive an initial scan of zonal price data within the city was undertaken with a view to establishing prima facie evidence of submarket existence.

In Scotland, details of housing transactions including price and financial source are stored in a public record, "The Register of Sasines". The Centre for Housing Research at Glasgow University has recorded all transactions in the City of Glasgow (constituting the core of the Clydeside conurbation) from 1972 to the present and geo-coded dwelling transactions to the nearest 5 metres. Patterns of small area price change can be identified and the database has been analysed using different grids and scales. A detailed report is available in Maclennan and Munro (1985), but already published data (Maclennan, 1982) indicates that there were marked differences in zonal appreciation rates between 1972–76, see Maps 1 and 2.

With the assumption that a qualitatively repetitive draw of dwellings is made from each grid square then price change indicate that attribute prices across areas are changing over time. By excluding new housing and by concentrating on unimproved dwelling stock, relative constancy of stock quality is assumed to exist within a given grid square. By definition, therefore, relative price changes imply relative change is some attribute prices. It is also clear from the Glasgow data that patterns of price change have a well defined spatial structure. Although the above procedure is quite crude it provides a prima facie case for the existence of submarkets and supports the case for a more detailed statistical analysis of housing prices in these locations.

The Hedonic Estimation Procedure

The first stage of the formal submarket identification procedure was concerned with grouping dwelling units into product groups on the basis of dwelling and neighbourhood characteristics. The Glasgow data on the characteristics relate to a representative (20 per cent) sample of 863 purchases in the city during a six month period (early to mid 1977). Groupings for the market were devised by factor analysis both with and without spatial contiguity constraints. In the Glasgow context there were four product groups with fewer than 25 observations. Since this raises problems in estimating hedonic attribute regressions these dwellings were reallocated to the most similar, larger groupings. At a manageable level of resolution (to preserve sample numbers within groupings and with computing costs in mind), the Glasgow analysis identified 5 main housing-neighbourhood types which, when mapped as in Map 2, generated 12 areas in the city with sample sizes running from 152 to 33 (and a median of 61). This procedure merely identifies housing "product groups" — it remains to be established whether significant attribute price differences exist and persist across these areas.

Preliminary house price regressions within each product group area were run to eliminate observed characteristics which had an insignificant impact on housing price variation. For instance, housing attributes such as inside toilet and kitchen, were so pervasively present that their influence would be measured in the regression constant term. In Glasgow, a surprisingly large number of neighbourhood variables relating to local public services (presence of schools, libraries, swimming baths, medical services, etc.) were also ubiquitous and were dropped from the index estimation procedure. The existence of multicollinearity between explanatory variables is a likely feature of housing markets and this requires us to treat the hedonic coefficients of correlated attributes with great caution. In this analysis, dwelling age and distance from CBD were highly correlated but since housing quality was not well correlated with age, dwelling age was dropped from the explanatory equation but distance from the city centre was retained. The other variables included did not appear to cause major collinearity problems with, in general, correlation coefficients of less than 0.3.

The present "state of the art" in identifying submarkets or in applying hedonic estimation techniques then suggests that Box-Cox tests of functional form should be used to select the appropriate form of the hedonic regression. Usually (as in Kirwan and Ball), the same functional form is tested for all potential submarkets. However, it should be noted that since differences in underlying supply and demand functions may be the source of variation in attribute prices it would be logically more consistent to select the appropriate statistical form for each product/area group. The Box-Cox tests outlined in Pollakowski (Pollakowski, 1982) were replicated for each of the product groups. We have two reservations, however, regarding this approach. First, we believe that some of our sample sizes are too small to conduct this test without violating the underlying statistical assumptions. Second, we have no behavioural basis on whether to accept the result of the statistical routines as being reasonable. We recall Kimenta's observation that "specification represents a commitment on our part concerning our prior kowledge and beliefs about the relationship that is being modelled" and that "specification of the model should not be dictated by mathematical or computational convenience". In a hedonic study over 59 American cities, Malpezzi et al (Malpezzi et al, 1980) argued for a loglinear specification on the grounds that such a formulation allowed for a joint determination of attribute expenditures within the regression, that is reduced problems of heteroscedasticity (vis-a-vis a linear formulation) and that the estimated regression coefficients had a straightforward interpretation (the coefficients are the percentage change induced in the dependent variable by a unit change in the independent variable). Thus, here we have reported the results arising from an application of a semi-log linear regression model to house prices observed in each of our product groups and we have, in spite of our theoretical reservations, estimated the same equation in each submarket. In Glasgow, for example, the Box-Cox method suggested that a linear specification would be more appropriate in 4 or the 12 zones. However, the pattern of differences in attribute prices between one zone and another did not change markedly (no submarkets were "created" or "eliminated") by adhering to a semi-log form. Frankly, we believe that in this area of research statistical techniques are now running well ahead of data suitable for their application, the simple and attractive idea of a hedonic price function is in fact rather difficult to estimate convincingly in the housing market.

The broad shape of the results from regressions based solely on housing-neighbourhood characteristics are indicated in Table 1 for Glasgow. This suggests that the areas with similar attribute price structures are;

1) Product groups 3, 4 and 5 in West Glasgow
2) Product group 2 throughout the city
3) Product group 1 in the west, centre and south
4) Product group 1 in the East End
5) Product group 3 in South Glasgow.
6) Product group 5 in South Glasgow.

Some comments on the analysis of Table 1 are noteworthy. First, where a particular attribute does not exist within a product group then there cannot be a price estimate for generally similar housing units but which differ in a few characteristics. Nor can comparisons be made when infrequent observation of an attribute produces a high standard error resulting in statistical non-significance. This missing or highly variable (small sample) attributes are excluded from our cross-group comparisons, for instance "detached house" and "no bathroom" characteristics in columns 1 and 2. The first set of product groups PG3W, PG4W and PG5W also illustrates some other problems in judging the existence of submarkets. For instance the "tenement flat" attribute test suggests that PG3W and PH4W have similar attribute prices and, in turn PG4W and PG5W are not significantly different. However, the attribute prices for this characteristic are significantly different between PG3W and PG5W. Fortunately this was the only instance of non-transitivity of significance in the tests undertaken and we have judged PG3W and PG5W to form a submarket along with PG4W.

The lower value product groups, PG1 and PG2, form different submarkets largely as a result of differences in attribute prices for rooms and for zonal tenure and transport variables. In the lower value ranges an additional room commands a particularly high premium and property prices, perhaps reflecting area uncertainties, become more sensitive (negatively) to the presence of council housing. Such factors also explain submarket variations within the lower price ranges, for instance the room space premium in PG1E is significantly less than for the rest of PG1, and PG1E displays particular sensitivity to tenure mix. Within the upper price bands, the south side product groups, PG3S and PG5S, have lower space premia than for similar products in the west of the city and, at the same time, markedly more sensitivity to distance from the CBD and to the presence of transport routes.

Persistence in Price Differences

To confirm submarket existence it is important to establish that observed price differences for attributes persist. After adjusting for price changes (in the overall price of housing) analysis indicates that the observed structures persisted over lengthy time periods (1 to 3 years).

Evidence of persistence is more difficult to establish in the Glasgow case as the hedonic regression analysis could not be repeated for successive years. Here the following procedure was used. For the product group areas identified in the 1977 grouping exercise, average prices (relative to the city mean) were estimated for 1976 and 1975. The estimates were not made for post 1977 years as after 1978 the city's tenement stock began to be affected by a large scale improvement programme. With the additional assumption that individual attribute prices in a zone change at the mean rate within the zone it was possible to assess whether significant price differences persisted. Again the pattern observed remains quite stable. Over the period studied, however, product group 3 in the west end became increasingly similar to 4 and 5 whilst the moderate quality tenement submarket (2) throughout the city converged with (3) but became progressively dissimilar to (1), the low value tenement sector. A study with more recent (1983) data suggerts considerable structural change in the Glasgow market from 1978–83 (Munro, 1985).

Explanations of Submarket Existence

In previous sections we have stressed that a variety of factors may create cross-area price differences. However, since the Glasgow tests were based on a household survey which investigated area housing preferences, search and bidding processes, expectations, financing arrangements and demand factors it was possible to examine how such variables varied across the different "submarkets" of that city. For brevity only the major conclusions are reported here.

We now consider how or why the additional factors introduced into the analysis may have a well-defined spatial or sub-market structure.

a **Financial Rationing.** This phenomenon has been widely discussed under the heading "redlining", (see Maclennan and Jones, 1985). Here it may be viewed as being an exogenous constraint on buyer behaviour which may generate price differences via restrictions on effective demand.

An analysis of loan finance patterns in Glasgow indicates that sub-market 1 has a distinctive financing structure (see Maclennan and Jones, 1983) with generally less than 20 per cent of transactions funded via conventional mortgages. The separation between the east end of Glasgow and the rest of this submarket largely arose from the fact that the 1977 survey indicated that less than 10 per cent of first time buyers in the city even considered the area as a potential location. That is, it was not in the perveived consumption possibility set. These finance and information factors appear to interact to depress attribute prices in the zone.

b **Expectations.** Expectations about future dwelling values or characteristics are not commonly recorded in housing surveys as housing attributes. They are included in all our empirical data. However, since expectations may have a well defined area structure we could expect them to produce observable and significant price differences paid on a standard dwelling.

Purchasers in Glasgow in 1977 were asked to indicate whether, in the three year period ahead, they expected their new neighbourhood to appreciate or depreciate relative to the city mean (in price and quality). The highest positive expectation scores were observed in submarket 2 throughout the city (indeed *all* purchasers in such zones had expectations of relative appreciation. Expectations in other zones, including zone 1, were largely neutral.

c **Information, Search and Seller Discrimination.** Previous research (Maclennan and Wood, 1982) has indicated that home buyers often have a spatially structured housing search process – that is search of the consumption possibilities schedule is restricted. Also search costs may differ within such areas. Both these factors lead to variation in price bids for similar properties in different locations. In addition, seller discrimination depends upon the capacity of sellers to receive, in some preferred or optimal selling period a series of bids. This capacity may vary, across space or time, depending upon the state of the market. That is, the form of exchange system may actually vary. For instance, new houses are usually sold in large numbers at fixed prices thus reducing seller discrimination. New and secondhand systems coexist in time. Also, it can be demonstrated that price and turnover behaviour varies throughout the market in response to macroeconomic (say interest rate changes) – not all parts of the market slow down or accelerate at the same pace or in the same period. Thus, variable price discriminating power may systematically, and persistently, influence dwelling prices paid for similar units (essentially rein-forcing preference and information factors).

Analysis revealed that the number of bids made by a purchaser to secure a purchase was the major determinant of total search costs (which for first time buyers amounted to around 8 per cent of dwelling prices). However, number of bids by a searcher was closely correlated with number of bids received by a seller, thus the search cost and price discrimination hypotheses cannot be tested separately. When average number of bids per purchaser was calculated across submarkets then the figure was particularly high in submarkets 2 and 3 (throughout the city) – averaging 4.5 bids per purchaser in the period studied. The figure was higher in submarket 4 (West) at 3.1, than in submarket 4 South (2.2) and was particularly low in submarket 1 at 1.8. Thus pressure of demand and seller power clearly varied across submarkets in a fashion consistent with the attribute price differences observed.

The association of demand groups with particular submarkets is discussed elsewhere (Maclennan and Wood, 1983). Here we briefly examine how housing market search patterns coincide with observed submarket structure. Lancaster observed that unless product groups have meaning for consumers then they are mere technical/statistical artefacts which are unhelpful in understanding consumer behaviour. From the Glasgow survey data it was possible to examine the spatial structure of consumer search patterns.

The search patterns of first time home-buyers who were over age 30 (usually with below average income and with a family) were restricted to submarkets 1 and 2 with households restricting search to a small set of neighbourhoods usually focused upon the initial search point. Other first time buyers, young singles or couples with professional and managerial occupations had a different search pattern. For most initial search took place in West submarket 3 or 2 with a spillover into south submarket 2 or 3 following extended failed search in the West End. The pattern for movers within the market (i.e. previous owners moving) was much more complex, thus comments are restricted here to consumers moving up-market from submarkets 2 or 3. For such groups search was restricted to submarkets 4 and 5 and there was a strong sectoral bias in the search pattern. Thus the spatial structure of search behaviour in the Glasgow housing market appears to be consistent with the submarket structure identified. The fact that indicators of market pressure, search behaviour and expectations differ significantly across the submarkets we have identified from hedonic estimates thus allays some of the fears expressed above regarding the inadequacy of hedonic specification and estimation methods.

CONCLUSIONS

The findings of this paper are time and place specific and they cannot be used to argue that submarkets are a lasting feature of all urban housing systems. However, they also imply that cross section econometric analyses of urban housing markets may be flawed, both in relation to model specification and estimation, if they set out with a strong assumption that competitive equilibrium prevails. This study shows that significant differences in housing attribute prices can persist beyond the real time periods over which most research is conducted. Our data also hints that price differences may be eroded over time and, hence, the pattern of submarket may alter over time. It is even possible that some form of equilibrium structure, but not based upon perfectly competitive market processes, may emerge over a longer period but such balance did not emerge within our study period.

The attribute price estimation procedure, regarding which some of our stated reservations remain, has been at the core of most studies of submarkets. The penultimate section of this paper, in examining bidding and search behaviour, draws attention to observable indicators of market tightness or slackness, which can be used to identify geographic or sectoral variations in excess demand. In this respect they form an important cross-check against hedonic house price based statifications of the market. Here, they indicated a pattern of cross sectional variation consistent with observed price differences.

An ideal test for the existence of submarkets would have departed from our procedure in two respects. First, a larger sample of purchasers would have been extracted at annual intervals over a longer period, perhaps as long as seven to ten years. Second, survey data on how households perceive and use housing characteristics would have led to a more confident specification of the hedonic regression equations, perhaps even allowing variation in functional forms estimated across product groups. We do not possess a database rich enough to undertake such research at the present time; we are continuing to collect further, and comparable, data for the Glasgow market.

REFERENCES

Ball, M., and R. Kirwan (1977) "Accessibility and Supply Constraints in an Urban Housing Market", *Urban Studies* 14: 11–32.

Butler, R.V. (1982) "The Specification of Hedonic Indexes for Urban Housing", *Land Economics* 58: 96–108.

Cain, G.C. (1976) "The Challenge of Segmented Labour Market Theories to Orthodox Theory", *Journal of Economic Literature* 1215–1250.

Clark, W.A.V. (ed.) (1982) *Modelling Housing Market Search.* London: Croom Helm.

Coddington, A. (1983) *Keynesian Economics – The Search for First Principles.* London: George Allen & Unwin.

Goodman, A.C. (1981) "Housing Submarkets within Urban Areas: Definitions and Evidence", *Journal of Regional Science* 21: 175–185.

Hey, J.D. (1982) *Economics in Disequilibrium.* Oxford: Martin Robertson.

Jevons, W.S. (1879) *The Theory of Political Economy.* London: Macmillan.

Kerr, C. (1953) "The Balkanisation of Labour Markets", *Review of Economics and Statistics.*

Kmenta, J. (1971) *Elements of Econometrics.* New York: Macmillan.

Lancaster, K. (1979) *Variety, Equity and Efficiency.* Oxford: Basil Blackwell.

Lowell, R.F. (1978) "Testing a Dual Labour Market Classification of Jobs", *Journal of Regional Science.*

Maclennan, D. (1982) *Housing Economics: An Applied Approach.* London: Longmans.

Maclennan, D., and C.A. Jones (1987) (forthcoming). "Building Societies and Credit Rationing: an empirical examination of redlining", *Urban Studies.*

Maclennan, D., and M. Munro (1987) (forthcoming). "Intraurban changes in housing prices: Glasgow 1972–1983", *Housing Studies.*

Maclennan, D., and G.A. Wood (1982) Chapters 5 and 7 in Clark, W.A.V. (ed.), *Modelling Housing Market Search.* London: Croom Helm.

Marshall, A. (1892) *Elements of Economics of Industry.* London: Macmillan.

Muth, R.F. (1977) "The Influence of Age of Dwellings on Housing Expenditures and on the Location of Households by Income", in Ingram, G.K. (ed.), *Residental Location and Urban Housing Markets.* Cambridge, Mass: N.B. E.R. and Ballinger.

Munro, M. (1986) *Testing for Segmentation in the Glasgow Private Housing Market.* Discussion Paper 8. Glasgow: Centre for Housing Research.

Phlips, L. (1983) *The Economics of Price Discrimination.* Cambridge: Cambridge University Press.

Pollakowski, H.O. (1982) *Urban Housing Markets and Residential Location.* Lexington: D.C. Heath.

Schnare, A.B., and R.J., Struyk (1976) "Segmentation in Urban Housing Markets", *Journal of Urban Economics* 3: 146–166.

Skinner, A. (ed.) (1974) *Adam Smith. The Wealth of Nations.* London: Penguin.

Straszheim, M.R. (1975) *An Econometric Analysis of the Urban Housing Market.* New York: N.B.E.R.

Weintraub, E.R. (1980) *Microfoundations.* Cambridge: Cambridge University Press.

Whitehead, C.M., and J. Odling-Smee (1975) "Long-Run Disequilibrium in the Housing Market", *Urban Studies* 12: 315–318.

Table 1. Area Product Groups in Glasgow.

Variable	PG3W	PG4W	PG5W	PG2	PG1W, CS	PG1E	PG35	PG55
Constant	9.047	9.21	9.32	8.31	7.6	7.31	8.86	7.33
Detached house	—	0.17	0.12	—	—	—	—	0.21
Semi-detached	—	0.11	0.13	0.09	—	—	—	0.14
Terraced	0.071	0.063	0.081	0.05	0.08	0.09	0.12	0.11
Tenement flat	0.05	0.041	0.06	0.06	0.03	0.04	0.06	0.04
No bathroom	0.15*	—	—	—	-0.21	-0.19	—	—
Two bathrooms	0.03*	0.06	0.07	—	—	—	—	0.08
Two public rooms	0.182	0.191	0.21	0.29	0.34	0.29	0.15	0.19
Three public rooms	0.31	0.283	0.295	0.33	0.37	0.34	0.23	0.25
Four public rooms	0.41	0.422	0.38	0.39	0.36	0.33	0.35	0.34
Five public rooms	0.47*	0.49	0.44	—	—	—	0.45	0.41
Six public rooms	0.50*	0.54*	0.49*	—	—	—	0.49	0.49
Seven public rooms	—	0.52*	0.55*	—	—	—	—	0.57
Central heating	0.06	0.071	0.075	0.05	0.09	—	0.09	0.11
Garden	0.08*	0.092	0.083	0.06	0.04	0.03	0.07	0.09
Garage	0.03	0.04	0.003	0.004	0.008	0.09	0.06	0.02
Distance from city centre	0.004	0.003	0.004	0.001	0.007	-0.002	0.003	-0.005
Per cent owner occupation in zone	0.0017	0.001*	0.002	0.003	0.004	0.006	0.003	0.001
Per cent council housing in zone	-0.002	0.001*	-0.003*	-0.005	-0.007	0.020	-0.004	-0.006
Distance to Nursery School	-0.007	-0.057	0.001	-0.0007	-0.0002	-0.001	-0.0012	0.002
Presence of Major Park	0.04	0.05	0.047	0.091	0.083	0.112	0.07	0.021
Bus routes in zone	0.037	0.042	0.046	0.002	-0.007	0.001	0.051	0.062
Railway, subway in zone	0.02	0.025	0.021	0.31	-0.002	0.003	0.042	0.055
Stone-cleaned	0.08	0.04*	0.09	0.12	0.096	0.051	0.07	0.02
R^2 adjusted	0.689	0.702	0.66	0.57	0.591	0.74	0.71	0.62
F for Equation	57.32	47.56	62.14	38.15	27.64	61.20	42.46	31.7
N	126	82	94	161	141	60	102	109

(1) Note, a house with one public room, kitchen and bathroom is taken to be the basic "housing" unit.

| Vn | 11.22 | 9.05 | 9.69 | 12.69 | 11.87 | 7 | 10 | 10.44 |

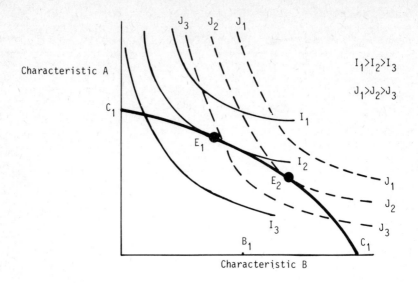

Fig. 1. Choice in Characteristics Space.

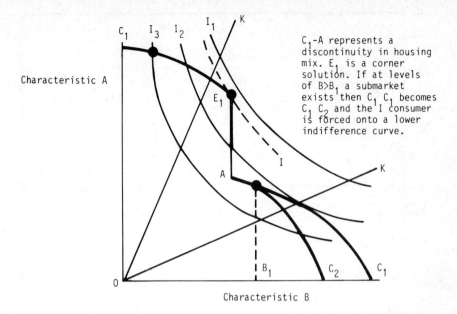

C_1-A represents a discontinuity in housing mix. E_1 is a corner solution. If at levels of $B > B_1$ a submarket exists then $C_1 C_1$ becomes $C_1 C_2$ and the I consumer is forced onto a lower indifference curve.

Characteristic B

KOK may indicate characteristic combination known to the consumer

Fig. 2. Discontinuities and Submarkets.

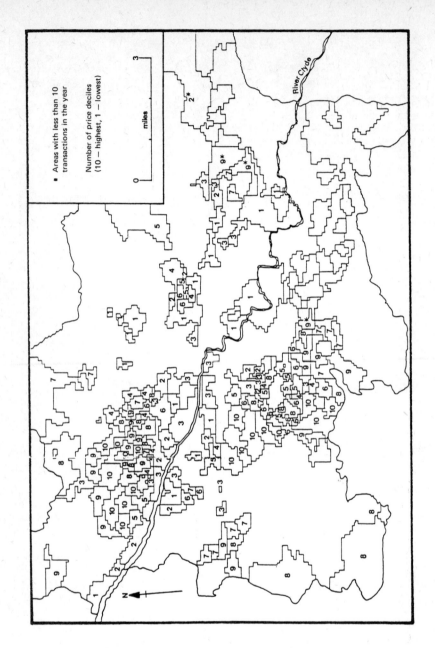

Map 1. House Price Deciles of Census Districts, 1983.

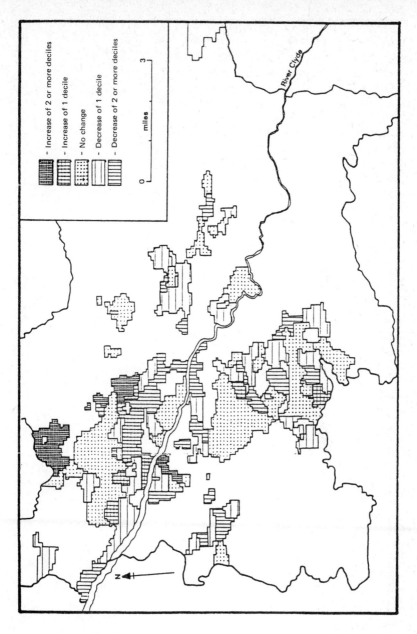

Map 2. Changes in the House Price Deciles of Census Districts, 1974–83.

Legend:
- Increase of 2 or more deciles
- Increase of 1 decile
- No change
- Decrease of 1 decile
- Decrease of 2 or more deciles

River Clyde

miles

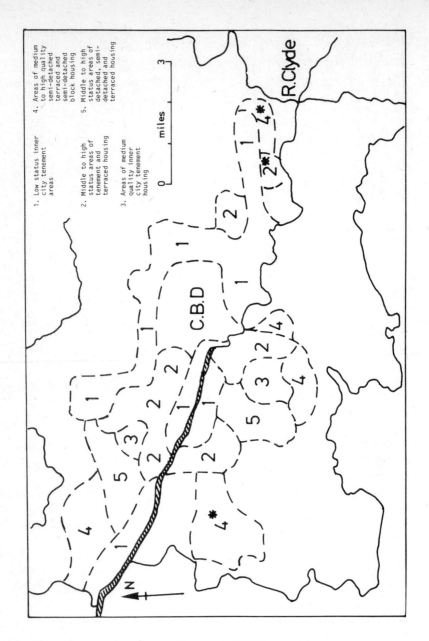

Map 3. Housing Products in Glasgow (1976/77 sample).

1. Low status inner city tenement areas

2. Middle to high status areas of tenement and terraced housing

3. Areas of medium quality inner city tenement housing

4. Areas of medium to high quality semi-detached terraced and semi-detached block housing

5. Middle to high status areas of detached, semi-detached and terraced housing

Housing Market Information and the Benefits of Housing Programs

5 3 - 70

John M. Quigley, University of California, Berkeley, USA

9320

INTRODUCTION

Housing market transactions differ from many other purchases of consumer durables in their complexity and in the importance of the public sector in affecting consumption. A wide and diverse collection of commodities are bought and sold in a single tied sale. In return for a monthly contract rent, or the amount specified to purchase a dwelling in fee simple, the consumer obtains a variety of structural characteristics, including size and quality attributes. Notable among the size attributes are parcel and living areas, numbers of rooms, bathrooms, garages and the like. Notable among the quality aspects of dwellings are their insulation and thermal properties, the vintage of construction, and the general state of repair.

However important these physical and structural components may be, household consumption of a variety of other goods is determined jointly with housing. Included in these goods are physical, locational, and neighborhood attributes, the character and quality of the local environment, and the public and social services provided to dwellings and their residents. Many of these attributes are difficult to measure precisely. Few of them are produced or marketed competitively; many are not marketed at all in any direct way.

The technical character of these components of housing also varies substantially. Some are essentially private goods, publicly supplied (e.g., refuse collection). Some are public goods subject to congestion (e.g., local parks), and some are pure public goods (e.g., noise levels, and the aesthetics of neighborhoods).

These goods also differ from the structural and physical characteristics of housing in the importance of government and local planning agencies in their allocation. Many of these collective commodities are supplied consciously by the public sector or arise as the result of regulation or regulatory oversight (or the neglect of regulatory oversight) by public authorities.

To an economist, these collective attributes of housing services provide the principal rationale for government policy in the housing market. Absent these externalities government housing policy would rest only upon the presumed "better tastes" of planners and public officials, their paternalistic motives, or the political ease of in-kind transfers.

The link between these attributes of residential life and the structure of housing prices suggests that housing market information can be used to "value" the diverse externalities in dense urban areas. This "valuation", in turn, implies that government decisions about increasing the supply of public goods or decreasing the supply of public bads can be informed by market-based estimates of the potential benefits of such activities.

The existence of some relationship between local externalities and market prices has been recognized in the economics literature for almost two decades. (The first paper I have been able to locate which investigates the empirical relationship is by Ronald Ridker [1967]). The theoretical basis for such investigations, however, was sketched out more than three decades ago. (The first paper I have been able to locate is by Nobel laureate Jan Tinbergen in 1956).

Since these initial investigations in the 1950's and 1960's, there has been an outpouring of research on these issues of valuation, not only by economists and planners but also by geographers, civil engineers, regional scientists and operations researchers. Despite these investigations and despite a number of high quality empirical analyses, there remains considerable controversy about just what is the appropriate theoretical framework for interpreting these relationships. Controversy abounds also in the appraisal of methodologies for estimating empirical relationships and for interpreting results as they relate to the benefits of any public program or government activity to improve housing amenities.

This paper provides a selective and non-technical review of these developments. In the following sections we sketch out and compare alternative strategies for the use of housing market information to estimate consumers' willingness to pay for public amenities. In addition, we compare the results of a wide variety of empirical studies which have attempted to estimate the benefits of the housing attributes provided collectively.[1] Finally, we speculate on factors which facilitate or retard the diffusion of these methodologies in the applied welfare economics actually practiced by government bureaus.

HOUSING PRICE INFORMATION

The point of departure for these investigations of consumers' willingness to pay for public goods is the analysis of price determination in the residential market. The tied purchase (or rent) of the housing commodity implies that the purchase or rental price (P) observed in the market reflects the housing characteristics ($H=[h_1, h_2, \ldots, h_I]$) and public goods and externalities ($A=[a_1, a_2, \ldots, a_J]$) enjoyed by housing consumers.

(1) $P = p(H, A)$

If the functional form for this relationship were linear, then the pricing of an observed housing and amenity package would be no different from the pricing of most other consumer goods. Marginal prices of all attributes would be constant and independent of the consumption of other aspects of the housing bundle. There is, however, ample reason to suspect that the housing price function is non-linear, since the costs of converting and reconfiguring existing dwellings are so large. With high conversion costs, it is entirely possible for a dwelling twice as large as another dwelling to rent for more or less than twice as much. High transformation costs sharply limit profitable arbitrage possibilities and can thereby insure that non-linear price schedules for housing attributes persist, even over a rather long run.

There is also good reason to believe that the prices of housing attributes are not independent of one another. For example, the unit price of increased quality probably depends upon the size and other amenities of a dwelling. Engineers, architects and quantity surveyors have postulated a variety of non-linear rules of thumb to estimate costs in new construction for dwellings with different sets of attributes. There is little reason to expect that the pricing structure of existing dwellings is less complex. In any case, the independence or separability of attribute prices is an empirical matter; the hypothesis of a lack of joint pricing can always be tested in a straightforward way for any housing market.

Under these circumstances the marginal price ρ of any attribute of housing h_i or environmental amenity a_j can be defined as

(2) $\rho_{a_{jk}} = \partial \rho / \partial a_{jk} = g(H_k, A_k)$

Note that the marginal price of the j th environmental amenity varies for each individual k, depending upon the entire vector of H and A chosen. Presumably competitive suppliers and demanders respond to these marginal prices, which represent the incremental cost of an additional unit of environmental amenity. It is important to note that if demanders are competitive, the marginal price represents the marginal rate of substitution of amenity for "other goods" (e.g., non-housing, non-amenity goods) regardless of the conditions underlying the supply of the amenity.

Since prices vary by individual, the demand curve for amenity a_j can be inferred from the empirical relationships

$$(3)\ a_{jk} = D(\rho_{h_{ik}}, \rho_{a_{jk}}, p_x, y_k \cdot P)$$

$$i = 1, 2, \ldots, I$$
$$j = 1, 2, \ldots, J$$

where p_x is the price of "other goods" (constant across individuals) and y_k is the income of individual k. Equation (3) represents the demand curve for amenity a_j estimated from observations on individuals' housing and amenity consumption, marginal prices, housing expenditure and income.

If this demand curve were known with any confidence, it could inform a wide variety of practical decisions made by local governments, regional authorities and central governments. Believable empirical counterparts to equation (3) could provide estimates of the market valuation of reductions in pollution, of improved access to recreational facilities and the like. Such estimates could provide measures of the market valuation of public subsidy programs and urban renewal projects, of increases in public services and could be used to evaluate a variety of housing-related government investments.

Quite obviously, the quantification of market benefits relative to costs and the verification that these benefits exceed costs need not be viewed as necessary in order to undertake public projects to upgrade or improve housing externalities. One can also imagine quite easily circumstances in which public programs were proposed even though aggregate market benefits fell short of costs.

Nevertheless, it should be clear, even to those who are not particularly enamored of market allocations, that serious estimates of market-based benefits would lead to better informed decisions about urban public projects.

THE WELFARE PROBLEM

A more formal statement of the consumer's problem is straightforward. Assume consumers have preferences over housing, amenities and other goods (x)

$$(4)\ U_k = U(H_k, A_k, x_k).$$

The household's budget constraint is

$$(5)\ y_k = p(H_k, A_k) + x_k,$$

where $p_x = 1$ is the numeraire.

Maximizing (4) subject to (5) yields

$$(6a) \quad \frac{\partial u/\partial h_{ik}}{\partial u/\partial x_k} = \partial p/\partial a_{ik} = \rho_{h_{ik}} \qquad i = 1, 2, \ldots, I$$

$$(6b) \quad \frac{\partial u/\partial a_{jk}}{\partial u/\partial x_k} = \partial p/\partial a_{jk} = \rho_{a_{jk}}. \qquad j = 1, 2, \ldots, J$$

Equation (6b) is the compensated (Hicksian) demand for amenity j - - the amount paid for an additional unit of a_j, holding the level of well-being constant.[2]

Since each consumer chooses one dwelling, the constant level of well-being is for consumer k:

$$(7) \quad U^\circ_k = U(H_k, A_k, y_k - p[H_k, A_k]),$$

and the amount the consumer would be willing to pay for other amounts of the housing-amenity package W_k is the solution to

$$(8) \quad U_k^\circ = U(H_k, A_k, y_k - W_k).$$

The willingness-to-pay for individual k depends upon his income and utility level and varies with the housing-amenity package.

$$(9) \quad W_k = W(U^\circ, y_k, H_k, A_k)$$
$$= W(p[H_k, A_k], y_k, H_k, A_k)$$

Two properties about the consumer's willingness to pay are observed from market data. First, at the equilibrium chosen by the consumer, the value of the willingness to pay function must equal the value of the hedonic function (W=P). Second, for each consumer, the partial derivative of the willingness to pay function must equal the partial derivative of the hedonic function $(\partial W/\partial a_i = \partial p/\partial a_i)$. Each observation on the choice of a housing-amenity package reveals a household's willingness to pay for amenity level a_i and the household's marginal willingness to pay for an additional unit a_i.

The competitive supplier's problem is analogous. Let C_k be the unit cost function for firm k

$$(4') \quad C_k = c(H_k, A_k, Z_k)$$

where Z_k are production function parameters for that firm and A_k is produced privately.

The firm maximizes unit profit Π

$$(5') \quad \Pi = p(H_k, A_k) - c(H_k, A_k, Z_k),$$

yielding first order conditions of the form

(6a') $\partial c / \partial h_{ik} = \partial p / \partial h_{ik} = \rho_{h_{ik}}$ $\qquad$ i = 1, 2, . . . , I

(6b') $\partial c / \partial a_{jk} = \partial p / \partial a_{jk} = \rho_{a_{jk}}$ $\qquad$ j = 1, 2, . . . , J

Let Ω_k be a function specifying the unit prices at which unit profits are constant for firm k,

(7') $\Omega_k = \omega(H, A, \Pi_k, Z_k) = \Pi^\circ_k - c(H, A, Z_k)$

Again, market data provide two pieces of information about these iso-profit offer functions. At each supplier's equilibrium, the value of the offer function must equal the value of the hedonic function ($\Omega = p$) and the derivatives of the cost function must equal the derivatives of the hedonic function ($\partial \Omega / \partial a_i = \partial p / \partial a_i$).

Each observation on the housing amenity package reveals a supplier's willingness to offer a private amenity level a_i for sale and the supplier's marginal willingness to supply an additional unit of a_i.

EMPIRICAL APPROACHES

Since these theoretical notions have been advanced and especially since the influential work of Rosen [1974], there has been an explosion of applications and empirical attempts to evaluate consumers' willingness to pay for amenities. Many of these are only loosely related to the foregoing theoretical treatment and many make implicit assumptions about the equilibrium process. This section reviews some of this work.

Early Studies

The earliest empirical applications of this framework for the evaluation of amenities were in analyses of air pollution (Ridker [1967], Ridker and Henning [1967]) and residential "blight" (Kain and Quigley [1970a, 1970b]). In these applications, regression models of the form of (1) were estimated using the average rents and housing values by census tract in a city or using samples of individual rental and owner-occupied dwellings. At the individual level, the willingness to pay Δ for an improvement in amenity a_1 from a_1^* to a_1^{**} was measured by the hedonic relation directly as

(10) $\Delta = p(H, [a_1^*, a_2, . . . , a_J]) - p(H, [a_1^{**}, a_2, . . . , a_J])$.

The market benefit to improved neighborhood air quality from a_1^* to a_1^{**} was computed as the sum of these quantities across the dwellings in the neighborhood.

As the analysis in the previous section indicates, this procedure is in general incorrect, and will overestimate consumers' willingness to pay for amenities. In fact, there is only one special case in which the procedure in (10) would yield accurate measurements of the benefits, namely if all households within the market were identical. In this special case, the hedonic function (1) and the willingness to pay function (9) would coincide, and (10) would provide an exact measure of benefits of some program to each housing consumer.

The most charitable interpretation of these early studies is that they could be used to identify correctly each household's willingness to pay for a marginal improvement in amenity (see Freeman [1974] or Small [1975] for details).

Despite these serious shortcomings, the flawed procedure outlined in (10) has been used in a variety of recent papers to estimate households' willingness to pay for public beaches, access, aircraft noise, etc. (These recent studies are noted by Follain and Jimenez [1985]).

Simultaneous Estimation

The original paper explicating the relationship between bid and offer functions and the price relationship (Rosen [1974]) includes an explicit recommendation for the econometric estimation of bid and offer functions: namely to estimate (1), differentiate it, and use the marginal prices to estimate equations 6a, 6b, 6a' and 6b' simultaneously. The suggestion is the estimation of

$$\rho\lambda = W(H, A, y, V_\lambda)$$

(11) $\lambda = 1, 2, \ldots, I + J$

$$\rho\lambda = \omega(H, A, Z_\lambda)$$

where ρ is an estimate of the marginal price obtained from (1) and (2), and V_λ and Z_λ are the identifying taste or cost parameters. Subject to this "garden variety" identification problem (in Rosen's terminology), estimation of $2(I + J)$ simultaneous equations will yield parameters of the compensated demand and offer functions.

There are apparently only two papers which have implemented this strategy using housing market information and which have presented simultaneous estimates of supply and demand parameters. Witte *et al* [1979] present a six-equation system estimating bid and offer curves for dwelling quality, dwelling size, and lot size, conditional upon prior estimation of the hedonic price function. Nelson [1978] presents estimates of a two-equation system measuring the compensated demand and the supply of air quality. The latter study is directly intended to provide estimates of the willingness to pay for environmental improvement. Three related issues arise in the estimation of the system described in (11).

The first involves the garden variety identification problem and the legitimacy of including some taste variables in the household bid for one or the other components of housing. It is quite difficult to specify the set of variables which identify the separate components of housing demand, say dwelling unit quality and neighborhood amenities.

The second derives from the prior estimation of the price relationship and the computation of its derivative. Since the dependent variable is computed from the H and A vectors via the regression, the only new information that arises from the computation of ρ is attributable to its non-linear functional form. For at least some functional forms, Brown and Rosen [1982] have shown that the system is unidentified.[3]

The third important issue is also inherent in the underlying methodology of the Rosen proposal. A comparison of W in equation (11) with the equation for willingness to pay, i.e., equation (9), indicates that it is misspecified. The marginal bid W for any amenity depends upon the consumption of housing (H) and amenity (A) attributes as well as "other goods". The latter term is income minus housing expenditures, y-P, not simply income, y. Thus as explicated by Epple [1984] in a very careful paper, estimation of (11) by simultaneous equation methods will yield inconsistent parameters of the willingness to pay function, at least if willingness to pay is defined as the compensating Hicksian variation.

These complications quite naturally suggest one approach to estimating the bid and offer curves which does not depend upon prior estimation of the hedonic price function or upon the differentiability of that function. As noted in a paper Son [1986], the bid and offer relations could be inferred from

$$P = W(H, A, y-P, V)$$
(12)
$$P = \Omega(H, A, Z)$$

subject to

$$\frac{\partial W}{\partial h_i} = \partial \Omega / \partial h_i \qquad\qquad i = 1, 2, \ldots, I$$

$$\frac{\partial W}{\partial a_j} = \partial \Omega / \partial h_j \qquad\qquad j = 1, 2, \ldots, J.$$

The two equation system in (12) could be estimated, consistently at least, subject to the coefficient restrictions noted by standard simultaneous equation methods.[4]

Fixed Supply Approaches

As noted in the introduction, a great many of the amenities which are important components of housing choice are not supplied competitively. For most of these components of housing, it may be quite sensible to view their supply as fixed according to some distribution within a housing market and as exogenous to any individual housing supplier or consumer. This assumption greatly simplifies the theoretical structure which must be imposed in order to evaluate consumers' willingness to pay for amenities, and may provide an adequate description of housing supplier behavior, at least when the public sector is the supplier.

Harrison and Rubinfeld [1978] use this simplified structure to estimate the willingness to pay for clean air. Papers by McDougal [1976] and Linneman [1980] use similar techniques to estimate consumers' willingness to pay for the services provided to dwellings by local government. The structure of these analyses is exemplified by the Harrison-Rubinfeld analysis of air pollution.

The authors estimate equation (1) from a sample of dwelling units, their characteristics, their sale prices, and the level of local air quality. They then postulate an inverse demand function of the form of equation (3), relating the level of air quality experienced by an individual household to its income and to the marginal price of air quality faced by that household. This equation is estimated by ordinary least squares on the assumption that air quality is inelastically suppled to each dwelling in the sample, and the authors include income (rather than income minus expenditures) in the model.

As noted above, the inclusion of y rather than y-P in the demand curve means that it cannot be interpreted as the compensated demand curve for air quality unless the marginal utility of money is constant. Also, as pointed out by Epple [1984], the assumption that supply is inelastic at each point is quite strong. If either condition, variable marginal utility of money or the supply assumption, is not met then the simple estimation strategy is inadequate.

Some of these objections are overcome if the form of utility function is specified directly. In that case, for a specific functional form the inverse of equation (3), i.e.,

$$(3') \; \rho_{a_j} = \mathrm{MRS}_{a_j, \; y - P} \qquad j = 1, 2, \ldots, J$$

can be estimated by an instrumental procedure. For at least several rather general utility functions (see Quigley [1982]), this procedure can be used to estimate the willingness to pay for amenities in a consistent manner.

For example if the utility function is of the generalized CES form

$$(13)\ U = [\Sigma \alpha_i h_i^{\beta_i} + \Sigma \alpha_j a_j^{\beta_j} + x^\epsilon]^{\psi}$$

then (3′) reduces to

$$(3'')\ \rho_{a_j} = (\alpha_j \beta_j / \epsilon)_{a_j}^{\beta_j - 1} [y - P]^{1 - \epsilon}$$

and the parameters are clearly estimable. The estimation of consumer demand under these conditions insures that the empirical results do satisfy the logical postulates of consumer choice. In constrast, the less well specified demand relationship in equation (3) need not satisfy this "integrability condition". Note, however, that the estimation of equation (3′) does depend upon the non-linearity of the market price function to achieve identification.

This approach is clearly related to the bid rent analyses undertaken by Wheaton [1977]. For example if (13) is the form of the utility function, then

$$(14)\ y - P = (U^{o\ 1/\phi} - \Sigma \alpha_i h_i^{\beta_i} - \Sigma \alpha_j a_j^{\beta_j})^{1/\epsilon},$$

which is, in principle, estimable, at least for samples of households with identical incomes or tastes. The Wheaton analysis is thus analogous to the proposal by Son [1986] under the assumption of a fixed supply of amenity.

PRACTICAL IMPLEMENTATION

As the foregoing discussion indicates, there has been a remarkable development during the past two decades in methodologies for estimating the market benefits of a broad variety of the housing-related amenities enjoyed in urban areas. This explosion of methodological research and empirical analysis has been fueled by advances in social scientific theory and statistical methodology, and by declines in the real costs of computation.

The economics and planning literature provides a rich set of substantive examples, not only of consumers' willingness to pay for environmental improvement, including clean air and a quiet milieu, but also for increased public safety, better schools, neighborhood quality, parks and recreational opportunities. It is not yet so clear, however, that these techniques have been used by planners and analysts in their evaluations of alternative policies for improving the housing and residential conditions of urban life. Definitive evidence on this is difficult to obtain, but I am aware of relatively few cases in which empirical analyses based upon these recent developments have been decisive, or even influential.

From one perspective, of course, this may be expected. The path from theoretical advance in economics to routine application has always been long, even when the theoretical advances could be shown to be privately profitable (e.g., linear programming). In cases where the profit is purely social, that is, measured in terms of a better balance between government expenditures and citizen preferences, the incentives for diffusion are certainly weaker.

This is not to imply that the data underlying conclusions about willingness to pay for externalities in the housing market has not been scrutinized professionally. On the contrary, it appears that these data and methodologies have been analyzed and picked over by other professionals to a rather remarkable extent. For example, the housing market data gathered and analyzed by Kain and Quigley [1970a, 1970b, 1975] have been reanalyzed, using more general models, by Galster [1977, 1979] and by Yinger [1978]. The housing market data gathered and analyzed by Harrison and Rubinfeld [1978] has been reexamined using more general statistical models in a recent monograph (Belsley, *et al* [1980]). This body of data and the problems of market valuation and willingness to pay has also been used quite recently to illustrate more powerful statistical optimization procedures, for example the alternating conditional expectation (ACE) model (see Brieman and Friedman [1985]).

These extensive investigations have not been undertaken, however, to evaluate the benefits of any real public program or to analyze the choices facing any public decision maker. Rather, they have been purely scientific and methodological investigations - - by mathematical statisticians, planners, economists and engineers - - whose purpose is to create better analytical tools.

These techniques are not yet diffused among practitioners and analysts. The abstraction of the willingness-to-pay argument may be too great, especially when the alternative in many instances is a physical damage function. Urban air quality is a good example. Statistical analyses relating morbidity or lost productivity to pollution (e.g., Lave and Seskin [1970], Mendelsohn and Orcutt [1979]) are easily motivated and readily interpreted, even though they are based upon extremely strong assumptions and even though the estimates appear to be quite fragile (see Atkinson, Crocker, and Murdock [1985]). In contrast, the behavioral assumptions imbedded in the willingness-to-pay measures reviewed here are susceptible to caricature (e.g., the assumption of purposeful behavior can be castigated as a requirement for "perfect" information in "perfect" markets, etc.).

The distinction between damage-based and willingness-to-pay based benefit measures would not be important if estimates derived from such approaches were similar. They are not. Theory predicts that benefits calculated as willingness-to-pay would be larger than damage-based benefits; empirical evidence suggests that they are larger by a factor of ten (Gerking and Schultze [1981]).

Rigorous benefit cost analyses are sometimes discounted because they quantify the obvious fact that the rich are better prepared to pay for almost anything than the poor. Indeed for most of the housing amentities discussed in this paper, the consumer demand estimates suggest an income elastic demand. In these cases, however, the practical implication of willingness to pay is somewhat different. The results of these analyses suggest that improved housing amenities could be provided to urban residents and financed by progressive taxes and that this would be a pareto improvement.

This is one of a precious few cases in which the analyst or planner evaluating public choices can simultaneously apply relatively innovative methodological techniques, conduct rigorous and hard-nosed dollar- (or kronor-) based measurement of intangible benefits, and be on the side of the angels when it comes to distributional considerations.

I think we should spread the word.

NOTES

1) A more extensive review of studies which have been directed towards the demand for housing attributes has recently been published by Follain and Jimenez [1985]. Besides the difference in emphasis, at some points there is a difference in interpretation between my analysis and that provided by Follain and Jimenez. Despite the extensive bibliography in the Follain-Jimenez paper (some 67 papers are listed in the bibliography), this paper notes some 33 additional research efforts devoted to valuing the externalities of housing. By any standard, the empirical work on these related topics has been prodigious.

2) Implicit in this statement of the problem and in all the empirical analyses derived from it is an assumption that there is sufficient variation in each amenity so that the p function is continuous with continuous first and second derivatives. (See Harrison and Rubinfeld [1978] for a discussion). The analysis also assumes that the housing market is "open" in the sense that change in amenity will induce immigration sufficient to keep utility levels exogenous. (See Quigley [1986] for an investigation of more complicated models in which housing markets are "closed"). The analysis also assumes that the market is in temporary equilibrium and, in particular, that the sizes of residential sites are not variable. (See Scotchmer [1985] for a discussion).

3) For example, suppose the hedonic function quadratic, as assumed by Witte *et al* [1979]. Then its derivative will be linear in the elements of H and A, and this will not permit estimation of (11) as a linear equation system.

4) Again, this is subject to the caveat noted by Brown and Rosen [1982]. The system is certainly not identifiable for any arbitrary functional forms for W and Ω.

REFERENCES

Abelson, P.W. (1979) "Property Prices and the Value of Amenities", *Journal of Environmental Economics and Management* 6: 11–28.

Abelson, P.W. and A. Markandya (1985) "The Interpretation of Capitalized Hedonic Prices in a Dynamic Environment", *Journal of Environmental Economics and Management* 12: 195–206.

Anas, A. and S.J. Eum (1984) "Hedonic Analysis of a Housing Market in Disequilibrium", *Journal of Urban Economics* 15: 87–106.

Anderson, J.E. (1985) "On Testing the Convexity of Hedonic Price Functions", *Journal of Urban Economics* 18: 334–337.

Anderson, R.J. and T. Crocker (1971) "Air Pollution and Residential Property Values", *Urban Studies* 8: 171–180.

(1972) "Air Pollution and Property Values: A Reply", *Review of Economics and Statistics* 54: 470–473.

Bayless, M. (1982) "Measuring the Benefits of Air Quality Improvements: A Hedonic Salary Approach", *Journal of Environmental Economics and Management* 9: 81–99.

Belsley, D. A., E. Kuh and Welsch, E. (1980) *Regression Diagnostics,* New York: John Wiley and Sons.

Blomquist, G. and L. Worley (1981) "Hedonic Prices, Demands for Urban Housing Amenities, and Benefit Estimates", *Journal of Urban Economics* 9: 212–221.

Bohm, P. (1979) "Estimating Willingness to Pay: Why and How?" *Scandinavian Journal of Economics* 81: 142–153.

Brieman, L. and J.H. Friedman (1985) "Estimating Optimal Transformations for Multiple Regression and Correlation", *Journal of the American Statistical Association* 80: 580–598.

Brookshire, D., M. Thayer, W. Schultze, and R. d'Arge (1982) "Valuing Public Goods: A Comparison of Survey and Hedonic Approaches", *American Economic Review* 72: 165–177.

Brown, J.N., and H.S. Rosen (1982) "On the Estimation of Structural Hedonic Price Models", *Econometrica* 50: 765–768.

Cassel, E., and R. Mendelsohn (1985) "The Choice of Functional Forms for Hedonic Price Equations: Comment", *Journal of Urban Economics* 18: 135–142.

Chinloy, P. (1979) "Hedonic Price and Depreciation Indexes for Residential Housing Again", *Journal of Urban Economics* 6: 272–273.

Clemmer, R.B. (1984) "Measuring Welfare Effects of In-Kind Transfers", *Journal of Urban Economics* 15: 45–65.

Cobb, S.A. (1977) "Site Rent, Air Quality, and the Demand for Amenities", *Journal of Environmental Economics and Management* 4: 214–218.

Cobb, S.A. (1984) "The Impact of Site Characteristics on Housing Cost Estimates", *Journal of Urban Economics* 15: 26–45.

Courant, P.N., and D.L. Rubinfeld (1978) "On the Measurement of Benefits in an Urban Context: Some General Equilibrium Issues", *Journal of Urban Economics* 5: 346–356.

Cropper, M.L., and A.S. Arriga-Salinas (1980) "Inter-city Wage Differentials and the Value of Air Quality", *Journal of Urban Economics* 8: 236–254.

Dale-Johnson, D. (1982) "An Alternative Approach to Housing Market Segmentation Using Hedonic Price Data", *Journal of Urban Economics* 11: 311–332.

Edlefsen, L.E. (1981) "The Comparative Statics of Hedonic Price Functions and Other Nonlinear Constraints", *Econometrica* 49: 1501–1520.

Ellickson, B. (1981) "An Alternative Test of the Hedonic Theory of Housing Markets", *Journal of Urban Economics* 9: 56–79.

Fisher, A. (1985) "The Hedonic Price Method for Valuing Environmental Resources: An Overview", mimeo.

Flowerdew, A.D.J. (1972) "The Cost of Airport Noise", *The Statistician* 21: 31–46.

Follain, J.R. and E. Jimenez (1985) "Estimating the Demand for Housing Characteristics: Survey and Critique", *Regional Science and Urban Economics* 15: 77–108.

Frankel, M. (1985) "Amenity Changes, Property Values, and Hedonic Prices in a Closed City", *Journal of Environmental Economics and Management* 12: 117–131.

Freeman, A.M. (1979) "Hedonic Prices, Property Values and Measuring Environmental Benefits: A Survey of the Issues", *Scandinavian Journal of Economics* 81: 154–173.

(1979) *The Benefits of Environmental Improvement: Theory and Practice*, Baltimore, MD: Johns Hopkins University Press for Resources for the Future, Inc.

(1979) "The Hedonic Approach to Measuring Demand for Neighborhood Characteristics", pp. 193–216 in D. Segal, (ed.), *The Economics of Neighborhood.* New York: Academic Press.

(1974) "On Estimating Air Pollution Control Benefits From Land Value Studies", *Journal of Environmental Economics and Management* 1: 74–83.

Galster, G.C. (1977) "A Bid-Rent Analysis of Housing Market Discrimination", *American Economic Review* 67: 144–155.

(1979) "Interracial Differences in Housing Preferences", *Regional Science Perspectives* 9: 1–17.

Gerber, R. (1985) "Existence and Description of Housing Market Equilibrium", *Regional Science and Urban Economics* 15: 383–401.

Goodman, A.C. (1978) "Hedonic Prices, Price Indices and Housing Markets", *Journal of Urban Economics* 5: 471–484.

Goodman, A.C., and Kawai, M. (1982) "Permanent Income, Hedonic Prices, and Demand for Housing: New Evidence", *Journal of Urban Economics* 12: 214–237.

Goodwin, S.A. (1977) "Measuring the Value of Housing Quality: A Note", *Journal of Regional Science* 17: 107–115.

Griliches, Z. (1961) "Hedonic Price Indexes for Automobiles: An Econometric Analysis of Quality Change", in *Price Statistics of the Federal Government*. Washington, DC: U.S. Government Printing Office.

Halvorsen, R., and H.O. Pollakowski (1981) "Choice of Functional Form for Hedonic Price Equations", *Journal of Urban Economics* 10: 37–49.

Harrison, D. Jr., and D.L. Rubinfeld (1978) "Hedonic Housing Prices and the Demand for Clean Air", *Journal of Environmental Economics and Management* 5: 81–102.

(1978) "The Distribution of Benefits from Improvements in Urban Air Quality", *Journal of Environmental Economics and Management* 5: 313–332.

Hausman, J.A. (1981) "Exact Consumer's Surplus and Deadweight Loss", *American Economic Review* 71: 662–676.

(1985) "The Econometrics of Nonlinear Budget Sets", *Econometrica* 53: 1255–1282.

Horowitz, J. (1984) "Identification and Stochastic Specification in Rosen's Hedonic Price Model", University of Iowa, mimeo.

Henderson, J.V. (1982) "Evaluating Consumer Amenities and Inter-regional Welfare Differences", *Journal of Urban Economics* 11: 32–59.

Jud, D., and J. Watts (1980) "Schools and Housing Value", *Land Economics* 57: 459–470.

Kain, J.F., and J.M. Quigley (1970a) "Measuring the Value of Housing Quality", *Journal of the American Statistical Association* 65: 532–548.

(1970b) "Evaluating the Quality of the Residential Environment", *Environment and Planning* 2: 23–32.

(1975) *Housing Markets and Racial Discrimination*. New York: Columbia University Press.

Kaufman, D., and J.M. Quigley "The Consumption Benefits of Investment in Urban Infrastructure", *Journal of Development Economics* (forthcoming).

Kanemoto, Y., and R. Makamura "A New Approach to the Estimation of Structural Equations in Hedonic Models", *Journal of Urban Economics* (forthcoming).

Kneese, A.V., and B.T. Boser (1972) *Environmental Quality Analysis: Theory and Method in the Social Sciences.* Baltimore, MD: The Johns Hopkins Press for Resources for the Future.

Lerman, S., and C.R. Kern (1983) "Hedonic Theory, Bid Rents, and Willingness-to-Pay: Some Extensions of Ellickson's Results", *Journal of Urban Economics* 13: 358–363.

Lind, R.C. (1973) "Spatial Equilibrium, the Theory of Rents, and the Management of Benefits from Public Programs", *Quarterly Journal of Economics* 84: 188–207.

Linneman, P. (1980) "Some Empirical Results on the Nature of the Hedonic Price Function for the Urban Housing Market", *Journal of Urban Economics* 8: 47–68.

(1981) "The Demand for Residence Site Characteristics", *Journal of Urban Economics* 9: 129–148.

Lucas, R. (1974) " Hedonic Price Functions", *Economic Inquiry* 8: 157–177.

Mark, J.H. (1980) "A Preference Approach to Measuring the Impact of Environmental Externalitites", *Land Economics* 56: 103–116.

McMillan, M.L. (1979) "Estimates of Households' Preferences for Environmental Quality and Other Housing Characteristics from a System of Demand Equations", *Scandinavian Journal of Economics* 81: 174–187.

Mieszkowski, P., and A.M. Saper (1978) "An Estimate of the Effects of Airport Noise on Property Values", *Journal of Urban Economics* 5: 425–440.

Muellbauer, J. (1974) "Household Production Theory, Quality, and the 'Hedonic Technique' ", *American Economic Review*: 977–994.

Murray, M.P. (1978) "Hedonic Prices and Composite Commodities", *Journal of Urban Economics* 5: 188–197.

(1983) "Mythical Demands and Mythical Supplies for Proper Estimation of Rosen's Hedonic Price Model", *Journal of Urban Economics* 14: 327–337

Mäler, K.-G. (1977) "A Note on the Use of Property Values in Estimating Marginal Willingness to Pay for Environmental Quality", *Journal of Environmental Economics and Management* 4: 355–369.

Nelson, J.P. (1979) "Airport Noise, Location Rent, and the Market for Residential Amenities", *Journal of Environmental Economics and Management* 6: 320–331.

(1978) "Residential Choice, Hedonic Prices, and the Demand for Urban Air Quality", *Journal of Urban Economics* 5: 357–369.

O'Byrne, P., J.P. Nelson., and J.J. Seneca (1985) "Housing Values, Census Estimates, Disequilibrium, and the Environmental Cost of Airport Noise: A Case Study of Atlanta", *Journal of Environmental Economics and Management* 12: 169–178.

Ostro, B.D. (1985) "The Effects of Air Pollution on Work Loss and Morbidity", *Journal of Environmental Economics and Management* 10: 371–382.

Palmquist, R.B. (1979) "Hedonic Price and Depreciation Indexes for Residential Housing: A Comment", *Journal of Urban Economics* 6: 267–271.

(1982) "Measuring Environmental Effects on Property Values Without Hedonic Regressions", *Journal of Urban Economics* 11: 333–347.

Phlips, L. (1974) *Applied Consumption Analysis.* Amsterdam: North-Holland Publishing Company.

Polinsky, A.M., and D.R. Rubinfeld (1977) "Property Values and the Benefits of Environmental Improvement", 154–180 in London W. (ed.), *Public Economics and the Quality of Life,* Johns Hopkins University Press.

Portney, P. (1981) "Housing Prices, Health Effects and Valuing Reductions in Risk of Death", *Journal of Environmental Economics and Management* 8: 72–78.

Quigley, J.M. (1982) "Nonlinear Budget Constraints and Consumer Demand: An Application to Public Programs for Residential Housing", *Journal of Urban Economics* 12: 177–201.

(1986) "The Evaluation of Complex Urban Policies", *Regional Science and Urban Economics* 16: 32–42.

Ridker, R.G. (1967) *Economic Cost of Air Pollution: Studies in Measurement.* New York: Praeger.

Ridker, R.G., and J.A. Henning (1967) "The Determinants of Residential Property Value with Special Reference to Air Pollution", *Review of Economics and Statistics* 49: 246–255.

Rosen, S. (1974) "Hedonic Prices and Implicit Markets: Product Differentiation in Pure Competition", *Journal of Political Economy* 82: 34–55.

Rowe, R.D., C. d'Arge, and D.S. Brookshire (1980) "An Experiment on the Economic Value of Visibility", *Journal of Environmental Economics and Management* 7: 1–19.

Schnare, A. (1973) "An Empirical Analysis of the Dimensions of Neighborhood Quality." Unpublished Ph.D. Dissertation, Harvard University.

Schulze, W., R. d'Arge, and D. Brookshire (1981) "Valuing Environmental Commodities: Some Recent Experiments", *Land Economics:* 151–172.

Scotchmer, S. (1985) "Hedonic Prices and Cost/Benefit Analysis", *Journal of Economic Theory* 37: 55–75.

Small, K. (1975) "Air Pollution and Property Values: Further Comment", *Review of Economics and Statistics* 57: 105–107.

Smith, B.A. (1978) "Measuring the Value of Urban Amenities", *Journal of Urban Economics* 5: 370–387.

Smith, V.K. (1983) "The Role of Site and Job Characteristics in Hedonic Wage Models", *Journal of Urban Economics* 13: 296–321.

Smith, V. (1979) "An Experimental Comparison of Three Public Good Decision Mechanisms", *Scandinavian Journal of Economics* 81: 198–215.

Son, J.Y. (1986) "Composite Good Market Models and Welfare Calculations." University of California, Berkeley, mimeo.

Tinbergen, J. (1956) "On The Theory of Income Distribution", *Weltwirschafthiches Archive* 77: 10–31.

Wieand, K.F. (1973) "Air Pollution and Property Values: A Study of the St. Louis Area", *Journal of Regional Science* 13: 91–93.

Williams, H.E. (1977) "Constraints of Theory and Practice in the Evaluation of Environmental Quality" *Urban Studies* 14: 365–369.

Witte, A., H. Sumka., and H. Erekson (1979) "An Estimate of a Structural Hedonic Price Model of the Housing Market: An Application of Rosen's Theory of Implicit Markets", *Econometrica* 47: 1151–1173.

Yinger, J.M. (1978) "The Black-White Price Differential in Housing: Some Further Evidence", *Land Economics* 54: 187–206.

The Economic Behavior of the Elderly in Housing Markets

$71 - 101$

U.S.
9320
9180

Raymond J. Struyk, The Urban Institute,
Washington, USA

This paper singles out one group of households — those headed by a person over the age of 64 -- for analysis of their housing consumption and the ways in which they adjust their housing in response to changes in their economic and demographic circumstances. One might well ask why it is appropriate to focus on this particular group at a conference dealing with broad issues of the economics of housing and housing policies at the national level.

There are several reasons why the housing of the elderly should command our attention, even in the present context. The first is that the elderly constitute a large and growing share of the population. Table 1 shows the percentage of the population in Europe, North America, and Japan at least 65 years of age in 1970, 1985, and projected to 2020. By

Table 1. Percentage of Population over Age 65 for Selected Regions and Japan 1970–2020.

	1970	1985	2020	Change 1970–2020
Eastern Europe	10.4	10.9	15.7	5.3
Northern Europe	12.7	14.8	17.7	5.0
Southern Europe	9.8	11.7	16.9	7.1
Western Europe	12.8	13.1	18.5	5.7
Northern America[a]	9.7	10.8	14.3	4.6
Japan	7.1	9.7	20.0	12.9
World Total	5.5	5.8	8.3	2.8

[a] Canada and the United States.

Source: United Nations, Department of International Economic and Social Affairs, *Demographic Indicators of Countries: Estimates and Projections Assessed in 1980* (New York: Author, document ST/ESA/SER.A/82, 1982), Annex II, various tables.

the last year, the elderly will account for almost one person in five in most of these areas. Generally, this represents an increase of about five percentage points over the fifty-year period; in Japan the increase is a staggering 13 percentage points. Moreover, the elderly will represent an even larger share of the households, since households headed by an elderly person are typically considerably smaller than other households. In the United States by the end of this period, the elderly will head nearly three out of every ten households.

With the elderly forming such a large share of households, the policy analyst has to know if their behavior in the housing market differs from that of other households if housing assistance programs are to be efficiently designed. Indeed, the behavior of this group can be expected to differ significantly from that of their younger counterparts. It seems likely that the housing and neighborhood environment should be of greater importance to the elderly than to other households because of the greater proportion of time the elderly spend at home and in their immediate neighborhoods. Another distinguishing characteristic of the housing consumption of the elderly is the frequent changes in the determinants of the optimal set or bundle of housing services that they would prefer to consume. From numerous studies of housing demand, we know that the preferred set depends on such factors as income level and asset holdings, household size and composition, and the health status of its members.

Among the elderly, these determinants can be expected to change, sometimes in rapid succession. One's spouse may die, functional mobility may become impaired, or income may be reduced due to death of a spouse or by the inflationary erosion of the value of some assets.[1] How each of these changes affects housing demand depends, of course, on the broader family environment. The onset of activity limitations for the male in a husband—wife household will have little effect, if the spouse is able to effectively compensate for the housekeeping functions performed by her husband and to attend to his now greater needs without undue strain. The onset of such limitations to someone living alone, however, may require the installation of special features -- grab bars, specialized sink hardware, and so forth -- and some personal assistance to make continued independent living feasible.

The determinants of the preferred bundle of housing services interact powerfully with another characteristic of the elderly: their lower propensity to make major housing adjustments. The low average mobility rates of the elderly are well known. These reflect the strong social ties and sense of place attachment built up over the course of decades which the elderly are understandably loath to disturb -- this phenomenon is termed "habit formation" by economists. Hence, adjustments are generally delayed and are often gradual. Homeowners in large dwellings who cannot afford to consume so much housing, may reduce maintenance or postpone making needed replacements. Renters in similar circumstances may continue to live in a unit, but only at the cost of spending an inordinate share of their incomes to do so.

A final aspect of the elderly's housing is that the definition of "housing" is broader than that typically used. For the elderly one must ask if the dwelling and its associated neighborhood are usable by the occupant. Beyond knowing that the unit is equipped with a serviceable bathtub and hot and cold water, one must know whether or not the members of the household can use it -- completely independently, with special equipment, or with personal assistance. An upstairs bedroom is of little use if its intended nocturnal occupant is incapable of negotiating the stairs.

The elderly also command our attention because as a group they are important in the policy arena. At least in the United States, and on the basis of limited information I believe elsewhere as well, they exhibit a higher incidence of the traditional housing problems of occupancy of deficient units and spending an "excessive" share of their income on housing. Hence, they have been the target of much attention by the housing ministries. In addition, however, the linkage between the provision of long-term care and the housing circumstances will grow in importance as the number of households headed by very old persons increases. In light of the great expense of providing care in institutions, developing alternative settings in which the housing environment is adjusted to facilitate continued independent living will be essential as a matter of national budget imperatives.

Finally, the potential for intergenerational conflict between young and old may emerge in the housing arena as well as in the broader sphere of income policies. For example, the legitimate aspirations of younger households to own their homes raises issues, concerning the extent to which older persons are occupying excessively large units. As discussed below, defining the self-interest of the young on this question is quite complex.

This paper examines the elderly in housing markets from three different perspectives, relying primarily on data from the United States. First, we look at the housing consumption of the elderly, concentrating on a few selected indicators. Second, we present information on the ways and frequency with which the elderly make changes to the bundle of housing services that they consume. In both of these sections, we use non-elderly households as a basis of comparison. The last section briefly discusses several prominent housing policy issues involving the elderly.

THE ELDERLY AND THEIR HOUSING IN THE UNITED STATES

This section focuses on two areas: the housing and housing-related problems that the elderly currently exhibit in the United States, and the extent to which the elderly in this country are "over housed".

Incidence of "Over Housing"

The question of whether a substantial group of the elderly are living in excessively large units has come to the fore in the United States in recent years. It is driven both by concern for the elderly occupants -- viewed as often occupying units that are a burden for them to properly maintain and to which they must allocate a large share of their income -- and by the knowledge that many of these homes could bee inhabited by larger families who, under current demand and supply conditions, cannot afford to purchase a home.[2] The issue of underutilization is assumed to emerge when children have left home or other household members have been lost through death or illness, but the remaining members stay in units they have occupied for many years.

The overall stake of younger households in shifting the elderly out of these units is, however, rather ambiguous. Since recent research has shown that (a) the elderly do not follow a life-cycle consumption pattern but bequest substantial sums to their children (Bernheim et al., 1985) and (b) home equity is a large portion of total assets, then relocating the elderly might lead to dissaving and small bequests. In any event, Lane and Feins (1985) have recently examined the extent of underutilization. The indicator of utilization used was the number of non-sleeping rooms (excluding bathrooms) plus the number of sleeping rooms in the unit compared to the number of persons in the household. They use this indicator to develop three standards of utilization: no underutilization, modest underutilization, and underutilization.[3]

In 1980, 35 percent of all elderly households were underutilizing their housing space and another 13 percent were characterized as modestly underutilizing their space.[4] A very large number of households is involved: 8.5 million. Households underutilizing their housing space have several distinct attributes: they are overwhelmingly homeowners (91 percent); half are persons living alone; half have lived in their homes more than 20 years; and 36 percent occupy units having seven or more rooms (Lane and Feins, 1985, Table 2).

This degree of underutilization obviously reflects the fact that the elderly on average are not adjusting their housing as they experience economic and demographic changes. In the next section we address the general question of housing adjustments.

Housing and Housing-related Needs

In considering the housing needs of the elderly it is useful to make the distinction between the traditional "housing problems" and the needs which arise from health problems and activity limitations. The traditional housing problems (called *dwelling-specific* problems hereafter) include deficiencies to the dwelling, spending an excessive share of income on housing, and living in over-crowded conditions. These are problems which can be measured in fairly straightforward ways and whose definition does not generally have a special dimension for the elderly.

Housing problems associated with activity limitations -- hereafter called *dwelling-use* problems -- are much less precisely defined. Indeed, activity limitations, used here as a shorthand label for the larger set of health-related problems, are better thought of as an indicator of a *potential* housing problem, since such problems can be effectively offset through personal help or unit modifications.[5] Thus, in trying to assemble counts of the number of elderly with housing-related problems, one must combine reasonably "hard" estimates of the traditional dwelling-specific problems with less direct, "softer" estimates of dwelling-use problems. Also difficult --this time because of data limitations -- is calculating the joint occurrence of dwelling-specific and supportive service needs.

In general, we find that the patterns of dwelling-specific and dwelling-use needs are quite different. Whereas dwelling-specific problems are strongly income-related and little associated with age, dwelling-use problems are related to age and physical impairments but not particularly to income.

Dwelling-specific Needs. Our focus here is on the incidence of physical deficiencies and excessive housing expenditure burdens in 1979. (See Table 2 for figures; definitions of these needs are consistent with those used by the government and they are listed in Annex A.) Moreover, we limit the population considered to those households *not* then participating in federal or state housing programs -- some 14.0 million elderly-headed households.

To interpret some of the figures in Table 2, knowing the distribution of households by tenure and by poverty status is essential. Table 3 provides this orientation. The tenure characteristics are generally familiar; relatively few elderly households are renters and the vast majority of elderly owners do not have mortgages. More non-elderly are renters and most homeowners still have mortgage debt. Interestingly, the incidence of poverty among renters is about the same for the elderly and non-elderly (about 27 percent), while among homeowners, the incidence of poverty is higher for the elderly (about 15 percent vs. 5 percent). It is worth noting that gross income

Table 2. Incidence of Housing Deficiencies and Excess Expenditures – 1979[a]

	Physically Deficient %	Excess Expenditures %	Deficient and Excess Expenditures %
Non-elderly			
Total	7.6	15.2	2.1
Renters	13.2	33.4	5.3
Owners w/Mortgage	3.1	7.9	0.5
Owners w/out	7.9	1.7	0.3
In Poverty	26.3	70.8	16.6
Renters	28.7	86.5	22.5
Owners w/Mortgage	17.1	73.2	10.1
Owners w/out	26.2	18.2	3.0
Elderly (65+)			
Total	11.5	18.4	2.4
Renters	17.2	55.3	7.8
Owners w/Mortgage	6.5	25.3	2.9
Owners w/out	10.1	4.5	0.4
In Poverty	29.0	41.0	8.7
Renters	31.0	74.9	17.7
Owners w/Mortgage	33.6	74.9	21.0
Owners w/out	27.4	17.7	2.3
Renters[b]			
Metro	12.1	58.8	6.9
Non-Metro Urban	21.6	54.6	7.3
Non-Metro Rural	40.1	37.3	13.3
Black	46.0	57.8	20.9
Other	13.3	55.0	6.0
Owners w/Mortgage[b]			
Metro	4.3	25.7	1.3
Non-Metro Urban	8.4	18.9	5.8
Non-Metro Rural	14.2	29.6	7.2
Black	24.7	44.3	12.5
Other	3.8	22.6	1.6
Owners w/out[b]			
Metro	6.8	5.1	0.4
Non-Metro Urban	8.4	4.4	0.0
Non-Metro Rural	18.3	3.4	0.8
Black	36.5	7.2	2.0
Other	8.3	4.4	0.3

[a] Only unassisted households are included in these figures; see Annex A for definitions.

[b] Elderly-headed households only.

Source: R. Struyk and M. Turner (1984), Table 3.

Table 3. Tenure Distribution and Incidence of Poverty by Tenure Status and Age of Household Head in 1979[a]

	Renters %	Owners with Mortgages %	Owners without Mortgages %	Total %
All Households				
Elderly	24	8	68	100
Non-elderly	34	43	23	100
Share of Tenure Group in Poverty				
Elderly	28	12	17	19
Non-elderly	26	3	8	9

[a] Only households not receiving housing assistance are included.
Source: Tabulations of Annual Housing Survey data.

is used in these and other calculations; hence, differences in the treatment of the elderly and non-elderly under the federal income tax system are not properly reflected. These differences increase the disposable income of the elderly compared to the non-elderly.

From the figures in Table 2, a fairly clear ranking emerges among the elderly running from those having the worst housing situation to those having the best. Impoverished renters and impoverished owners with mortgages are at the low end and non-poverty owners with mortgages and without mortgages are at the higher end. Differences by location exhibit a familiar pattern, with the incidence of deficiencies rising steadily as one examines successively more rural locations. This pattern holds across all tenure groups. The incidence of excessive expenditures is more varied, but generally tends to be lower in rural areas.

The relative disadvantages of black households is strikingly clear. Their units exhibit extremely high levels of deficiencies. The incidence of excessive expenditures is also higher for blacks than for other households, especially among renters, but the differences are generally small in comparison to the divergence in dwelling deficiency rates between the races. Finally, although not shown in the table, there is little difference in the rate of deficiencies among the elderly aged 65—74 and those 75 years old and over (Struyk—Soldo, 1980, Table 3—6).

Comparing the elderly with the non-elderly, one sees that the incidence of dwelling deficiencies is about the same among poor households (at about 28 percent) but higher for the elderly overall (11 vs. 8 percent). As to excessive expenditures on housing, a similar pattern is evident with the poor having similar incidences (except that the incidence for non-elderly renters exceeds that of the elderly), and the elderly overall have higher incidences of high expenditures in every income group. However, after allowing for differences in the tax treatment of non-poor households, the incidence of excessive expenditures for the elderly and non-elderly may be quite similar.

To summarize, in 1979 there were about 1.61 million elderly-headed households living in dwellings that would be characterized as being physically deficient and about 2.58 million spending an excessive share of income on housing.[6] Since only about 340,000 have these problems in common -- meaning that many are spending a large fraction of their incomes to live in decent housing -- a total of about 3.85 million have a dwelling-specific housing problem. This is 28 percent of all elderly households. The incidence among those below the poverty line is much greater: of the 2.66 million elderly-headed households in this group, 61 percent have at least one of these problems.

Dwelling-use Problems. While it has been long observed that those whose activities are limited by health problems or disabilities are less able to function effectively in their homes without assistance, national housing policy in the United States has only recognized this fact to a limited extent. In considering policy options for aiding those with such problems, clearly one must know the size of population needing assistance. A key point to note at the outset is that dwelling-use problems can be ameliorated by supportive services, modifications made to the unit that facilitate its use, or both.

Here we give two estimates of the number of households with dwelling-use problems needing help, which are intended to bracket the actual number. The more generous definition is one which counts all of those who have a functional impairment due to disability or health problems. Applying this type of criterion to data from the 1979 National Health Interview Survey, one finds that about 12 percent of persons age 65 and over have a need for some form of supportive services in their homes -- 7 percent of those age 65 to 74, and 21 percent of those age 75 and over.[7] If the same rate applies to elderly-headed households, this implies about 2.0 million households are in this category.[8]

The incidence of need defined in this way is greater for women than for men (in both age groups), greater for blacks than for others, and apparently greater for those with lower incomes. I say apparently because it is possible that many of those with low incomes in 1979 had spent their way down to this level through having to spend accumulated assets for medical and supportive care in recent years. (In the U.S., some government assistance for long-torm care is available only to households with low incomes and low asset holdings.)

A more conservative estimate of the number needing supportive services can be obtained if we look at the share of those who have a functional limitation who are receiving formal care services, i.e., services provided by an agency, whether paid for by the recipient or not. This type of calculation has the advantage of deleting those who receive essential services only from family members, neighbors, and friends. Nationally, about 25 percent of the elderly who report a functional limitation are receiving formal services. Applying this rate to the 2 million households noted above yields a figure of about 500,000 households who require support services provided by a formal agency.

This figure, however, is probably too low for two reasons. First, certainly not all those who need such services are receiving them. Second, some persons are now in long-term care institutions who would not be there if such services had been available to them. Evidence of this appears in the analysis of the determinants of institutionalization. Those who live alone are institutionalized at higher rates compared to elderly in multi-person households, even after controlling for health status and activity limitations (Weissert and Scanlon, 1983).

All in all, one might take an estimate on the order of 750,000 elderly-headed households as needing formal supportive services. Additionally, one and one-half times that number now need and receive informal services -- either from sources within the household or from outside. Public policy should be structured so as to complement informal services, not replace them.

It is also important to note that when one examines the determinants of the likelihood of a person receiving formal supportive services, the dominant factors are the extent of the person's disability and the absence of informal services. Interestingly, after controlling for these conditions, income by itself is not an important factor, suggesting that over some range public programs and informal assistance are reaching many of those in greatest need of supportive services (Soldo, 1983). Thus, service recipiency seems to be largely determined by incapacity, lack of informal assistance, the availability of formal services, and, in some cases, the ability to pay for them.

Dwelling Modifications. The need for some types of supportive services can be eliminated by various changes to the dwelling which can compensate for particular functional impairments. These range from the installation of grab-bars and easy-to-grasp doorknobs and other hardware to specially equipped telephones to bathrooms and kitchens remodeled to accommodate wheelchair use. In other cases, such modifications can reduce the need for supportive services and thus complement their provision. The best estimate of the probable need for modified dwellings -- beyond those already occupied by some 700,000 elderly-headed households -- is on the order of one million units (Struyk, 1982). As indicated above, these are not in addition to the count of those needing some type of support services. If we assume that the needed modifications are concentrated among the 750,000 households with the greatest impairments (who are also those most likely to be receiving formal supportive services), then about 250,000 households need to occupy units with some special features who are not also receiving formal supportive services. (Unit modifications are discussed further below.)

The Overlap Between Dwelling-specific and Dwelling-use Problems. Newman has used data from a supplement to the Annual Housing Survey to estimate that about 17 percent of the elderly-headed households with a person having an activity limitation reside in a unit that is physically deficient.[9] Note that this rate is substantially higher than the 10 percent rate for elderly-headed households with no members with such limitations, suggesting that households with an impaired member have greater difficulty maintaining or affording decent housing.[10] This rate implies that in 1979 there were some 340,000 households in the group with both dwelling deficiencies and dwelling-use problems.

Similar calculations can be done for the overlap between those with excessive housing expenditures and a member with an activity limitation. This yields an estimate of 540,000 households with the combined problems.[11] Again, those households with an impaired member have a higher incidence of this problem than do other elderly households without such a member.

Summary

The figures in Table 4 summarize the information compiled on the number of elderly-headed households with various housing-related needs. As implied earlier, these are order-of-magnitude estimates designed to give a general picture of the present situation. An encouraging point is that very probably less than a million households are characterized as having both dwelling-specific and dwelling-use needs. This is only about 6 percent of elderly headed households of 1981, suggesting that it is a group that it should be possible to assist. On the other hand, there are large additional groups that have one or the other type of need. Against this, though, is the fact that some of the households included in these counts do not need financial assistance. Finally, a cautionary note: these figures are for 1979. The sharp increases in the number of elderly that will occur in the years

Table 4. Summary of Housing Needs of Elderly-Headed Households, 1979.

Type of Need	Thousands of Households	As Percent of Total Elderly Households
Dwelling-Specific Needs		
Deficient dwelling	1,610	11.5
Excessive housing expenditures	2,580	18.4
Dwelling-Use Needs		
Supportive services		
Generous estimate	2,000	14.2
Stringent estimate	750	5.4
Dwelling Modifications		
Including those needing supporting services, stringent definition	1,000	7.1
Excluding those needing supportive services, stringent defintion	250	1.8
Overlap Between Dwelling-Specific and Dwelling-Use Problems		
Supportive services (generous definition) and:		
Deficient dwelling	340	2.4
Excessive housing expenditures	540	3.9
Supportive services (stringent difinition) and:		
Deficient dwelling	128	.9
Excessive housing expenditures	140	1.0

ahead, as well as the greater share that will be in the older, more frail group of elderly is well-known and should be kept in mind when thinking about possible policy interventions.

BEHAVIOR OF THE ELDERLY IN THE HOUSING MARKET

To design public interventions to deal efficiently with the problems just outlined one must know how the elderly are likely to respond to various incentives. This section first reviews available econometric evidence on the behavior of the elderly as consumers of housing services and investors in housing assets. It then goes on to survey the evidence on the ways in which they adjust their housing consumption in response to various economic and demographic changes. We give primary attention to those studies which have provided separate estimates for the elderly and the non-elderly.

Housing Demand

Perhaps surprisingly, there have been few housing demand studies which considered the elderly as a separate group. Most studies simply include a dummy variable for the age of the head of household as an explanatory variable. This summary concentrates on those studies which have considered elderly households as a distinct population.

Quite divergent results have been obtained from these studies, and the critical factor explaining the differences is whether the population studied was composed only of recent movers or of all households. Where recent movers are the population analyzed — on the ground that those have recently made an adjustment will be near their equilibrium housing consumption — price and income elasticities of demand for the elderly are similar to those of the non-elderly (Reschovsky, 1982). On the other hand, divergent results in studies of several aspects of housing demand are documented where all households are included in the analysis. These include multinominal logit estimates of the demand for various housing bundles (Boersch–Supan, 1983)[12]; analysis of the likelihood of households enrolled in a housing allowance program becoming recipients (Zais et al., 1982); and, estimates of tenure choice probability models (Struyk, 1976). Thus, mobility takes on special importance as a way of effecting housing change.

Housing Adjustments

Households can adjust their homes through two distinct paths: switching dwellings by relocating, and modifying the unit initially inhabited to better meet their housing needs. Of course, the magnitude of change typically feasible from modifying a unit will be less than that possible by switching units, especially for units in multifamily structures. This section examines what is known about both of these approaches for elderly American households.

The general conceptual framework explaining the causes of housing adjustments, involving the idea of "consumption disequilibrium," is well-known and applies equally well to relocation and in-place adjustments. Sociologists, like Rossi (1955) and Speare et al. (1974) summarize the process beginning with dissatisfaction with the present unit. The household makes its decision on the basis of (1) the magnitude of the dissatisfactions, (2) the expected satisfaction with an alternative, and (3) the cost of making the adjustment. Economists [e.g., Goodman (1976), Cronin (1980), Reschovsky (1982)] construct a model in which households obtain "utility" from a particular unit but must discount the utility by the costs associated with attaining it. Net present values of alternatives are compared and the unit providing the household with the greatest present value is selected. The approaches of both disciplines are driven by the present bundle of housing services no longer being close to the optimal or best currently available bundle, given costs. (Cf. Quigley and Weinberg, 1977).

Relocation. The lower mobility rates of the elderly are widely appreciated.[13] Moreover, this phenomenon seems to hold across countries. For example, the figures in Table 5 from Schneider et al. (1985) are the mobility rates of husband—wife households in the U.S. and West Germany in the late 1970s, with the samples for both countries having been adjusted so as to exclude households whose mobility might be effected by housing programs or living in circumstances present in only one country, e.g., mobile homes in the U.S. The much lower mobility rates of households headed by someone age 65 or older is vividly evident for both homeowners and renters in both countries.[14] Moreover, West Germans are seen to have much lower mobility rates than Americans.

Table 5. Residential Mobility Rates for Husband-Wife Households without Children in the United States and West Germany by Age of Household Head[a].

| | Percent of households moving in last year | | | |
| | Homeowners | | Renters | |
Age	Germany	U.S.	Germany	U.S.
Under 30	b)	b)	32.3	57.0
30—44	3.8	19.4	19.0	43.1
45—64	1.0	6.4	7.6	21.7
65+	.8	3.6	4.7	12.5

a) For samples of households matched on general characteristics; e.g.,
sample excludes those receiving housing assistance and those living in
mobile homes.
b) Group is less than 2.5 percent of households in tenure group.
Source: Schneider et al. (1985), Table 3.

In reviewing the results of a number of analyses of the mobility of elderly households, Newman et al. (1984) classified the reasons given to explain low mobility into four groups:

1. Strong psychological attachment to the current residence as a result of spatial and social relationships built over many years, i.e., habit formation;

2. lack of knowledge concerning housing alternatives or inability to search for new housing due to poor health or no transportation;

3. the absence of suitable housing alternatives within the search space defined by the household; and,

4. incorrect assessment of the costs of current housing due to under-evaluation of the opportunity costs on home equity; also, miscalculation of actual transactions costs including searching and moving expenses.

To date no compelling evidence supporting any of these hypotheses has been produced despite several studies of elderly mobility [e.g., Golant (1972), Lawton et al. (1983), Reschovsky (1982)].[14]

On the other hand, some insights into elderly mobility come from a recent analysis by Meyer and Spear (1985) which used a 10 year longitudinal data file. For one thing, this analysis shows mobility rates rising after age 70, consistent with the elderly seeking units that are better suited to their needs or moving in with those who can help them as the extent of disequilibrium becomes very great. Secondly, Meyer–Speare differentiate among six types of "destinations" of moves, e.g., shifting locally to attain greater assistance -- perhaps moving in with a child. They find that age, income, marital status pre-move tenure, and health differentially effect the likelihood of moving to a particular destination. All of this suggests that greater care in studying distinct subpopulations yield greater understanding of mobility.[16]

Comparatively little research has been done on the determinants of the types of housing changes made when the elderly do relocate, owing in good part to the lack of appropriate time series data sets. Struyk (1980) used the two-panel national Survey of Low-Income and Disabled to perform a detailed analysis for the lower-income population. Housing consumption was characterized by: unit size (number of rooms); the presence of basic plumbing and mechanical systems; tenure; and, the ratio of (out-of-pocket) housing expenses to income.

The analysis of broad patterns revealed remarkably little consistency. There were, for example, a substantial number of households moving into larger units as well as those shifting to smaller ones. These findings, combined with the general similarity of the characteristics of relocating and stationary households that was also documented, underscore the complexity of fully analyzing the determinants of specific kinds of housing adjustments that are effected upon relocation.

Several consistent patterns did emerge, however, from the multivariate analyses. The household's familial situation -- both within the home and in terms of proximity to children, in the base year and changes over the observation period -- significantly affect the type of adjustments made. Different marital statuses, for example, are associated with differential changes made by renters in dwelling size, condition, and housing expense burden.

Both owners and renters in the base year who relocated were found to shift to units without major deficiencies, after controlling for other factors. Similary, after holding changes in family situation and other conditions fixed, both tenure groups were found to move to smaller units.

On the other hand, the relation between the housing expense to income ratio and base year income was seen to differ sharply for the two tenure groups. As expected, those who were initially homeowners (often with no mortgage debt) were found to increase housing expence-to-income ratios upward as incomes rose. Renters, by contrast, used the relocation to effect a reduction in rent-income ratios, with bigger reductions coming at higher incomes.

A shift from homeownership to rental tenure was found to be significantly and positively related to an increase in the number of activity limitations on the part of the head of household and to be positively related to the proximity of children in the area, presumably reflecting assistance expected from the children. Furthermore, high rents in an area significantly discouraged a change to rental tenure.

Overall the results consistently point to the relocating households being in substantial disequilibrium with respect to housing consumption prior to the move and to their making highly rational adjustements.[17)]

In-place Adjustments. Compared to the documentation on residential mobility, little is known about how households adapt their units to better suit their needs. A recently completed study (Struyk and Katsura, 1985) filled this void partially by following panels of about 200 elderly and non-elderly homeowners for five years and recording several types of housing adjustments as well as information on household composition, economic position, housing quality, formal and informal supportive service received, activity limitations of family members, and other data. Some care must be exercised in interpreting these data because sample households are not representative of all households, being drawn from fourteen neighborhoods in seven large cities.

Four adjustments were studied: (a) taking in a roomer or boarder; (b) changing the use of rooms; (c) making modifications to the dwelling to permit physically impaired households to make fuller use of the unit; and, (d) changes in the pattern of dwelling maintenance and improvement.

The incidence of the various housing adjustments is summarized in Table 6 separately for households headed by an elderly person and those headed by a non-elderly person. The rates are for the last two years of the approximately five year observation period. Only a very small percentage of households had a roomer or boarder present or changed the use of rooms within their homes over this period. A rather surprisingly high 10 percent of elderly headed and 5 percent of the non-elderly headed households undertook modifications to their homes to facilitate their use by a physically impaired family member. Taken together, these figures indicate that about 8 percent of elderly headed and 6 percent of non-elderly headed households make one of the first three types of housing adjustment *each year*.

Table 6. Incidence of Housing Adjustments by Age of Household Head.

	Elderly-headed households, %	Non-elderly headed households, %
Roomer or boarder present, in last 2 years	3	1
At least one room use change in last 2 years	5	6
Dwelling modified to assist impaired person, last 2 years	10	5
Dwelling repairs and improvements over last 2 years:		
made repairs in both years	69	80
made moderate sized repair in at least one year[a]	77	83
made major repair in at least one year[b]	19	22
only small or no repairs in both years	20	14
no repairs	5	3

[a] Moderate repairs are those costing between S100 and S1000, inclusive.

[b] Major repairs or improvements are those costing over S1,000.

Source: Struyk and Katsura (1985) Table 1.2.

These rates can be put into perspective by noting that about 3.3 percent of the elderly and 13 percent of the non-elderly homeowners adjust their housing circumstances by changing residence each year.[18] Hence, rates of in-place adjustments for the elderly are at least double those achieved by relocating. In contrast, the non-elderly relocate more often than they make these types of in-place adjustments.

Repairs and improvements are associated with the types of adjustments just reviewed and with longer term strategies of housing upkeep and investment. One hypothesis considered was that there is a cohort of elderly homeowners who, because of economic or health circumstances, decides implicitly to draw down on the equity in their homes through a program of undermaintenance. Similarly, the analysts were interested in which households persistently are investing in their homes. The last two rows of figures in Table 6 show that 20 percent of the elderly in our sample under undertook little or no repair activity over two years and that they were somewhat more likely to do this than their non-elderly counterparts; however, the differences between the two groups are not large. The elderly as a group are undertaking repair and improvements -- even large improvements to their homes -- at quite high rates. Still, they undertake fewer such repairs and investments and each year they spend less than their more youthful counterparts. The overall pattern is one in which properties are indeed largely being maintained, and disinvesting households are a definite minority and comparable in size with the non-elderly.

A final point concerns the extent to which multiple types of adjustments are being made by the same households. Even when the adjustments made over the full five year period were examined, little evidence of households making more than one type of housing change was found. The only exception to this was among those making major improvements to their homes and those modifying their homes to facilitate its use by an impaired member where a clear pattern of overlap was evident.

Another part of this work employed multivariate techniques with the goal of identifying the broad relationships present between each of the housing adjustments and the factors we have hypothesized to causally effect the occurrence of such adjustments. The ability to successfully carry out these analyses was somewhat limited by the small sample sizes involved and the small number of some adjustments that were observed over the five-year period. Nevertheless, some distinct patterns did emerge. Because the patterns for the elderly differ from those for the non-elderly, the focus in this summary is on the findings for households headed by an elderly person.

Changes in the *use of rooms* withing a dwelling were found to be systematically driven by the activity limitations of the household members. While severe limitations on the part of a spouse have especially powerful effects, limitations explerienced by the respondent and the presence in the household of someone else with physical impairments also significantly increase the likelihood of room use changes. On the other hand, the receipt of help by the spouse from outside of the home is a strong offsetting factor. Men living alone are over 10 percent more likely to make such room use changes than other types of households. Finally, economic circumstances do not appear to play an important role in determining whether housing adjustments of this type are undertaken.

The multivariate models estimated to explain the probability that a household would *take in a roomer or boarder* over the period yielded quite weak results, indicating the lack of systematic association between this type of housing adjustment and the factors hypothesized to be causal agents. Still, it was found that if the respondent had explerienced severe mobility limitations and had been receiving some help from outside the home for an extended period, the likelihood of having boarders in the home is sharply higher than for others. Changes in these statuses over the period reduce this likelihood, presumably such changes prevent other households in this situation from executing possible plans to take in a roomer. Multiperson households and men living alone appear to be more willing to take a boarder than elderly women living alone, after controlling for other factors. This finding is consistent with women being concerned about having strangers in their homes. There is also some indication that incomes falling over the period -- not low initial incomes -- may be a factor pushing households to accept boarders.

The likelihood that an elderly household will *modify its dwelling so as to be more useful to a physically impaired household member* is also determined significantly by the presence of members with activity limitations. Again, such limitations on the part of the spouse are especially important. Both activity limitations per se and the use by the spouse of special equipment to assist with mobility (e.g., walker, wheelchair) are strongly correlated with this type of adjustment. Counterbalancing the limitations to some degree are the receipt of services and the presence of social support outside of the home: starting to see at least one child once or more each week, having meals brought to the home over an extended period, and regularly attending a senior center all lower the probability that a modification will be made.

Economic position (as measured by income and net wealth) does not play much of a role in determining the likelihood of this type of housing adjustment occurring, suggesting that one way or another those households who badly needed to make dwelling modifications do get them done. Additionally, changes in the economic position of households over the full observation period were consistently not significant determinants of such changes. Additionally, for the elderly the configuration of multistory homes did not effect the likelihood of an adjustment being made, although for the non-elderly the presence of both a bedroom and a bathroom on the first floor of such a unit reduces the likelihood of a modification by about 7 percent.[19]

Summary

The foregoing provides an interesting view of the differences in the housing adjustments and behavior in the housing market of households headed by an elderly person compared to those headed by a non-elderly person. The penchant to "adjust in-place" appears to be substantially greater for elderly American homeowners compared to their more youthful counterparts. For the elderly, homeownership is an "absorbing state," and as such a key factor in explaining mobility and wealth accumulation. This pattern may be even more pronounced in some European countries where mobility patterns for the elderly are even lower than in the United States. Differences in residential mobility appear to hold the key to housing consumption distinctions between the elderly and non-elderly.

In terms of the responsiveness of the elderly to price signals and to changes in incomes, the results appear to depend critically on the population begin studied. When estimates involve populations that include recent movers as well as those with longer tenures, sharp differences are found between the elderly and non-elderly. On the other hand, when only populations of recent movers are considered, much more similar values for income and price elasticities are found. This implies that once households decide to relocate, they tend to respond similarly to the same economic factors.

A POLICY FRAMEWORK

In previous sections we have seen that dwelling-specific and dwelling-use problems often occur independently. Nevertheless, in a substantial minority of all cases, they occur together. Moreover, it seems probable that as dwelling-use problems become more acute, the incidence of dwelling-specific problems will increase rapidly. Activity limitations by a family member (and the energy required of others in the household to provide informal care) means that dwelling upkeep will likely be diminished. Likewise, drawing down on assets to pay medical bills and for formal care will lower incomes, possibly to the point at which housing expenditures become "excessive." We have also seen that the elderly are likely to respond rather differently to programmatic incentives than their non-elderly counterparts.

The challenge is to design a set of policy interventions that is flexible enough to deal with the variety of need mixes and ability-to-pay circumstances that will be encountered. If policies are properly designed, it may well permit savings in the total public resources going to the elderly as better options to both long- and short-term institutional care are utilized. In a number of instances, for example, in-home services have been found to defer institutionalization and to reduce the number and length of visits to acute-care hospitals.

Three principles should guide the design of the general policy response. First, cost-effectiveness -- using broadly defined benefits and costs -- is essential. In this calculation, costs include the substantial transactions costs experienced by the elderly. In the case of long-term care, they also include costs incurred by assisting additional households beyond those to whom the assistance is actually directed, i.e. serving those who otherwise would have received informal assistance is viewed as a cost. Particularly at issue is the substitution of formal for informal supportive services. On the other hand, benefits are also multifarious. Freeing informal caregivers to work in the market may result in greater productivity. Arrangements in which the elderly living in communal arrangements provide assistance to each other provide benefits in promoting independence. Of course, the major benefits flow from reduced institutionalization, and fewer economic resources for the housing the elderly from timely adjustments.[20]

Second, to the maximum extent feasible, the programs should be constructed to permit a range of choice to the elderly in terms of the solution adopted: remaining a homeowner or shifting to rental quarters; community-based versus institutionally-based services. Naturally, the recipient may have to pay a larger share of the cost for more expensive solutions; but the choice should still be present.

Third, the options should be structured so as to foster timely adjustments in the "housing-bundle" selected. As noted at the beginning of this paper, the housing needs of the elderly can be highly dynamic. Solutions offered in responding to those needs ought to encourage timely changes in the basic housing situation -- for example, from living alone in a single-family home to an apartment in a congregate housing project. At the same time, given the reluctance of the elderly to relocate, the new arrangements themselves might be such as to accommodate several levels of assistance.

The key idea behind the framework set forth here is that it is essential to tailor solutions to fit each of a range of housing-related needs. As needs change, alternative appropriate solutions should be available. To achieve this matching requires that one differentiate both among types of housing needs and among recipient populations. The various types of housing-associated needs were discussed at length above. Three household attributes seem key: economic resources (and hence the ability to pay for services), mode of tenure, i.e., owner-occupancy versus renting, and the type of structure -- single vs. multiunit structures. The latter strongly affects the efficiency with which many support services can be provided, and tenure effects the range of options available for coping with dwelling deficiencies and excessive housing expenditures.

Going beyond the principles just enunciated is rather difficult in the present context, since realistic discussions of policy alternatives run quickly into the details of the ways in which a particular country (the U.S. in this case) has organized its housing and related social policies in the past to assist the elderly.[21] In this instance, I have decided to discuss three points, all of which have the common feature of fostering timely adjustments -- probably through switching dwellings. More specifically, the focus is on those lower income households who are eligible for government assistance with their housing-and-supportive services requirements.

The first area to be addressed here is providing assistance to elderly households with dwelling-specific problems. Consider the following facts. First, data from the Housing Allowance Supply Experiment indicate that under an entitlement program the elderly became recipients of voucher-type assistance at lower rates than the non-elderly (Struyk–Soldo, 1980, Table 7–10). Two separate factors contributed to this result: (a) the elderly enrolled at lower rates than the non-elderly; and, (b) although a higher share of the elderly were able to initially qualify the unit in which they were living at enrollment, those who did not qualify the unit had a significantly lower likelihood of eventually receiving payments under the program (Zais et al., 1982, Chapter 6).[22] The latter factor is certainly consistent with the low propensity of the elderly to adjust their housing through relocating. The second fact to consider is that there has not been a significant problem in renting units to the elderly in newly constructed subsidized housing projects. At least in the U.S. this is not too surprising because the subsidy involved in such projects is generally very large.[23] This suggests that mobility can be induced if the incentives are great enough. (Of course, the question remains as to whether those who participate are most appropriately housed in such projects.)

Overall in the U.S. we have the conundrum of the elderly participating in traditional housing programs at high rates compared to the non-elderly, while at the same time displaying a low average willingness to move. The solution to this riddle seems to be that (a) the programs are not generally available to eligible households but rather are restricted to a fraction who would participate so that (b) those who are the "willing movers" -- who perhaps have the greatest housing disequilibrium and the most to gain financially by participating -- are those who participate. The possible difficulties with social (or project-based) housing programs, in terms of serving households with dwelling-specific problems, might become clear if all eligible households were entitled to receive assistance. In this case the effects of lower propensities to move on the part of the elderly would be sharply more evident and would deter program effectiveness. Countries with entitlement housing programs may have already confronted such problems. A careful analysis comparing elderly participants and nonparticipants might well provide very valuable information on the magnitude of the transactions costs perceived by nonparticipants.[24]

The second point concerns the frail population, those with dwelling-use problems, some of whom have dwelling-specific problems as well. In particular, the point deals with reconciling goals of fostering timely housing adjustments with permitting the household as much choice as possible. As noted, the evidence is very strong that the elderly -- especially homeowners -- will prefer to remain in the units they have occupied for an extended period, even though these dwellings may be poorly matched to their current housing needs and that the units might be more fully utilized by other households. It would seem that the general principle should be to provide such households with an entitlement sufficient to obtain the necessary support services in the lowest cost arrangement; if a household chooses to remain in its home where services are more expensive to provide, it would pay the difference. Use of "reverse annuity mortgages" might be especially suited for allowing homeowners to pay these additional expences.[25]

For example, a congregate housing facility might be the most efficient environment in which to provide a daily meal service and housekeeping assistance to a frail elderly widow. She may elect, however, to remain in her single-family home and still receive these services from public agencies. In this case she would pay the extra cost of travel time and expenses, etc. involved in providing help in her home. As the volume of services needed increased, and presumably the extra cost of providing them in the scattered single-family homes, the incentives for shifting to the lower cost alternative living arrangement would also rise. To date this principle has not been followed in the provision of such services in the U.S., and we do not have good information on perceived net benefits from such shifts. Again, the experience of other countries might be informative.

The final point is really a hypothesis. The hypothesis is that mobility rates of the elderly are especially dependent on the supply of suitable alternatives available. These alternatives probably constitute a particular subset of all housing and living arrangements. Some obvious examples include: rental units within the same neighborhood as that where the homeowner has been living; rental living arrangements with only limited support services, or where a menu of services is potentially available but only paid for if used; arrangements in which limited communal living exists both for social interaction reasons and to permit some savings in the cost of living. The proximate presence of such options would lower information and search costs and might well dramatically reduce the "psychic cost" of relocation which seems to be so large a part of total transactions costs for the elderly.

In sum, it may be fair to characterize the elderly as focusing more on the transactions costs than on the benefits of relocating. A question that comparative research might focus upon is the impact of the availability of various alternative housing bundles on the timing and type of housing adjustments made by frail elderly.

NOTES

* The author gratefully acknowledges comments on a draft from Robert Buckley, Sandra Newman, and Margery Turner.

1) For evidence on the movement of the elderly in and out of poverty, see Holden et al. (1986).

2) This argument gets rather more complicated upon additional reflection. First, elderly homeowners are disproportionately living in central cities, and it is far from clear that there would be a demand for these units even if they were on the market. More generally, however, for the increase in the supply of existing units on the market to cause the price of housing to fall (and thus make owner occupancy more affordable) would require that there be quite limited substitution between the demand for new and existing units. If there were high substitution, then the fall in demand for new units would result in lower production of such units and the overall supply would remain about the same. Since many existing units are less costly than new ones because they provide a smaller and different bundle of housing services than new units, substitution may in fact be limited.

3) See Annex A for the definition of underutilization.

4) These results are similar to those obtained by Reschovsky (1982, p. 26) using continuous measures of disequilibrium based on comparisons of housing consumption of recent mover and longerenured households.

5) Limitations on the activities of the elderly can mean that they are unable to utilize fully the dwelling. For example, they may be unable to use the kitchen and bathroom without assistance (possibly because they are inconveniently located in relation to living and sleeping areas), unable to properly clean and maintain their home, unable to go shopping without help. On the other hand, these limitations may be effectively offset by the assistance provided by other family members or neighbors or by modifications to the dwelling itself. Unfortunately, the only general measures of housing needs arising from activity limitations focus on the limitations themselves, not on the services the household must do without because of them.

6) Less detailed estimates using somewhat different definitions for deficiencies by Irby (1984) with 1981 data show about 1.2 million elderly househoulds in deficient units and 2.55 million with excessive expenditures.

7) See Annex A for the actual definition employed, and Annex Table B for more complete figures. This discussion is based on work by Soldo (1983). For further consideration of such estimates see Manton and Soldo (1985).

8) This procedure seems to be reasonable, given that using a similar definition of impairment Newman (1985) found about 13 percent of the elderly-headed households had at least one member with such an impediment.

9) Newman (1985) uses the same definition of dwelling deficiencies used earlier in this paper. Figures are for 1978.

10) Together with the information on the determinants of the receipt of support services it also implies that the services received do not have much effect on dwelling conditions.

11) In doing this calculation, the rate was applied only to those elderly-headed households not participating in a housing program, the general assumption being that they would not have excessive expenditures on housing.

12) Weisbrod et al., (1982) have estimated more elaborate housing choice demand models for elderly households. These estimates are only for elderly-headed households and unfortunately the authors only report the logit coefficients, not the corresponding elasticities.

13) We are really interested in local mobility, not migration. For an analysis of elderly migration determinants see Fournier et al. (1985).

14) Other studies documenting the lower mobility rates of the elderly include Butler et al. (1969), Kain & Quigley (1975), Morrison (1967), MacMillain (1983).

15) Reschovsky, for example, included in his age-stratified models of the probability of a household relocating a variable which measured

the extent of the disequilibrium prior to the move between the equilibrium housing consumption (as indicated by the choices of recently moving households) and current consumption. His models yielded inconsistent results as to the effect of the extent of disequilibrium. Reschovsky employs the Hicksian concept of consumer surplus to measure the benefits (extent of disequilibrium) from relocating, based on parameters of an estimated Stone–Geary utility function.

[16)] Newman (1975) examines the housing adjustment of the disabled elderly with considerable effect.

[17)] Merrill (1984) has analyzed the changes in home equity accumulation by elderly homeowners that occurred over a 10-year period as some of the households included in the sample relocated.

[18)] Schneider, Stahl, and Struyk (1985), Table 2.4; tabulation of figures from the Annual Housing Survey for 1978.

[19)] The analysis of repairs and improvements differs qualitatively from the other housing adjustments under consideration because they are not readily identifiable one-time events. Rather, households may change their level of activity and maintain it over a period of years, with the effects of such shifts only gradually becoming evident. The findings in this area can be illustrated for the probability of a household undertaking some repair or improvement activity in both of the final years of the observation period and the probability that in both years, given that it undertook repairs, the household spent more than the median amount expended for repairs among sample households making some reapirs.

The economic position of the household was clearly more important for repairs and improvements than for the other adjustments. Especially with regard to the likelihood of spending more than the median amount, income level at the start of the two year period over which the repair activity of the dependent variable is defined was important. Households in the lowest income quartile are about 25 percent less likely to spend more than the median amount in successive years than a household in the highest income quartile. Dwelling conditions played less of a causal role than anticipated. Substantial dwelling defects present at the baseline (year 1)

turn out to be a good predictor of the *lack* future repair activity in the final two years. T presence of problems with leaking basemen heating systems and the like -- measured ea year during the period -- were found to exe little measurable influence on repair activity.

In general, activity limitations and receipt social support and assistance from outside of t home were wound to be less important in e plaining repairs than they are for other housi adjustments. But some of these effects are ca tured by the household undertaking a dwelli modification which does significantly raise t probability of a sustained high level of rep activity. Living arrangements (and impli levels of potential support within the hom were found to have only limited influence repair activity.

[20)] Achieving cost-effectiveness in the U.S. m also well require a degree of coordinati among services far beyond that now occurri especially between housing and support s vices which are presently administered indepe dently in most cases.

[21)] For a general description of current U national housing policies for the elderly see Z et al. (1982), Chapter 3. For a survey of lo initiatives to serve this group, see Myers (198

[22)] Rent subsidy programs in the U.S. requ that the unit meet minimum physical standa as a condition for receiving the first payme Units are reinspected annually.

[23)] See Mayo and Barnbrock (1985). Tur (1982) notes that some older, less desira projects (which would embody lower subsidi are having some rent-up difficulties in so parts of the country.

[24)] Some analyses of this type for all hou holds was undertaken as part of the Hous Allowance Demand Experiment, in study the response of households to different s allowance offers.

[25)] For an overview of the potential of th instruments see Jacobs (1982).

REFERENCES

Anthony, A.S. (1984) Prepared Statement in U.S. Special Committee on Aging, *Sheltering America's Aged: Options for Housing and Services.* Washington, D.D.: U.S. Government Printing Office, Senate Housing 98—875.

Bernheim, B.D., A. Schleifer, and L. Summers (1985) "The Strategic Bequest Motive", *Journal of Political Economy,* Vol. 93: 1045—75.

Boersch—Supan (1983) "Do Falling Housing Prices Encourage Household Formation?" Cambridge: Department of Economics, MIT, processed.

Burke, P. (1984) *Trends in Subsidized Housing, 1974—81.* Washington, D.C.: Divison of Housing and Demographic Analysis, U.S. Department of Housing and Urban Development.

Butler, E., F. Chapin, G. Hemmens, E. Kaiser, M. Stegman, and S. Weiss (1969) *Moving Behavior and Residential Choice: A National Survey.* Washington, D.C.: Highway Research Board.

Cronin, F. (1980) *Search and Reseidential Mobility: Part I, Economic Models of Decisions to Search and to Move Among Low Income Households.* Washington, D.C.: Urban Institute, Paper 249—27.

Drews, R. (1982) *Rural Housing Programs: Long Term Costs and Their Treatment in the Federal Budget.* Washington, D.C.: Congressional Budget Office.

Feins, J., and C.S. White, Jr. (1978) *The Ratio of Shelter Expenditures to Income.* Cambridge: Abt Associates.

Fournier, G., D. Rasmussen, and W. Serow (1985) "Elderly Migration as a Response to Economic Incentives." Tallahasee, Fla.: Department of Economics, Florida State University.

Golant, S. (1972) *The Residential Location and Spatial Behavior of the Elderly.* Chicago, Ill.: University of Chicago, Department of Geography.

Gold, M. (1984) *The Older American's Guide to Housing and Living Arrangements.* Washington, D.C.: Institute for Consumer Policy Research.

Goodman, J.L., Jr. (1976) "Housing Consumption Disequilibrium and Local Residential Mobility", *Environmental and Planning A.* 8: 855—74.

Holden, K.C., R.V. Burkhauser, and D.A. Myers (1986) "Income Transitions at Older Stages of Life: The Dynamics of Poverty", *The Gerontologist,* 26: 292—97.

Irby, I. (1984) *Housing Problems in 1981: A Synopsis.* Washington, D.C.: Housing and Demographic Analysis Division, U.S. Department of Housing and Urban Development.

Jacobs, B. (1982) "An Overview of the National Potential for Home Equity Conversion into Income for the Elderly." Rochester: Public Policy Analysis Program, University of Rochester.

Kain, J., and J. Quigley (1975) *Housing Markets and Racial Discrimination.* New York: National Bureau of Economic Research.

Kingsley, G.T., and Schlegel, P.M. (1982) *Housing Allowances and Administrative Efficiency.* Santa Monica: The Rand Corporation, N-1741-HUD.

Lane, T., and J. Feins (1985) "Are the Elderly Overhoused? Definitions of Space Utilization and Policy Implications", *The Gerontologist,* 25: 243–50.

Lawton, M. (1976) "The Inner-city Resident: To Move or Not to Move", *The Gerontologist,* 13: 443–448.

Lawton, M.P. (1985) "The Relevance of Impairments to Age – Targeting of Housing Assistance", *The Gerontologist,* 25: 31–4.

Levine, M. (1982) *Housing Assistance Program Options.* Washington, D.C.: Congressional Budget Office.

MacMillan, J. (1980) *Mobility in the Housing Allowance Demand Experiment.* Cambridge: Abt Associates.

Manton, K., and B. Soldo (1985) "Dynamics of Health Changes in the Oldest Old", *Milbank Memorial Fund Quarterly/Health and Society,* 63: 206–85.

Mayo, S., and J. Barnbrock (1985) "Rental Housing Subsidy Programs in West Germany and the United States: A Comparative Program Evaluation," in K. Stahl and R. Struyk (eds.), *U.S. and West German Housing Markets.* Washington, D.C.: The Urban Institute Press.

Merrill, S.R. (1984) "Home Equity and the Elderly", pp. 197–224 in H. Aaron and G. Burtless (eds.), *Retirement and Economic Behavior.* Washington, D.C.: The Brookings Institution.

Meyer, J.W., and A. Speare, Jr. (1985) "Distinctively Elderly Mobility: Types and Determinants", *Economic Geography,* 61: 79–86.

Miller, L.S., and L. Walter (1983) "The Comparative Evaluation of the Multipurpose Senior Services Projet -- 1981." Berkeley: The University of California.

Morrison, P. (1967) "Duration of Residence and Prospective Migration: The Evaluation of a Stochastic Model", *Demography,* IV: 533–561.

Myers, P. (1982) *Aging in Place: Strategies to Help the Elderly Stay in Revitalizing Neighborhoods.* Washington, D.C.: The Conservation Foundation.

Newman, S. (1976) "The Housing Adjustments of the Disabled Elderly", *The Gerontologist,* 16: 312–17.

(1985) "Housing and Long-Term Care: The Suitability of the Elderly's Housing to the Provision of In-Home Services", *The Gerontologist,* 25: 35–40.

Newman, S., Zais, J., and Struyk, R. (1984) "Housing Older America", pp. 17–55 in I. Altman, J. Wohlwill, and M.P. Lawton (eds.), *The Physical Environment and The Elderly.* New York: Plenum Press.

Quigley, J., and D. Weinberg (1977) "Intra-Metropolitan Residential Mobility", *International Regional Science Review,* 2: 41–66.

Reschovsky, J. (1982) *Aging in Place: An Investigation of the Housing Consumption and Residential Mobility of the Elderly.* Ann Arbor, Michigan: University of Michigan, doctoral dissertation.

Rossi, P. (1955) *Why Families Move.* New York: The Free Press.

Schneider, W., K. Stahl, and R. Struyk (1985) "Residential Mobility", pp. 23–54 in K. Stahl, and R. Struyk (eds.), *U.S. and German Housing Markets: Comparative Economic Analysis.* Washington, D.C.: The Urban Institute Press.

Sherwood, S., J.N. Morris, C.C. Sherwood, S. Morris, E. Bernstein, and E. Gorstein (1985) *Final Report of the Evaluation of Congregate Housing Services Program.* Boston: Hebrew Rehabilitation Center for the Aging.

Soldo, B. (1983) "A National Perspective on the Home Care Population." Washington, D.C.: Georgetown University, Center for Population Research, Working Paper in Demography CPR 83–4.

Speare, A., S. Goldstein, and W. Frey (1974) *Residential Mobility, Migration, and Metropolitan Change.* Cambridge, Mass: Ballinger.

Struyk, R. (1982) "The Demand for Specially Adapted Housing by Elderly-Headed Households." Washington, D.C.: Urban Institute Project Report 3014–1.

(1984a) "Home Energy Costs and the Housing of the Poor and the Elderly", pp. 35–84 in A. Downs, and K. Bradbury (eds.), *Energy Costs, Urban Development and Housing.* Washington, D.C.: Brookings Institution.

(1984) "Housing-Related Needs of the Elderly Americans and Possible Federal Responses", pp. 52–87 in U.S. Senate Special Committee on Aging, *Sheltering America's Aged: Options for Housing and Services.* Washington, D.C.: U.S. Government Printing Office, Senate Hearing 98–875.

(1976) *Urban Homeownership.* Cambridge: Lexington Books.

Struyk, R., and B. Soldo (1980) *Improving the Elderly's Housing.* Cambridge: Ballinger Publishing Company.

Struyk, R., and J. Zais (1982) "Providing Special Dwelling Features for the Elderly with Health and Mobility Problems." Washington, D.C.: The Urban Institute.

Struyk, R., and H. Katsura (1985) *Aging at Home: How the Elderly Adjust Their Housing Without Moving.* Washington, D.C.: Urban Institute Report 3166–04.

Struyk, R., and M. Turner (1984) "Changes in the Housing Situation of the Elderly", *Journal of Housing for the Elderly,* 2:3–20.

Turner, M. (1985) "Building Housing for the Low-Income Elderly: Cost Containment and Modest Design in The Section 202 Program", *The Gerontologist,* 25:271–79.

Weisbrod, G.E., J. Berkovec, J. Royce Ginn, S. Lerman, H. Pollakowski, and P. Reid (1982) *Residential Mobility and Housing Choices of Older Americans.* Cambridge: Cambridge Systematics.

Weissert, W., and W. Scanlon (1983) "Determinants of Institutionalization of the Aged." Washington, D.C.: Urban Institute Working Paper, 1466–21.

Zais, J., R. Struyk, and T. Thibodeau (1982) *Housing Assistance for the Elderly.* Washington, D.C.: The Urban Institute Press.

ANNEX A, DEFINITIONS

1. **Dwelling deficiency.** See Table A–1. Specifics of the definition were dictated by the data available in the Annual Housing Survey. This definition is the same as that employed by the U.S. Department of Housing and Urban Development (HUD).

2. **Excessive Housing Expenditures.** Here we follow HUD's lead so that our results will be consistent with other tabulations. Excessive burden is defined separately for renters and homeowners. For renters, gross rent (*contract rent* plus utilities paid by the tenant) above 30 percent of gross household income is considered excessive. For owner-occupants, out-of-pocket expenditures for housing (excluding expenditures for maintenance and improvements) above 40 percent of family income is considered excessive. The higher standard for homeowners is based on the tax advantages accuring to homeowners and on the capital gains-producing investment embodied in their housing expenditures. (See Feins and White (1978) for more discussion of this point.)

3. **Need for supportive services.** Two definitions are used, based on data in the 1979 National Health Interview Survey. The "generous" definition, developed by Soldo (1983) includes any person with at least one of the following:

○ needed or received help with at least one of the seven Activities of Daily Living (ADL)
○ needed or received help with at least one of the four Instrumental Activities of Daily Living (IADL)
○ was not able to perform one or more of the ADL functions
○ stayed in bed all or most of the time
○ needed help with urinary or bowel devices.

The "stringent" definition includes those persons in the group defined by "generous" definition who receive formal home care services.

4. **Housing Utilization.**[1] The standard consists of three levels of utilization as measured by this indicator. The first level, "No Underutilization," includes units having two or fewer non-sleeping rooms plus one bedroom or fewer for each person with the household. This measure assumes that each person in a household can reasonably utilize one bedroom and that at least two non-sleeping rooms are needed for common household use. Therefore, a one-person household with up to three rooms is not underutilizing space, nor is a married couple or other two-person household with up to four rooms. Crowded housing units (less than one room per person) are also in this No Underutilization category. However, only 1% of the elderly households who moved out of their units were subject to crowding.

The second level, "Modest Under Utilization," designates housing units with two non-sleeping rooms and one bedroom more than is required for the size of the household, or more than two non-sleeping rooms and the appropriate number of bedrooms (one bedroom per person). Therefore, an individual living alone in two rooms plus two bedroom falls into this category, as do married couples with two non-sleeping rooms and three bedrooms.

The third level, "Underutilization," consists of units with one extra bedroom for the size of household plus more than two non-sleeping rooms, or two non-sleeping rooms plus more than one extra bedroom. Thus, single-person households with three rooms (e.g., kitchen, living room, dining room) plus two bedrooms or more, couples with three or more rooms plus three bedrooms, and couples with more than three bedrooms are all defined as underutilizing their housing.

---

[1]From Lane and Feins (1985), p. 244.

Table A—1. Deficiencies which Cause a Housing Unit to be Judged Physically Inadequate — Based upon AHS Items, Revised Definition (1981). (HUD/Simonson Definition.)

Type of Deficiency	Description of Deficiency
Plumbing	1. *Lacks or shares some or all plumbing facilities.* The unit must have hot and cold piped water, a flush toilet, and a bathtub or shower - - all inside the structure and for exclusive use of the unit.
	2. *Lacks adequate provision for sewage disposal.* The unit must be connected with a public sewer, septic tank, cesspool, or chemical toilet. (Units with this deficiency are almost invariably defined as having a plumbing deficiency as well.)
Kitchen	3. *Lacks or shares some or all kitchen facilities.* The unit must have an installed sink with piped water, a range or cookstove, and a mechanical refrigerator - - all inside the structure and for exclusive use of the unit.
Physical Structure	4. *Has three or more of five structural problems:* leaking roof; open cracks or holes in interior walls or ceiling; holes in the interior floors; either peeling paint or broken plaster over one square foot of an interior wall; evidence of mice or rats in last 90 days.
Common Areas	5. *Has three or more of four common area problems:* no light fixtures (or no working light fixtures) in common hallway; loose, broken, or missing stairs; broken or missing stair railings; no elevator in building (for units two or more floors from main building entrance in buildings four or more stories high).
Heating	6. *Has unvented room heaters which burn oil or gas.* If unit is heated mainly by room heaters burning gas, oil, or kerosene, the heaters must have flue or vent.
Electrical	7. *Lacks electricity.*
	8. *Has three out of three signs of electrical inadequacy:* One or more rooms without a working wall outlet; fuses blown or circuit breakers tripped three or more times during last 90 days; exposed wiring in house.

Source: Simonson (1981), pp. 84—85.

Table A-2. Prevalence Rate per 1000 65+ of Need for Home Care [a] for Select Characteristics, by Age 1979.

Characteristics	Total	Age 65-74	75+
Total	121.0	69.9	211.0
Race			
White	116.0	64.0	207.0
Black	168.0	127.0	245.0
Other	148.0	82.0	320.0
Sex			
Male	91.0	55.3	166.6
Female	141.0	81.1	237.2
Region			
Northeast	129.0	78.0	219.0
North Central	104.0	54.0	188.0
South	130.0	80.0	221.0
West	118.0	62.0	216.0
Place of Residence			
Central City, SMSA	123.0	77.0	204.0
SMSA, not Central City	113.0	64.0	203.0
Rural, nonfarm	132.0	74.0	230.0
Rural, farm	72.0	25.0	164.0
Living Arrangements			
Alone	124.0	77.0	177.0
With Non-Relative	246.0	132.0	392.0
With Spouse	82.0	55.0	163.0
With Other Relative	243.0	134.0	346.0
Medical (Last 12 Months)			
Yes	292.0	195.0	412.0
No	105.0	60.0	189.0
Personal Income (In 1978 dollars)			
S 2,000	175.0	b)	b)
S 2- 2,999	287.0	b)	b)
S 3- 3,999	200.0	b)	b)
S 4- 4,999	102.0	b)	b)
S 5- 5,999	59.0	b)	b)
S 6- 6,999	46.0	b)	b)
S 7- 9,999	56.0	b)	b)
S 10-14,999	21.0	b)	b)
S 15,000+	28.0	b)	b)

[a] Consult Annex A for definition.

[b] Insufficient number of cases for reliable estimation.

Source: Estimates from the 1979 National Health Interview Survey prepared by Soldo (1983).

Research on Housing Politics and Housing Policy

Introduction

Lennart J. Lundqvist, The National Swedish
Institute for Building Research, Gävle

To a large extent, political research on housing has been focussed on
housing policy, and its content and effects. In particular, housing policy
has been studied as another example of welfare statism. The research has
been centred more on the effects of housing policies on the functioning
of the housing market, and the distribution of housing welfare among
social classes and household groups, than on the politics of housing.
While there are traces of this earlier direction in the keynote addresses,
there is, however, an explicit wish to study the politics of the housing
question in a more systematic way than before.

David Donnison directs our attention to the *inputs* into housing politics.
He shows how our perceptions of social phenomena creep into how housing
problems are defined, how measures are engineered and administered, and
how this chain of attitudes and actions tends to have severely discriminating
effects on the distribution of housing welfare. However, he also points to
the importance of research; facts coming from systematic and un-biassed
investigations can help in restructuring perceptions, and thus policies.

Still, however, facts must be interpreted. Here values enter policy discussions. And according to Donnison, value preferences will always differ,
derived as they are from infinitely varied human experience. Thus, the
least we should strive for is to involve those whose welfare is at stake in
the decisions to be made. This should be done, he says, not just as a matter
of justice, but because reality will be misunderstood if the perceptions of
those people are not taken into account. Even if Donnison does not say so,
his example of the new Glasgow policy for the homeless implies that the
content of housing policy will change with the entrance of new actors on
the arena.

However, *Ulf Torgersen's* discussion of the peculiarities of housing policy *content* shows that once housing is provided on certain terms for a certain group, this comes to be taken for "granted". Unlike other welfare services, housing is not something taken away from the recipient when he or she is no longer formally eligible for it. To some extent, this may be an effect of the crudeness of welfare indicators, but it means that policy measures once intended to achieve a distribution of housing welfare similar to that of other welfare services will eventually lead to inequalities, and to social divisions along housing tenure lines. In the end, housing policy will thus give birth to strong interest groups, defending systems of support and subsidies favouring their housing status.

In his examples of tenure-biassed policies in Great Britain, Norway and Sweden, Torgersen shows how favours given to homeownership may lead to social inequalities. He ends on a rather pessimistic note concerning whether the principles of tenure and equal distribution of welfare can be reconciled in housing. And even if he does not explicitly draw such a conclusion, he seems to imply that housing policies tend to create constituencies whose political strength is such as to preclude dramatic changes towards a more welfare-oriented policy.

Drawing on what she interprets as a common change towards privatization in housing policy content, *Carolyn Adams* wants to find out whether this has any effect on the *relations* among actors in housing politics. In particular, she analyzes whether increased government reliance on support to housing consumption (housing allowances, tax deductions for homeowners) — rather than direct production has altered the well-established corporatist structures in housing politics.

With examples from several welfare states, Carolyn Adams shows that the powerful positions gained by the construction industry during the earlier, production-oriented policy era have in fact been retained. The assumption that the consumer-inclined privatization tendency would bring organized housing consumer interests to the fore in policy-making is not substantiated by empirical evidence. However, the politics of housing is moving to new arenas, particularly into tax and finance policy arenas. Here, producer interests must compete with other producer groups for policy influence, while consumer interests continue to play a marginal role. Her conclusion is that it is how well housing producers fare in this competition, and not any assumed or showns strength of housing consumer interests, that will determine how much resources are devoted to housing in the future.

According to *Nathan Schwartz,* the relations among housing policy actors, and thereby much of the content of policy, can be explained by analyzing the *arenas* – national, local and others – and *tools* of policy. He says that policies which subsidize housing consumption in the United States – by emphasizing market approaches – make for "arena-less" implementation of policy. These tools also deprive consumers of subsidized housing of supportive interest groups strong enough to influence policy-making. This precarious situation is further compounded by the highly visible budgeting forms, leaving subsidized programs like housing allowances very susceptible to budget cuts.

On the other hand, tax subsidies to home owners make for arena-less implementation. Here, however, institutional forces behind policy – financial institutions, builders – are strong and able to maintain support on the national arena where such tax policies are decided. Furthermore, the tax deductions are invisible in the budget process, thus rendering them politically less vulnerable. Schwartz also shows how British housing policy, with its national policy-making but local implementation and the diversity of policy tools works against the local arenas becoming influential in housing policy. Any local initiative – such as the Glasgow program described by Donnison – can thus be prevented from reaching national attention, unless a wide range of support can be gained. For this support to occur, the issue must cut across the different local implementation program lines.

Interpreted in this way, these key-note addresses thus imply a reality far away from that envisaged by the architects of the "social" housing policy instigated in the early post-war period. Housing policy is dominated by values other than those seen as the core of such a social policy. As indicated by Torgersen, that policy has resulted in well entrenched interest groups, defending their tenure-based privileges. And as shown by both Adams and Schwartz, producer interests may find it more compatible with their self-interest to join forces with the dominant home-owner segment than with the rental sector.

No doubt, much of the change in the direction of housing policy content is based on our perceptions of what constitutes the problem – or problems – in housing. As David Donnison shows, research can lay these perceptions open, and induce change. Hopefully, these chapters, and the others in this volume, will stimulate future housing research.

Poverty, Power and Stigma: The Case of the Single Homeless

U.K.

Glasgow

9320

9140

David Donnison, Town and Regional
Planning, University of Glasgow, Scotland

INTRODUCTION

In the first part of this paper I shall reflect on the ways in which we think
and talk about human needs, and on the policy responses to which those
thoughts and words are apt to lead — taking homeless men as a case study
of these processes. I shall argue that our perceptions of poor people encourage assumptions and policy responses which reinforce the exclusion
of these people from society's mainstream. In the second part of the paper
I shall show how one city broke out of this pattern in its treatment of
homeless people, and discuss the implications of that achievement. In the
third and final part of the paper I offer some broader conclusions for
policy makers and students of the policy making process.

SEEING AND DOING

Imagine a scene which is familiar in the big cities of many affluent countries. A middle aged man, wearing a rather dirty old coat and down-at-heel
shoes and carrying a bulging plastic bag, walks slowly along the street. The
street too is rather old, dirty and down-at-heel. The man stops at each of
the refuse bins he passes, and fumbles through them; for cigarette ends,
you guess. There is something heavy in the pocket of his coat. It might be
a bottle.

How would you describe this man? As a "dosser" or a "wino" perhaps?
Or as a "transient" or "tramp"? Or simply as a "homeless man"? We have
no word to describe him — because we have no way of perceiving him —
which does not carry implications of various kinds: implications about the
problems (if any) that we are perceiving, about their urgency, and about
the responses which it would be appropriate to make to them.

Take the word "dosser" for a start. It goes back more than two hundred years and means one who sleeps in a doss-house or common lodging house. Less hostile than "wino" — an American term used to describe people in an advanced stage of alcoholism — it is the kind of word that is often used to describe homeless people by residents living in the kind of neighbourhood we have imagined. It suggests that the man may have problems, and may *be* a problem to others, but these problems should be dealt with somewhere else. As words like "transient" or "tramp" imply even more strongly, to label a man a "dosser" suggests that he is probably on the move and without local roots. That suggests that his needs, whatever they may be, are not the responsibility of the conventional, local housing services (for he does not live in — indeed, may not be capable of living in — that kind of housing). Neither are they the responsibility of the home help or home nursing services or the conventional social work services (for he has no home, and may have left town by tomorrow). For these services the "dosser" is not a problem, he is a solution: almost by definition, he makes no demands on their resources. "Dossers" may however be a problem for other services: for the hostels which shelter them, for the social assistance service to which they may turn for money, or for the police.

To call this person a "homeless man" is to use words which imply fewer assumptions: people may associate the term with other characteristics, but all it really tells us is that he is homeless; so he may want a house. More often, however, the British talk about the "single homeless" (implying that these people have no families, and should perhaps not be entitled to the ordinary forms of housing for which families are given priority).

The "homeless and rootless" is another British term — a phrase heavy with assumptions: the assumption, for example, that the man we are considering is not likely to vote at elections, or even to be on the electoral register, and that he is not really entitled to the public services available to, and paid for by, the resident voters and taxpayers.

These are simple examples of the ways in which perception creates language which in turn helps to shape perception. There is a whole library of books and journals about those processes. They remind us that perceiving is a skill which has to be learnt. It is not "given" — not simply the reception of a set of sense data fed into everyone's nerve endings in a uniform fashion. We have to interpret these stimuli in order to "make sense" of what would otherwise be the buzzing and blooming confusion of the world. Our interpretations depend upon guesses which we have to make about what we actually see (*is* that really a bottle which makes a bulge in the man's pocket?) and about the context or meaning of objects and events — the circumstances surrounding them. (We may guess, for example, that the man does not want, or could not cope with, ordinary housing.)

The words we use to express our initial perceptions then convey further suggestions — about the nature of the problem under discussion, about its urgency, about the kinds or response which would be appropriate, and therefore about the directions in which solutions should be sought. It may seem natural, for example, that "winos" need hostels for alcoholics, that "tramps" and "transients" need temporary shelter — probably on the edge of towns, well away from their nicer suburbs.

Our "solutions" then shape and reinforce public perceptions of the problems for which they have been fashioned. Voluntary organisations build hostels and night shelters for "dossers" who are turned out every morning and given no assurance that they will be allowed in again the following evening. In some cities these men are compelled to collect social assistance payments from offices which specialise in dealing with those who have "no fixed abode" — offices in whose waiting rooms the men only meet others with a life style similar to their own. The central government runs resettlement units for these men, and the trade unions representing their staff fiercely resist proposals for transferring their functions to local housing authorities. Indeed, the staff of many of these services become highly skilled at dealing with the problems of alcoholism and human dereliction — problems which such a regime is likely to create, or at least to perpetuate. They mount campaigns and form pressure groups seeking funds for more night shelters, more hostels, more experts on alcoholism...

Meanwhile the rest of the population — respectable residents, worrying about the safety of their children, the reputation of their street and the value of their property — fiercely oppose the development of any service which might attract "dossers" to their own neighbourhoods. Thus hostels, services for addicts and social security offices specialising in the "N.F.A. cases" are pushed into remote or unattractive quarters where the homeless are more completely excluded from the rest of society and more visibly labelled and stigmatised.

The human situation with which this analysis began is a small example of a much larger issue: an example of poverty. Poverty arises from, and contributes to, various forms of exclusion from society's mainstream. It also arises from, and contributes to, various forms of powerlessness. And our perceptions of the poor, if they are humiliating and stigmatising, are also causes and effects of exclusion and powerlessness. Thus poverty, exclusion, powerlessness and stigma are inextricably linked to each other. They must be tackled together, for we cannot eliminate one unless we eliminate the others too. Public services which were designed only to meet the most urgent material needs — night shelters, hostels for addicts, social security officers dealing only with the "N.F.A. cases" — too often reinforce exclusion, loss of power and humiliating stigma, and thereby perpetuate poverty too.

NEW PERCEPTIONS; NEW POLICIES

Although they have been slightly caricatured in my account, the perceptions and policies I have described are reasonably typical of the situation in many cities in Britain and in other countries. The way in which these things work can be better understood if we study the experience of a city which has broken out of this pattern. Glasgow is one of several such cities in Britain. (Similar things are happening in Aberdeen, Leeds and London.) What follows is not intended to be a carefully weighed history of Glasgow's experience: I have deliberately picked out the crucial events in the story in order to examine their significance. That emphasis on the more creative steps which have been taken inevitably makes this account read like propaganda on behalf of Glasgow. So I must stress that while this account is true, it is not the whole truth: there is still a lot of pain, a lot of mistakes and much that is saddening about this city's treatment of homeless people.

One of the first steps taken to launch new policies in Glasgow was a survey of homeless people which was designed to find out who they were and how they perceived their own needs. In the event, insufficient women were included among those interviewed and the report on this research dealt only with men. A study of homeless women was therefore made later. The main findings of these two studies have been quoted time and again since then. These are some of them.

The oddly dressed, elderly men, sometimes under the influence of drink, who hang about in the streets and sleep on park benches, typify for many people the homeless. That is because they are the most visible representatives of the group. But if you look, not at the "stock" of those visibly homeless tonight, but at the "flow" of those who become homeless at some point in the year, a different picture emerges. Most of the flow are young – in their twenties or even younger. Many are women. This finding helps to transform public perceptions of the older men who form the majority of the stock of homeless: no longer a bizarre out-group, they are a minority of a much larger number of quite ordinary people who become homeless at some time in their lives. Those most visible to the public are the few who did not find a way back into more settled living conditions.

Most of those who are currently homeless, and even more of those who become homeless during the year, are "local" people who were born in the city or have lived in or near Glasgow for many years, and do not intend to move away. They have, on the face of it, as good a claim as anyone else to the services provided for the city's people. Although most of them expect little or no help from their relatives, a large proportion of these people – despite the fact that they are called the "single" homeless – are in fact married, or have been at some time; but their relationships broke up. Often that was the reason why they became homeless. Only a small minority of them have a drink problem. Most of them are registered in the usual way with a doctor in the health service. In short, they are a much more "ordinary" group of people than the popular stereotype would suggest.

How do they perceive their own needs? The great majority of them want to live in ordinary housing like everyone else, and most believe they are capable of doing so. The minority who want to remain in hostels are those who have spent most years in them. Given time, it seems that hostels generate a demand for their own services.

As these surveys were made, the Housing Department of Glasgow District Council began rehousing these men in ordinary public housing in many different parts of town, closing the worst of the old lodging houses and hostels, and improving the remainder. That rehousing programme was easier to bring about here than in some other cities because Glasgow has the biggest stock of public housing in Britain. Nevertheless it was fiercely opposed by many people, expert in running hostels for the homeless, who sincerely believed that these men would not be capable of living independently in a flat of their own.

Meanwhile, the Social Work Department of the Strathclyde Region (within which Glasgow is the largest city) set up a special unit to help those of the homeless who sought their aid. About one third of those rehoused did so. The help most frequently given was advice about how to furnish and manage a home, how to buy food and cook it, how to get payments for furniture from the social security office, and so on. Most of this help was provided, not by social workers but by "home advisors" — women with long experience of running their own households in similar neighbourhoods.

Hostels run by voluntary agencies, often with help from unpaid volunteers, continued. But voluntary workers expert in dealing with problems like alcoholism began increasingly to work within the hostels provided by the local authority, rather than setting up hostels of their own.

The momentum of these changes was carried forward by The Glasgow Council for the Single Homeless (GCSH) on which were represented all the agencies, statutory and voluntary, national and local, concerned with the single homeless in Glasgow. Although this was, legally speaking, an independent charity which raised its own funds for research and published reports critical of public authorities in the city, it was staffed and administered by the Housing Department: GCSH had no formal authority, but its influence was considerable because the agencies represented on it agreed that they would seek their colleagues' advice about any proposal for new developments in their own services for the homeless before introducing changes. Several important modifications in their policies were brought about by discussions around the GCSH table. Likewise when resident action groups tried to exclude services for the homeless from their neighbourhoods, GCSH had enough influence to defend these projects successfully before the city's Planning Committee.

The respect accorded to this Council owed a great deal to leading politicians from the District's Housing Committee and the Region's Social Work Committee who participated regularly in its discussions. That called for a good deal of patient statesmanship, for they had the difficult task of defending their services when these were criticised by GCSH, and defending GCSH when their political colleagues responded angrily to these criticisms.

Equally important in some ways was a regular lunch club run by the Region's special unit for the homeless. GCSH represented the bosses of the agencies working in this field. The lunch club brought together for regular discussions the staff working in the front lines – housing officials, pressure group spokesmen, home advisors, Salvation Army workers, hostel wardens, social workers, prison welfare officers, research workers and so on. A movement was being created on behalf of the homeless.

No mention has yet been made of any initiatives taken by the homeless themselves. They were a long time in coming. Among the politicians and the professionals, even the most radical and passionate advocates of the cause of the homeless were reluctant to involve them directly in the work of GCSH. The break-through was made easier when the Region's Welfare Rights Service started working with the men still living in hostels and found them well able to participate in a campaign for social security benefits which eventually netted a million pounds in back pay for them, and a million pounds more each year thereafter. Before long the Hostels Action Committee – consisting of representatives from most of the city's hostels – was sending a spokesman to GCSH and bringing large numbers of hostel residents to public meetings organised by the Council. That gave the professionals a glimpse of their services as perceived from the other side of the counter – a glimpse which was probably more salutory than specific proposals put forward by the homeless. ("I tell my people: *never* see a social worker by yourself. Take a friend with you: They behave differently when you have a witness.") Such remarks, made without aggressive intent as a casual comment on life as these men knew it, helped to transform the assumptions and attitudes of all concerned.

So what, at the end of the day, did all this achieve? Since the end of this day is still a long way off, no more than an interim report can be given. It would include the more generous provision which Glasgow has made for rehousing single people in public housing before there is any danger that they become homeless; the rehousing in ordinary rented flats of well over a thousand people from hostels; the closure of some of the worst of those hostels, and the improvement of others; the fact that most of those rehoused from hostels are still living in their flats, and presenting no more problems of rent arrears or troubles with neighbours than the average public tenant; the continuing queue of hostel dwellers asking to be rehoused; the creation of a new, small, well-staffed reception unit for homeless women, brought about despite fierce initial opposition from the community council representing the neighbours; the attempt now being made to transform policies for the single homeless throughout Britain, in which the experience of Glasgow is much quoted... and many other things.

CONCLUSIONS

I draw conclusions from this story, first of a practical kind for those concerned with housing and poverty, and then of a more theoretical nature for those concerned with broader questions of policy analysis.

The practical lessons to be learnt from this story are that we can most effectively improve the opportunities and living conditions of the poorest people if we are at the same time determined to remove the humiliating stigma imposed on them by a fearful and hostile public, to bring them into the mainstream of society rather than excluding them, and to give them responsibility and power whenever we can, rather than keeping them dependent, medicalised or criminalised. Poverty, exclusion, powerlessness and stigma are imposed on people together and have to be removed together.

Social solidarity has to be our goal if we are genuinely determined to reduce poverty. If some groups need special treatment, that should be offered (like the home advisor service in this case) for the purpose of helping marginal people to move into the mainstream, not on terms which reinforce their exclusion (like the low-grade night shelters run by some charities and church groups, or the social security offices which deal only with N.F.A. cases). That will call for changes in public perceptions of the poor which public policies may obstruct (by depriving homeless people of any secure resting place, for example, and compelling them to wander about the streets all day as visible and squalid examples of ostracised humanity). Or public policy may help to bring about benign changes in public perceptions. (Public hostility to hostel dwellers is due partly to hostility to the hostels themselves — which are equally unpopular with many of their residents. Rehousing them in ordinary housing helps other people to see those who were homeless as ordinary citizens entitled to the same treatment as everyone else.)

These arguments also have more profound implications for policy analysis. Here I only have space to touch briefly on three related issues.

Many of us were taught that "is" never entails "ought"; facts by themselves never lead to conclusions about action; and it is of course true that empirical evidence alone never leads conclusively to one specific prescription for action. But "facts" do not hang from the trees like fruit, waiting to be gathered. They are man-made interpretations of our perceptions; and perceiving and interpreting are skills which have to be learnt – and can therefore be relearnt to produce different results. What we actually see are not objectively unique clusters of sense data perceived by everyone in the same way. What we see is a "dosser", a "tramp" or a "homeless man", and these perceptions come loaded with different meanings and policy implications. Although our interpretations do not entail unique conclusions for action, they go far to define the character and urgency of the problems we believe ourselves to be dealing with, and the range of responses which seem relevant to them.

It follows that we must learn to look critically at our perceptions and the interpretations we make of them – not in the hope of reaching some value-free, universally acceptable formula, but to clarify the experiences which provide the context and source of these interpretations, to check their validity and authenticity, and to shed myth, romance and prejudice so far as we can.

If this analysis casts doubt on the meaning and status of "facts", it must also pose questions about values – which leads to the second point I wish to make. Much of the economic theory which provides the tools of policy analysis is founded on the Utilitarian idea that people's preferences should constitute the basic unit of computation and the fundamental criteria for policy decisions. But preferences are derived from a lifetime of experience, and as people's lives unfold their preferences may change. Indeed, one of the main aims of a policy decision may be to bring such changes about: to create an environment which will make new preferences possible. (To integrate homeless people who were hitherto excluded and stigmatised, for example, so that people's attitudes towards them will change as they begin to think of them, not as "dossers", but as neighbours and fellow citizens.) Should we then evaluate the policy according to the values which held sway before it was implemented, or according to those which follow afterwards? Can we predict what will follow with any confidence? There can be no authoritative answer to those questions.

It follows that policy makers and the experts who advise them have to make and defend their own choices. Their values and preferences are not seperable from that work – like dogs to be exercised in the evenings and at week-ends when their owners are off duty. They are an essential part of the weekday professional equipment of such people, and should be more publicly recognised as such.

The third point which follows from these is that perceptions of "facts" and value preferences, being derived from infinitely varied human experience, will always differ. So how do we take decisions which compel us to choose between conflicting perceptions? I have one conclusion to offer.

Let us remember that we shall always be likely to misinterpret the world if we do not take account of the perceptions of those whose welfare is at stake in the decisions to be made. If those people are poor, their perceptions are likely to be disregarded because they lack power. That is why they are poor. So special steps will always have to be taken to give them a voice. (In the case of Glasgow's homeless people, surveys were made. Public perceptions of their character, situation, needs and aspirations proved to be a long way from the truth. The attempt to gain a more authentic perception of these things was one of the starting points for changes in policy.) But surveys are only a beginning. The people for whom decisions are being made should somehow be given a voice in the proceedings – and in academic seminars and conferences about their needs, too – not just as a matter of justice but because we are liable to misunderstand reality if their perceptions are not taken into account. Theirs is not the only voice which must be heard, but it is the most important one.

Housing: the Wobbly Pillar under the Welfare State

Ulf Torgersen, Institute for Political Science, Oslo University, Norway

INTRODUCTION: THE PURPOSE OF THE PAPER

Let me at once state the main theme of the lecture. I believe that some of the characteristics of housing policy and its variations are best described in terms of the uneasy relationship between welfare state purposes and housing policy, and the way in which other purposes are introduced and mixed with the welfare state designs. I believe that housing always will occupy a special and awkward position in welfare thinking due to the special nature of the commodity in question. I also believe that this problem does not necessarily have determinate consequences; rather it is a predicament which gives the policy-makers a certain menu of troubles, from which they may choose, and from which they have to choose. For this reason I shall start by setting out *the institutional peculiarity of housing as part of the welfare state.* I shall move on by way of emphasizing that housing policy, unlike the other fields of welfare state endeavour, will contain much that is rather different from this perspective, and that *the isolation of the welfare aspect is bound to present problems.* In this connection I shall argue that the more the welfare state concerns are tied to and involved in other egalitarian or redistributory·purposes, the more we will see the welfare concerns in trouble; *welfare concerns will suffer from multi-purpose kindness.* I shall illustrate this assumption by showing how well three different welfare-oriented housing policies seem to fare, with particular reference to *the role housing tenures play in the schemes of things in England, Norway and Sweden.* I do not intend to go beyond this brief presentation but I believe that it will be sufficient for the substantiation of the assumption that the autonomy of the welfare state aspects of housing constitutes a very important variable when one wants to describe housing policy.

THE INSTITUTIONAL PECULIARITY OF HOUSING AS A
WELFARE STATE COMPONENT

When we talk of the relationship of "housing" to the "welfare state", we are mentioning two entities of a somewhat problematic nature. "Housing" certainly is no unified field of policy; but more of these fissionary tendencies later. The "welfare state" is no simple term either, and some of the vagueness is related to housing.

On the general and programmatic level, there is no problem. The welfare state is concerned with the provision of goods, of services and/or resources necessary to a life without glaring wants, and with the mobilization of public effort to that end. From this definition housing certainly cannot *a priori* be excluded and obviously deserves a place in the list of relevant domains. Still, housing is often excluded from otherwise rather catholic surveys of the welfare state and its various aspects. Quite frequently it is included in the normal lists of social services, but for instance Michael Walzer's interesting review of equality in different spheres of life in his *Spheres of Justice* does not mention housing along with the many other objects of concern. The vagueness is pinpointed by the British sociologist Thomas Marshall, who in his highly respected book *Social Policy* (possibly the best textbook of its kind in the UK) admits housing within the province of the welfare state. However, he quickly adds: "But these responsibilities are not precisely defined in terms which would give the citizen a legally enforcable right to be housed." The care with which Marshall sets off housing from the rest of the social services is clear and we can do no better than to elaborate on his dictum. Let us see what we can make of it.

The three other domains, pensions, schooling, and health, have a number of common characteristics. In all these areas fairly clear *standards* have been extracted from vaguer notions of need, and these standards define when the institutions in charge are responsible and which course of action they must take. The standards may be embodied in statutes, found in administrative routines or derived from canons of medical science, but regardless of sources they are reasonably clear and the pressure of legalization and bureaucratization — important qualities of the welfare state — represents a further impulse in that direction. Lack of conformity to such standards is increasingly subject to *legal action* from the prospective recipient. The action of the agencies of the welfare state in these three areas is supposed to be *immediate and without delay*, whether it is the provision of schooling for children of the appropriate age, medical care in case of sickness or infirmity, or pensions where old age is reached or other conditions are present. When queues occur, they are considered a serious flaw in the system. Those responsible are *trained bodies of professionals*, often subdivided into proliferating specialities; these occupational categories have been growing alongside the welfare state. What they dispense is *continuous delivery of service, cash or temporary access to equipment*. Such provisions normally cannot be, and where they can, *may not be forwarded for money or other remunerations*. In many cases, though not exclusively, such provisions are supplied only by the welfare state agencies. Each of these three domains are thus not just a type of human concern, but a *fairly unified institutional complex*, with well-defined borders, *esprit de corps* and a national director.

In all these respects the domain of housing sticks out like a sore thumb. Standards of housing exist, and represent guidelines for construction and to some extent for demolition, but the minimum standards that require the public authorities to take action are quite a distance below what is considered a reasonable standard. No such double standard-level can be found in other areas of the welfare state, though pensions have some similarities. There is, except for such critical cases, no immediate action in the provision of help. This area also has less of a body of professionals. What they provide is not so much running supply of cash or service, but a single operation, whether it is a municipal apartment, a long term loan or the like. Housing subsidies and similar kinds of temporary support are also there but the "once-and-for-all"-kind of help looms large. The result of such help may result in ownership of, or long term disposition of a house, with considerable market value. These efforts to help people get an acceptable dwelling are of course likely to be assembled administratively, but the multiplicity of measures may often result in their separation between different governmental departments: the presence of a department of housing is not a fact of all European governments, and – as we shall comment upon later – need not be confined to the welfare state aspect of housing.

The causes of this is fairly simple; housing as commodity or good is very different from other goods, and we do not accept that housing once acquired, and the terms at which it is acquired, is subject to withdrawal or change of terms. Notions of rights in present conditions evolve and solidify: a municipal dwelling provided because of pressing need will not be withdrawn no matter how prosperous the recipient might become, and the increase of rent or its equivalents will be much less easily accepted than the increase of prices on other goods or services. These and other conditions serve to make housing an odd man out in the welfare company. In order to emphasize the difference one may possibly indulge in a minor piece of social science fiction; if one had organized housing in the form of a massive and large national house, with adjustable walls, a house in which dwelling was inexpensive or free, and where the exit of a relative or the birth of a new baby (to mention a few of the standard operating procedures) would lead to wall-adjustment by carpenters following application and administrative decision — then one would have a reasonable approximation to the normal welfare state thinking. I take it that its absence from anything practiced in societies with welfare states brings home the general point.

THE CRUDENESS OF WELFARE INDICATORS

Let us now inspect in somewhat more detail the problems one faces in the choice of welfare routines. If one attempts to find indicators that are supposed to single out individuals or households falling below some standard of housing, and also try to establish some form of economic support aimed at making that piece of housing available if the resources are not available, which often they are not, one will be faced with a number of recurring problems. They can best be classified under the following headlines:

a) **The indicators of need will have to be reasonably crude measures,** as all indicators are. In the UK the municipal housing projects were restricted to the "working class" or "artisans" and it was just after the Second World War that members of the middle class were formally eligible for housing in such housing estates. This obviously created some problems since the question of need did not necessarily respect class boundaries.

b) **Indicators will necessarily change with respect to crudeness over time.** An example from the Oslo Co-operative Housing Association may serve as the prototype. In the first years after the Second World War, the people who enlisted as members of that organization and consequently as applicants for housing in one of their estates were on the whole people in need of housing. But exactly because this Association enjoyed the support of the authorities, new groups applied for membership, and those who are now eligible because of seniority on the list of members are mainly people who are homeowners.

c) **Positions on such waiting lists, the right to continue to possess such housing facilities, and the right to continue to benefit from loans given on reasonable terms will be difficult to dismantle as they pass on to heirs, or as the conditions for this type of benefits otherwise disappear.** Such rights cannot easily be established and dismantled without incurring considerable animosity and distress, since such benefits, once conferred, will tend to be taken for granted.

d) **The actual benefit derived from such grants or favours may change in value, since their value will depend upon conditions external to the welfare-**

oriented agency. The value of some type of loan may undergo serious changes as the economy is subject to changes. Certain loans may become more of a boon because of inflation, and consequently represent more of a benefit than the public authorities had intended. Other benefits may experience a contrary development. Since a particular dwelling may change in attractiveness and market value for a number of reasons this is a recurring aspect of systems of housing welfare.

e) A certain degree of distortion of indicators will occur because the agencies may want to confer not just a piece of housing of quality to the needy ones, but also an environment of quality. For this reason they will like to include categories of households where the need is less pronounced and in this way create more balanced social milieus. A dwelling does not have value just as a physical structure fit to keep the rain out and protect from outsiders looking in, but also as access to collective goods, among which one may class the environment, and maybe particularly the social environment.

I think that in most systems where one has tried with some seriousness to incorporate some welfare state considerations in housing policy one will have encountered one or more of these problems, and possibly more, since I do not claim to have covered the intire repertoire of slightly wayward measures. In themselves they will mean that the purpose of the various measures will in a fairly consistent way be somewhat off the mark. This does not mean that they should be written off as completely ineffective or that they are at completely cross purposes with welfare concerns. But the deviation from a strict welfare priority will be sufficiently noticable to attract attention. Indeed, such attention may also be considered desirable, since a more inclusive category of beneficiaries may be a way of ensuring the continued life and popularity of the measures. We shall for this reason take a closer look at the measures within housing politics including categories that are so wide that the conception of "welfare" cannot circumscribe the purpose, and where other goals are pursued in conjunction with or in conflict with those of welfare provision.

HOUSING POLICY AND MULTI-PURPOSE KINDNESS

The extension of housing policy beyond the welfare conception can appear in many forms. In many cases it is hardly correct to conceive of it as an extension, since the measures may have been shaped by an altogether different kind of thinking. Let us try to enumerate some of the various ways in which humane purposes may appear as supplements to or substitutes for welfare state thinking.

In some cases the two purposes live uneasily side by side. I think the prime example is the British municipal housing system. It was originally conceived of as a kind of cheap housing for people who did not have good housing and who were not well equipped with economic resources. But the Labour government, e.g. the Minister of Housing, Aneurin Bevan, did not see the public housing sector as a boon for the needy but a way of housing the nation, and expressed this vision in rather eloquent language. While the municipal apartments have primarily been reserved for the ones in need of housing, and cheap housing as well, this concern has not been the only one. A number of criteria and purposes has been added, and coexisted with the concern for other social goals. A survey of attitudes to the selling of British council houses was carried out by my colleague Lars Gulbrandsen and myself in 1980. It revealed a considerable split in the opinion; some would reserve the housing for the needy, some would extend it further, and some considered it to be something that ought to be available to everybody. Moreover, those who had the latter opinion also wanted to sell these houses off to the tenants; the combination of opinions in the population consequently differed from the one among the elite in British politics. Such comparatively confused combinations of welfare state purposes and somewhat different ones must be regarded as good examples of mixed intentions.

In some cases an idea which to some degree is related to welfare state thinking is applied across the board, and not trimmed to the more limited task. The welfare state may properly be seen as a repudiation of the free operation of the market, since it conceives of needs independent of the products of the market, and designs measures to supplement the market. But the hostility to the market is often given broad support in a fairly general way. This propensity may have rather unexpected consequences, since measures to counteract the market can benefit the most varied social categories, and the redistributive aspects of such measures, let alone welfare state-aspects, may be rather absent. To this should be added that there is nothing that keeps individuals from claiming the evil of the market forces when this will improve their position with regard to the acquisition of cheap housing, but at the same time keeps them from claiming their right to sell the cheaply acquired piece of real estate at the current free market value. Attempts to keep such tendencies in check by insisting on the control of such sales to keep the possessor from reaping a profit from the public subsidies are normally very complicated to design, hard to enforce, and resisted by recourse to a number of comparisons to other categories of more fortunate beneficiaries of public support.

In some cases purposes outside the province of housing are invoked in order to trim some public measure that might at least be a part of more purposeful organization of housing benefits. It is generally assumed among Norwegian economists that the housing taxes in Norway are rather low. This has been pointed out with envy by the Danish tax evader and former politician, Mogens Glistrup, and with reproach by the professional staff of the OECD. But any improvement in this has been warded off by reference to the consequences this allegedly would have for the *pensioners*. An increase in the housing taxation would, it was claimed, have the undersirable effect of increasing the taxes of the men and women of old age, and this again might mean that they could not afford to stay in the house where they had lived most of their adult life. Viewed in another way, this is essentially a question of the adequacy of the pensions. There probably would not be too many difficulties in allowing that kind of taxes to accumulate, only to be paid the municipality at the moment this piece of property was inherited. It could of course also be handled by some simple rule of tax exemption for the aged. The very same low taxation, in conjunction with the rule that allows a taxpayer to deduct interests without any upper magnitude limit from one's income, has also led to the rapid accumulation of housing property on the part of the people with high incomes. This serves as a housing subsidy and is tolerated as a *substitute for less progressive taxation*, but is of course defended with recourse to such principles as the importance of housing and the sanctity of homes. In the demand for more "flat" mortgages – mortgages where the sum of the principal and the interest stays very low during the first years (and, one surmises, hopefully disappears because of inflation later) is included a wish to *increase the child allowance*, since it is the family expenditures that most frequently are cited as the trouble for which this type of mortgage is supposed to be a suitable remedy. These three measures are all measures that have some impact on the distribution of housing and its cost to the household, but they have other targets as the essential ones, and thus mix the purposes.

I have not discussed the logic of public opinion in the propagation and maintenance of such measures. Quite frequently they conform to the following pattern. Some kind of measure is introduced for reasons that we may not go into. It is shown to have some strange effects, but it is maintained by pointing to some special subgroup, to whom the reform of the measure would be highly problematic. Rather than to remove it and replace it with some more narrow-gauged one, normally a subsidy of some kind, or a tax deduction geared to the specific problem at hand, the measure is allowed to stay on the statute books. It is not my intention to state that such measures run counter to the purpose proclaimed. Rather I would claim that to some extent, it does its job, but also has a number of confusing side effects, the general consequence being that it requires quite some effort to unravel who gets what in which way. Possibly the middle class gets away with some benefits, but a very strong additional random element is to be suspected.

TENURE BIAS AS A CONTEXT OF PURPOSE MIXTURE

We have so far just mentioned some examples of political measures in the two preceding sections. I shall now proceed to sketch the context in which many of the wayward measures occur, and this I believe to be what I shall call *the tenure bias*. Different systems of housing policy are in some way organized around ideas of the relative value or importance of the different tenure forms. As tenure forms I count *homeownership, co-operative housing, municipal housing* and *private renting*. The tenure bias would be expressed in notions about what is really the "best" or the "most worthly" kind of tenure, and notions about what kind of tenure represents the purposes and ideals of the welfare state and related principles.

If we look at Norway, Sweden and the UK, we find rather clear differences with reagard to tenure bias. *Norway* considers, briefly expressed, renting, be it private or public, to be a low form of human housing, historically uncommon except for the rise of this variety of tenure as a consequence of urbanization. It is due to be replaced by other forms of ownership, with no clear preference for the co-operative or non-co-operative variety. Both the latter are considered agents of the welfare state. *Britain* is more complex: it has never bothered about co-operative housing, and the value of private renting is low. Labour had no clear preference for anyone tenure, while the present Tory government, probably with considerable support, thinks that homeownership is the thing to be encouraged as congenial to be independent life man should aspire to. As the tool of the welfare state, however, the council sector would collect most of the votes. *Sweden* differs from both these systems since it is without any particularly pronounced tenure preference. It certainly is in line with the Social Democratic temper that there is a large co-operative sector, and a considerable municipal sector as well. Still it would neither be correct to say that home-ownership is just tolerated, nor that it is considered the wave of the future. Sweden is, at least compared to the other two countries, fairly tenure-neutral. Now let us see how these rather different systems influence the ability to disentangle the purposes and the policy measures from each other.

In *Norway* the post-war purpose was to organize the exodus from the Egypt of private tenancy, and at the same time build more houses, but not too big or too well-equipped ones. Public renting was practically absent, and reduced still more. Both the private homes and the co-operative estates were financed by the Norwegian State Housing Bank, which granted very reasonable loans; the interest as well as the principal was very small. Control of private renting was introduced, and price control of both private homes financed by the Housing Bank and the co-operative homes was part of the scheme. These measures worked for some time, but around the end of the 1960's they became unstuck. The alternative was a tighter co-ordination of the measures — which would have required more controls than previously and in a less control-oriented climate. The Housing Bank experienced that the old houses were practically mortgage-free, and cost very little, and one tried to transfer some of the money to the new dwellings. Large sections of the population were hostile to the housing taxation, which disappeared as the tax assessments did not follow the inflationary price increase. The price control was effective only to some extent, and hardly in the homeownership sector. To work out a comprehensive new policy to replace the many attempts that had tried to help different groups in different ways would have required superhuman political strength. Instead the different measures were replaced by a relaxation of controls in many areas and a very marked trimming of redistributive ambitions.

In *Sweden* the purpose was not conceived as a crusade to abolish renting, nor to establish one variety of housing as the prime tool of the welfare state. Swedish housing policy was not designed to bring ever larger groups into the Canaan of homeownership, whether of a Tory or Social Democratic-populist variety. The ambition of the Social Democratic policy, a policy with considerable support beyond that camp, was to promote the building of new dwellings of a wide variety of tenures and the consistent manipulation of the market in order to establish a comparatively similar expenditure level for tenants in different forms of tenure. One worked *through* the market rather than against it. While this type of policy has had its problems, it has on the whole created fewer problems than the Norwegian brand. Through the importance of the municipal renting sector and some auxiliary devices this fairly simple end has been accomplished rather well, and there have been no concerted efforts to change this combination of absence of tenure bias and dominance of public and semi-public tenure. Moreover other measures with more explicit aims at helping subcategories have been added, but they have not seriously interfered with this main design, which does not preclude considerable subsidies to the sector as a whole.

In the *UK* changes in the main concept of the housing supply have occurred, and the present government has been involved in a consistent efford to reduce the public sector, which by European standards is fairly large and consists only of municipal housing. This bias towards the private homeowning sector, a bias which also has a component of dislike of expenditures to the public sector, and on the whole towards favorable treatment of the homeowners, has left the British housing policy with neither the many faceted, through ill-coordinated populist zeal of the Norwegian case, nor the bias-free system coordination of the market of the Swedish variety. There is not in any of the two other countries the same strong feeling that there is one acceptable tenure form which is also extremely strongly correlated with social status. In none of the other countries is class and voting behaviour that strongly linked to modes of tenure. To the extent that welfare measures are included in the differential treatment of tenures they are, however, operative through the public sector mainly.

The three systems thus exhibit very different combinations of qualities and very different combinations of purposes. It appears to me that the Swedish system allows for the simplest device for combining a fairly clean and well-functionning market and fairly specific welfare measures. The Norwegian system used many devices that aimed at many things simultaneously and for that reason both commanded broad support and were very difficult to change or adjust to other measures. The British system seems to be stuck in a combination of a wish to reduce the public sector through favours given to the private, and the need to give considerable support to the latter exactly because the split along tenure lines emphasizes social inequality rather than softens the class distinctions.

WELFARE ASPIRATIONS AND HOMEOWNER DOMINANCE

Let us conclude with a few remarks on the welfare problems in a society with a predominace of private tenure. The UK aspires to become such a society and Norway is well on the way towards becoming one, particularly since the later rescinding of the market controls have left the co-operative sector in much the same position as the homeowners. It is a fairly widespread notion among politicians with a conservative bent that the free property market has also taken care of the often different levels of running housing expenditures deriving from highly different anti-market measures, some of which are notoriously ineffective. If this was so, the need for intervention would be fairly marginal, though certainly important.

I belive this to be wrong. The elimination of price restrictions on the property market and the elimination of special, protected markets, can make the property market function better. But it can not ensure a degree of equality of housing expenditures among dwellings of the same general size and quality because it cannot ensure the same degree of mortgage load on the different dwellings. Add to this the highly different amounts of inherited housing property owned by the different households. The spectacular growth of the stock of private housing property after the World War II in Norway has only just begun to pass on to the next generation, but in the unsystematic way which is the wont of such undirected processes. Cheap loans with limited expenditures at the outset cannot really solve this problem, since these loans will have to be paid back some time. It seems as if the choice really is between the acceptance of fairly comprehensive dwelling subsidies, or the acceptance of considerable social inequalities, possibly charged on the social expenditure account. The unwillingness to offset great differences in running expenditures linked to great variations in inherited housing property may be considerable, but so may be the reluctance to accept such equalities. It is possible that rather than to work out a systematic way to tackle these issues, the choice will be a series of stop-gap operations. We may thus have both a free property market and more hectic patchwork activity than ever.

The Politics
of Privatization

127-55

U.S., W. Europe

9320

9110

6140

Carolyn Teich Adams, Geography and Urban
Studies, Temple University, Philadelphia,
USA

Privatization is the single most pervasive trend in national housing policies
in the industrialized West. Throughout Western Europe and North America,
national governments are turning increasingly to private financing, private
construction, and private ownership of the national housing stock. This
shift is most visible in those countries that have traditionally held to what
David Donnison has labeled "supplementary" housing policies, or policies
whose aims were limited to bolstering the private housing market and
providing shelter for groups that could not be served by private builders
(Donnison 1967). In two such countries, Britain and the U.S., conservative governments have gone so far as to begin selling off government-owned
housing units to their occupants. And even in countries which had previously pursued more "comprehensive" housing policies aimed at planning
and controlling the *total* volume of housebuilding in the economy, governments are relying more on private capital markets to finance housing while
encouraging higher levels of homeownership. Some observers have used the
label "commodification" to describe this trend toward extension of the
private market in housing, and the accompanying retreat from socialized,
subsidized housing (Harloe 1981).

Obviously the policy of privatization carries some crucial implications
for the operation of housing markets, some of which have been explored
by housing researchers. Most of their work focuses on the question of how
the increasing reliance on the private market affects the distribution of
housing services to different groups and classes in society (Harloe and
Paris 1984, Magri 1977, Achtenberg and Marcuse 1983, Forrest and
Murie 1983).

My theme in this paper is somewhat different from theirs. I am concerned primarily with the consequences of privatization for the policy-
making process, and more specifically with the question of whether the

privatization of housing policy is reconcilable with the corporatist structures of policymaking that have developed in the housing field during the postwar period. During the 1950s and 1960s the massive production programmes undertaken by many European governments have created a set of institutional relationships and roles which can reasonably be characterized as "corporatist" in nature. Webs of interdependence linking public officials, financial institutions and housebuilders, both nonprofit and profitmaking, have developed over the years in response to governmental interventionism. My question is: will governments' moves to withdraw from the housing market under a policy of privatization significantly change the structure of that policymaking process?

Political scientists, especially American political scientists, are typically interested in the question of how politics affects policy -- that is, how the interplay among classes, parties, interest groups and influential individuals shapes governmental outputs. This emphasis in political studies in the U.S. has sometimes been attributed to the pluralist ideology which sees politics as an open competition among interests and the state as little more than the arena within which the contest is played. Pluralist reseachers are chiefly interested in identifying winners and losers in the formulation of particular policies. Neo-Marxists share with pluralists the view of government as merely an instrument, though of course they see it as an instrument of ruling elites rather than of interest groups broadly defined.

My focus in this paper is not on the classic political scientist's question of how politics shapes policy, but rather on the opposite question: how policy shapes politics. Specifically, the subject is how a policy of privatization shapes the policymaking process in the housing field. Our starting point is an assumption that departs from both pluralist and neo-Marxist schools: government is more than an instrument which receives and processes demands from its environment. Government also reaches into the environment to mold the configuration of interests in society. Rather than simply responding to political demands, public officials shape those demands by legitimizing some interests while excluding others, and by locating different policy processes in particular arenas having their own sets of rules, participants, levels of bureaucratic control, etc. (For example, tax policies are made in quite different areanas than social welfare policies.) Governmental policy choices are not only influenced by, but also influence, the structure of interests in the affected sectors of society.

CORPORATISM AND POSTWAR PRODUCTION PROGRAMS

There is no better illustration of the reciprocal power relations between governments and interest associations than the corporatist models of policymaking which have emerged in Western Europe in the last several decades. In many spheres of activity commentators have recognized new forms of political and economic relationships which do not conform to our traditional understanding of democratic politics. The principal feature of these new political forms is the growing interdependence between government and certain functional interest associations whose designated representatives are incorporated into governmental decisionmaking. The role of these organized interests is not limited to simply pressing their demands on public officials. They also assume responsibility for implementing public policy and for persuading their members to accept the decisions jointly arrived at. Corporatism may be defined as

> a mode of political representation and state intervention involving the attribution of public status to interest groups and other organizations involved in regular negotiations with the state within stable, formal or informal institutional contexts, and charged to some extent with the execution of public policy... In other words, organized interests whose cooperation is vital not only gain privileged access to the policy process, but also have a measure of public authority delegated to them (Craig and Harrison 1984: 76–77).

Direct bargaining between functional interests and bureaucratic officials usually takes place behind the scenes and frequently by-passes democratically-elected legislatures. I do not intend to imply that corporatism, where it exists, necessarily supercedes all democratic forms. In fact, corporatist arrangements may prevail in some policy sectors while the politics in other domains remains pluralistic in character (Cawson 1982, Harrison 1984). Lehmbruch has coined the term "liberal corporatism" to connote a mixed system of governance in which corporatist features coexist with liberal democracy (Lehmbruch 1979). And Martin has even speculated that liberal corporatism and pluralism are not qualitatively different forms but simply different points on a continuum. In corporatism groups have a larger and more formalized role in designing and administering public policy. But corporatism should not be viewed as a radically new model of governing since pluralist liberal models have always provided opportunities for political bargaining that by-passed legislatures (Martin 1983).

In which policy sectors are corporatist models most common? The term most often refers to tripartite bargaining involving government, labor and management, in the fields of economic planning, industrial relations and incomes policy. But it can also be applied to the provision of some social welfare benefits, of which housing is the most obvious example. The social welfare fields are most likely to reflect a set of institutional arrangements that Cawson has labeled "meso-corporatism," involving a more restricted range of issues than does the higher-level "macro-corporatism," and not necessarily tripartite in form (Cawson 1985:11).

The strong ties between governments and producer groups in the housing sphere are largely a reflection of the widespread emphasis after World War II on massive construction to meet the acute housing shortages existing throughout Europe. Those shortages, arising from war damage, wartime diversion of resources away from housing, and large-scale demographic shifts, brought governments into the housing field on a scale unknown before the war. Achieving their production goals depended on working through the housebuilding industry, traditionally a fragmented industry composed of large numbers of small producers. Not surprisingly, governments preferred to deal with comprehensive interest associations that would be in a position to negotiate for diverse interests (for example, both large and small builders) and to persuade their members to accept the agreements negotiated on their behalf. They thus sought out such comprehensive associations and used the power of the state to bolster the associations' position.

It is easiest to discern these public/private linkages in situations where government itself was the purchaser of housing services and therefore worked directly with industry in the construction of public housing. Britain's postwar Labour government, for example, embarked on a program of public construction that cemented the bonds between government and building interests. Following a vigorous campaign in the immediate postwar years (completing 190,000 units of public housing in the year of 1948 alone), subsequent British governments (even Conservative ones) managed to maintain a high rate of production over most of the postwar period. From 1946 to 1976, British local housing authorities built at the impressive rate of 143,000 units per year (Merret 1979: Chapter 9). During that period local governments, which were the bodies responsible for building and managing public housing in Britain, developed close working relationships with the housebuilding industry -- bonds that were sometimes even stronger than the officials' ties to their own constituencies. Dunleavy's study of several local housing authorities concluded that neither public opinion nor parliamentary politics played an important role in the high-rise boom in British public housing in the 1960s; instead, the causes for the boom can be traced to the shared understandings and interests of housebuilders and public officials. Intense pressure on local authorities by major contractors led to increasing control over public housing by these firms, whose architects by the mid-1960s were designing over 20 per cent of all public housing and nearly 70 per cent of industrialized housing (Dunleavy 1981; see also Dickens and Goodwin 1981).

On the continent in France, West Germany, Sweden, and the Netherlands, postwar governments adopted labor unions, religious groups, voluntary and cooperative societies as their primary instruments for the provision of housing. Backing these non-profit enterprises with low-interest government loans, public authorities in these countries made it possible for them to secure further loans from private credit sources. Many of these nongovernmental builders became large, highly professional enterprises with far-flung interests throughout the particular nation in which they operated. Working through such companies gave governments more leverage over costs and building standards in a greater number and variety of projects than they could have gained by working in more fragmented housing markets. Hence it was in the interest of public authorities to encourage their formation.

Perhaps the most dramatic example of government initiatives to structure the political environment by encouraging industry associations is that of postwar Sweden. In a sense, the Social Democrats actually created Sweden's producer lobby by sponsoring the growth of SABO, an association of nonprofit building corporations, as well as the massive expansion of the cooperatives, HSB and Svenska Riksbyggen. By manipulating interest rates, the Social Democrats moved quckly after World War II to channel private credit away from mortgages and to establish the government as the primary credit source for homebuilding. In its role as banker to homebuilders, the government proceeded to give preference to nonprofit housing associations in distributing loans and to encourage the formation of national associations to represent them. According to Headey,

> the nonprofit building corporations, which were in effect created by the (Swedish) government, HSB, Svenska Riksbyggen and the construction workers' trade union have all gained additional members, resources and influence because of central government programmes and municipal contracts (Headey 1978:81).

France's postwar government was also instrumental in building the capacity within the construction industry to carry out its postwar programme. Typical of much of French industry, the construction sector in the 1950s was composed of small, traditionbound firms which resisted introducing new building technologies and materials. The national *Ministère de la Construction et du Logement* sponsored research into new construction techniques and materials and used its leverage to encourage the merger of small firms into larger ones as well as to promote the use of modern financial and management practices by housebuilders (Pearsall 1984). Like Sweden, France provided low-interest loans to nonprofit housing societies (known in France as HLMs, or *habitations à loyer modéré)* which dominated construction well into the 1960s.

West Germany's government has played an active role, not only by bolstering the position of certain industry associations, but by influencing their internal organization as well. A comparative study of the structure of housebuilding associations in Britain and West Germany argued that many of the important differences observed in the two nations' interest associations could be explained by differing governmental structures and actions since World War II. Unlike their British counterparts, German national officials will often refuse to talk to individual firms, no matter how large, referring them to their own associations. Naturally this practice enhances the position of the peak associations in the German system. German officials have few qualms about trying to mold interest associations in ways that are useful to the government. British civil servants, on the other hand, generally treat business interest associations as voluntary bodies whose organization is a matter for firms to decide among themselves (Grant and Streeck 1985).

Interestingly, housing policy in the U.S. approximates more closely a corporatist model than do most realms of American policymaking. By and large, the American political process does not display the corporatist tendencies that we have observed in postwar Europe. One reason is that there are few peak associations which have enough coverage to be formally recognized as speaking for their constituents. Thus there are few examples in the U.S. of formal incorporation of interest associations into the policy process (Salisbury 1979). Nonetheless the influence of interest groups over policy is sometimes substantial, and this is nowhere more apparent than in the housing field.

As one of the best-organized lobbies in the nation, the housing coalition has had a direct influence on American policy since the 1930s, when the effort to create federal subsidies for home ownership was spearheaded by the major financial institutions connected with the housing industry (the Mortgage Bankers Association, the American Bankers Association, the U.S. Savings and Loan Association, and the National Association of Mutual Savings Banks) and by the major building industry organization (the National Association of Home Builders). This industry coalition has persisted with few basic changes up to the present day, continuing to operate as a clientele group supporting national mortgage insurance programs and favourable credit conditions for homeownership, and (since the mid-1960s) supporting subsidies for social housing as well. The activities of this powerful lobby have extended beyond the legislature into a direct working relationship with bureaucratic officials in which industry groups have supplied personnel and written guidelines for federal agencies (Checkoway 1980, Lilley 1973).

The American situation, however, does not qualify as geniuine corporatism because it does not display the *reciprocity* between government and interest associations that defines corporatist models. Compared with the U.S., the more direct control exerted by most European governments over their domestic credit institutions and their larger share of the total investment in residential construction have placed them in a far stronger bargaining position vis-a-vis private builders.

THE TREND TOWARD PRIVATIZATION

No aspect of housing policy has drawn more comment in recent years than the trend toward privatization -- a trend that is also observable in other social welfare areas, including health care, transportation, and education. Yet for all the commentary on the subject, there are no universally-accepted definitions of the term. Indeed, as Donnison has pointed out, "it is a word which should be heavily escorted by inverted commas as a reminder that its meaning is at best uncertain and often tendentious" (Donnison 1984). In the British context, which is surely the most vivid example to date of the privatization of housing, the word is associated with the government's campaign to sell off public housing units to the tenants who occupy them. The Thatcher Government has proclaimed its intent to bolster political democracy by encouraging property ownership, a goal which involves transferring a significant portion of the nation's public housing stock into private hands. In a similar, though more limited move, the Reagan administration in the U.S. created in 1986 a demonstration program to sell several thousand public housing units to their occupants.

The high visibility of these policy shifts, particularly in Britain, has fueled a misconception that privatization as a policy is attributable to the ascendence of neo-liberal political sentiments. Such a conclusion is easy to draw from the public rhetoric of conservative parties throughout the industrialized West -- a rhetoric which stresses the need for governments to withdraw from the provision of goods and services, allowing private markets to take over these functions. But there are two problems with this tendency to identify privatization with the rising fortunes of conservative parties in the 1980s: (1) privatization as a policy has been pursued by governments other than conservative-controlled governments, and (2) privatization does *not* withdraw government from the market; it merely changes the nature of governmental intervention.

When we look at the industrialized West as a whole, it seems clear that the privatization of housing policy, though only recently discovered and labeled, represents a trend that is several decades old. If by privatization we mean a shift away from direct government financing and/or production of housing units, toward housing that is produced by the private market, then privatization is a widespread and longstanding strategy of Western governments. Note that this definition of the term does not necessarily imply that governments withdraw from markets entirely, leaving consumers to pay for a good or service from their private incomes. In fact, privatization usually involves large-scale transfers to consumers to subsidize their purchase of private housing.

The trend toward privatization began several decades ago when governments no longer faced the severe shortages of the early postwar period. And it began, not with the owner-occupied segment but with the rental segment of the market. As the housing shortage receded, public debate in many of the nations of Western Europe began to focus on housing affordability as the major housing issue. Inflation and rising construction costs affected all income groups and segments of the market, pushing questions of equity in the distribution of housing costs and opportunities to the fore (Priemus 1983, Heclo and Madsen 1986). Production subsidies gave governments little leverage on these problems of distribution and affordability because they could not be used to target particular types of households. Increasingly, governments turned to housing allowances to supplement construction programs. Sweden, the Netherlands, West Germany and France all reduced the size of their production programs in the 1970s while expanding the coverage of housing allowances (Howenstine 1986).

West Germany made the earliest postwar moves toward privatizing the housing market in the early 1960s, just as soon as the postwar housing emergency had begun to subside. Rent control and tenant protections were phased out, and the *Wohngeld*, Germany's version of housing allowances, was significantly expanded in 1965. So quick were the Germans to shift toward a private market approach that some observers have interpreted that country's social construction program of the 1950s as a temporary aberration rather than a significant policy change (Marcuse 1982).

France's experience offers another example, albeit more gradual, of a shift away from production subsidies and toward allowances. Despite the creation of massive supply subsidies through the HLM movement in the early postwar period, French policymakers began in the 1960s to offer less and less favorable financial terms for the HLMs, steadily increasing the interest rates charged to HLMs for the allowances (*aide à la personne*) to replace production subsidies (*aide à la pierre*) was finally articulated in several major reports published in 1975. The most influential of them, the Barre report, was named for the chair of a government-appointed study commission and future prime minister. France's policy of subsidizing construction, Barre argued, mainly benefited the better-off groups in French society. His conclusion, that market forces should play the principal role in housing provision, was embodied in the Housing Act of 1977, which both reduced government expenditures for construction and channeled subsidies directly to householders through allowances (Pearsall 1984:39).

The increased reliance on allowances by West Germany, France and other Western governments constitutes one form of privatization because it assigns to the private market the responsibility for producing rental housing, while government merely provides a cash transfer to tenants who choose among housing alternatives in the open market. Another important policy instrument to promote privatization is the tax expenditure, which goes to owners instead of renters. Tax expenditures may be defined as losses of tax revenue attributable to provisions of tax laws that allow special exclusions, exceptions, or deductions from gross income, or provide special credits, preferential tax rates, or deferral of tax liability. Normally these tax concessions take the form of government forgiveness of taxes on that portion of income devoted to paying interest on mortgage loans. So widespread and large is this form of subsidy to housing that it has created what one observer called a "second welfare state" coexisting with the more widely recognized "first" welfare state (Headey 1978:24).

The U.S. is perhaps the premier example of the use of tax expenditures to subsidize housing. The mass income tax, first adopted during World War I, has provided enormous incentives to homeowners, including deductions for interest payments and property taxes, deferral or exclusion of capital gains on home sales, and a decision not to tax imputed rent. In addition to subsidizing homeownership, the U.S. government also uses tax expenditures as a spur to suppliers of low-income, multi-family housing; by allowing owners to accelerate the depreciation of their rental properties, the government creates the opportunity for declaring tax losses. These tax concessions to owners of rental property were significantly increased in 1981 by the Economic Recovery Tax Act, enhancing the profitability for all owners of housing developments, including social housing built for low-income families. As of 1985, tax expenditures comprised the bulk of federal subsidies to housing; homeowner deductions cost the government $49.3 billion and investor deductions another $5.8 billion, while the total direct expenditures for all social housing programs amounted to only about one-fourth as much (Dolbeare 1985:34).

Britain, too, has a longstanding tax policy allowing full deductibility of interest payments on mortgages. In addition, owner-occupiers have been free from capital gains tax and capital transfer tax and, from 1963 onward, free from tax on imputed rent. As in the U.S., the subsidy granted to property owners via the tax expenditure is far in excess of direct subsidies to the tenants in social housing. In 1982/83, for example, the average owner-occupier received a subsidy of 366 pounds per year, compared with an average subsidy to council tenants of only 206 pounds (Balchin 1985:239). Clearly, among the nations included in this discussion, Britain and the U.S. are normally perceived as the bastions of home ownership. They would therefore be expected to offer the largest tax concessions to property owners. But what about the governments on the continent? Table 1 shows that even in these countries, tax expenditures constitute a sizeable proportion of housing subsidies, though they do not always go exclusively to owner-occupiers. In West Germany, for example, the impressive tax expenditures go more to the owners of rental properties than to owner-occupiers. For German rental housing, all capital gains remain untaxed so long as they are reinvested in real property.

Table 1. Composition of Housing Subsidies in Selected Countries.

	Housing Allowances	Tax Concessions	Producer	Other
France (1984)	22%	43%	35%	0%
West Germany (1978)	9%	50%	21%	20%
Netherlands (1983)	27%	27%	34%	12%
Sweden (1981)	24%	47%	29%	0%

Source: E. Jay Howenstine, *Housing Vouchers: A Comparative International Analysis* New Brunswick: Rutgers University Center for Urban Policy Research, 1986, pp. 110–111.

The relative proportions of subsidies going to renters versus owners has, of course, been hotly debated in a number of the nations under scrutiny here, but the tax expenditure remains a primary vehicle of government support for the housing market. Even the Swedish government, whose ruling Social Democrats in the early 1970s openly challenged the fairness to renters of these tax concessions, ultimately concluded that its best course of action would be to *increase* the subsidies going to renters rather than to *reduce* those available to homeowners (Heidenheimer et al. 1983:112).

Yet another manifestation of the gradual privatization of housing policy has been the withdrawal of governments from the role of primary lender, shifting to private capital markets the responsibility for providing the credit needed to build social housing. Here too, West Germany led other European nations. Immediately after the war, the government had taken the lead in making large capital loans and grants to nonprofit builders of social housing. As early as 1956, however, national legislation authorized a shift away from the government's role as banker, toward government subsidies to assist nonprofits in repaying loans to private credit sources. By 1967 government outlays for this latter type of subsidy exceeded those for government-provided loans and grants. When the legislature extended subsidies to higher-income households in 1967, it employed only the device of subsidizing privately-secured loans. "Thus, private capital, now more significantly available, played an ever-increasing role in the housing field, including subsidized housing" (Marcuse 1982:96).

France moved in the same direction, starting a few years later than West Germany. During the 1950s and 1960s most of the funds flowing into the housing market came from government sources. The vast majority of units constructed were government-financed, either as HLMs or as subsidized private dwellings (*secteur aidé*). However, once the French government succeeded in organizing an effective mortgage market in the mid-1960s, banks and other private financial institutions began to take over as the main sources of housing funds. Government activity shifted toward providing subsidies to reduce the interest on loans supplied by private credit sources. By 1975 the banks advanced almost half of the credit used to finance the construction and purchase of housing in France (Bandyopadhya 1984:167). The Housing Act of 1977 carried this trend even further.

The French have pioneered in the use of mixed-economy corporations (*sociétés d'économie mixte*) as a device for securing private capital to support the construction of social housing. Introduced in the 1950s, these public/private corporations brought together representatives of local government (who usually controlled 65 per cent of the votes on governing boards) with private sector investors holding the remaining shares. Although such organizations can boast considerable success in promoting housing development, they have a less impressive record in achieving their social welfare goals. Their history is one of gradual retreat from their initial mandate to create social housing; increasingly they have financed middle-income housing and economic development projects instead of low-income housing (Eisinger 1982).

The effect on the housing market of the various privatizing strategies outlined above is predictable. Table 2 shows the widespread decline during the 1970s in the proportion of units produced by government and by other nonprofit suppliers. In every one of the nations listed, the private builders' share of production rose during the last decade.

Far from being products of conservative political ascendancy, the various policy instruments sketched above have been employed by politicians of both left and right. Indeed, we can go far in explaining their growing popularity by recognizing their appeal to parties of vastly different ideological stripes. Housing allowances are seen by politicians of the left as a way to equalize access to housing for their working class constituents. Politicians on the right are prone to support allowances because they assign the primary responsibility for housebuilding to the private market. Much the same analysis applies to tax expenditures for owner-occupiers, which have brought such significant benefits to working class home owners that politicians of the left have consistently managed to overlook their regressive nature, while those on the right applaud their effectiveness in stimulating property ownership. The political consensus surrounding tax expenditures

Table 2. Dwellings Completed, by Type of Investor, 1970 and 1980.

	National, County and Local Governments, %	Nonprofits, %	Private Builders, %
France			
1970	.7	32.2	67.1
1980	.8	20.6	78.6
West Germany			
1970	2.3	18.4	79.3
1980	1.5	8.6	89.8
Netherlands			
1970	16.3	31.6	52.1
1978	2.7	27.7	69.6
Sweden			
1970	4.3	53.9	41.8
1980	2.4	33.3	64.2
Britain			
1970	48.6	3.3	48.1
1980	36.1	11.2	52.7
United States			
1970	2.3	0.0	97.9
1980	.5	0.0	99.5

Source: United Nations Economic Commission for Europe, *Annual Bulletin of Housing and Building Statistics for Europe.*

has been unassailable even in countries with the strongest socialist parties. Despite the recent partisan conflict in Britain over the Conservatives' effort to sell off council housing, the general pattern in Britain over the past 25 years has been one of party convergence on government subsidies to home-ownership (McLeay 1984). France's Socialist Party made it clear from 1948 onward that it supported measures to bolster private ownership, largely because the gravity of the housing shortage made virtually all housing schemes acceptable. Ultimately even the French Communist Party abandoned its earlier opposition to owner occupation (DuClaud-Williams 1978:216, 245). In West Germany it was the Social Democrats who took the initiative in 1977 to extend tax concessions to the purchase of existing houses (as opposed to newly-constructed dwellings). Up to that time the government had restricted tax subsidies to newly-built housing as a stimulus to construction; the extension by the socialists in 1977 vastly increased the housing stock to which these incentives apply (Harloe 1981:37).

It is perhaps not so surprising that traditional socialists and conservatives find indirect subsidies to renters and property owners an acceptable alternative to direct government support of producers. What is somewhat more difficult to comprehend is the willingness of neo-liberal, or supply-side ideologists, in the Reagan and Thatcher regimes to support these costly subsidy programs. After all, supply-siders would normally oppose large-scale subsidies to consumption, preferring instead to channel government support to what they consider to be the more "productive" sector of the economy. Yet here again, the nature of these indirect subsidies allows multiple interpretations. Using a certain logic, adherents to supply-side economics can justify them as subsidies to suppliers. As economists frequently point out, homeowners are not only the consumers of their housing; they are also its suppliers. (This is the basis for the argument in favor of taxing homeowners on the imputed rent that they collect as "landlords" to themselves.) Some policy analysts have argued that housing allowances as well are really subsidies to suppliers (private landlords), since they permit rent increases that could not otherwise be imposed on tenants (Marcuse 1982: 95). Viewed from this perspective, the indirect subsidies that are the centerpiece of privatization in housing have an understandable appeal for neo-liberals.

IS PRIVATIZATION COMPATIBLE WITH CORPORATISM?

The Persistence of Government/Producer Linkages

The interdependent relationships which have linked Western governments to producer and financer groups in the postwar period are largely a product of the strong production emphasis in housing policies. The political commitment to a massive expansion of the housing stocks of these countries bred a system of bargaining over policy that benefited governments, labor, housebuilding firms and financial institutions, furnishing a classic example of the way in which policy sometimes shapes the policymaking process.

Will the shift in housing policy, away from direct subsidies to production and toward indirect subsidies to transactions carried out in the private market, undermine these corporatist arrangements? It would certainly seem plausible that a policy which trades direct intervention for indirect subsidies to the market would require far less institutionalized bargaining between government and producer groups. One might even argue that privatization embodies a clear rejection of corporatism, insofar as it seeks to limit government direction of the economy and expand market freedom.

Privatization might be seen to weaken corporatist arrangements in several important ways. First, it provides less incentive for producers to organize themselves into peak associations. Under corporatism the promise of official incorporation into the policy process creates incentives for producers to join peak associations and to accept guidance from sector leaders.

But when governments shift to subsidizing consumers (either through housing allowances or tax concessions), then producer groups are no longer assured that direct benefits will result from their collaboration with government. The benefits they receive will come only indirectly, mediated by the market.

On the government's side there is a similar prospect for diminishing returns from corporatism because government wields less control over production in a privatized economy. Subsidies to consumers, no matter how massive, do not yield the same opportunities for governments to influence how much housing is built, of which different types and prices, in which locations, on what schedules. Rather than reviewing production plans and schedules, public officials distribute entitlements that go to broad categories of beneficiaries. Indeed, politicians advocating privatization often defend it precisely on the grounds that it replaces government controls with market self-regulation. This was explicit, for example, when the Dutch government adopted a policy of "liberalization" in 1969, gradually removing many government regulations concerning volume of production, quality, price and geographical location of housing, and replacing them with the free market as a regulator (Van Weesep 1984).

The tensions that may arise between governments and private sector institutions under privatization are illustrated by Britain's experience with the building societies, the private nonprofit bodies which dominate the financing of owner-occupied housing in that country. As a result of the societies' independent status, government exercises little direct control over the structure of housing opportunity in the owner-occupied sector. The building societies have created and administer their own rationing devices by, for example, refusing to lend in certain areas, refusing to lend on houses over a certain age, lending only to those who have had deposits with the society for a minimum period of time, and limiting loans to a proportion of the property value. When criticized for any of these practices, the societies invariably reply that their first obligation is to protect the investments of their depositors, rather than to pursue social goals.

To look at the U.S., which has historically pursued the most thoroughly privatized housing policies of any Western nation, one might easily conclude that such policies are incompatible with corporatism. Although the American housebuilding industry wields enormous influence over public policy, there are few signs of any reciprocal control exercised by government. For the most part government has simply supported the industry in its pursuit of a consistently high volume of construction (Checkoway 1980). But there are two problems with using the American case to draw the conclusion that privatization and corporatism are inimical to one another. First, as noted earlier, housing is a sector in which corporatist tendencies are actually *strong* relative to other sectors in the American economy. Second, although they did promote large-scale production, especially of suburban housing, postwar policies in the U.S. were more aimed at stimulating the economy than addressing the housing problems of particular groups or regions. Consequently, federal officials never sought the kinds of controls over production that characterized European policy systems. It is not clear that the government could not have achieved some greater degree of influence over the industry, had that been its goal (though of course one would never expect to see the same level of intervention in the U.S. as in the more statist systems of Europe).

A nation in which corporatism and privatization appear to have flourished together in the postwar period is West Germany. Marcuse has described the basic goal of Germany's postwar housing policies as permitting "maximum scope and support to the private housing industry (property owners, builders, suppliers, finance, management) with governmental regulation and subsidy limited to supporting that industry, except for those situations in which other overriding priorities exist" (Marcuse 1982:88) In the years immediately following the war, of course, the government recognized a need to exert strong public control in order to overcome the critical shortages. But as early as the mid-1950s the Christian Democrats began shifting housing policy to the "normal" focus on the private market. Ever since then, with the exception of a brief period of renewed governmental activism in the late 1960s, an underlying assumption of private sector primacy has guided German policymakers.

Yet its commitment to the private market has not prevented the German government from intervening systematically in the housebuilding industry, especially to support and protect the small-scale artisan segment of the industry. Artisan firms are represented by a peak association (*Zentralverband des Deutschen Baugewerbes*) which represents about 80 per cent of the firms in the industry. Its high level of coverage (impressive for so fragmented an industry) is in part due to the legal and financial assistance it receives from government. A national law regulating artisan firms (*Handwerksrecht*) requires that they employ certified artisans and that they belong to regional "chambers of artisans" which offer training programs and technical assistance to members. The government also subsidizes low-interest loans to help certified artisans in setting up their own businesses. The over-all effect of public intervention is to segment the market and limit competition, all with the intent of protecting these small businesses (Grant and Streeck 1985). The German government also bargains directly with the other important peak association in the industry representing large industrial builders (*Hauptverband der Deutschen Bauindustrie*), though its ties to the HDB are not so close as to the artisans' association.

Even so zealous an advocate of privatization as the Thatcher government in Britain does not appear to find its commitment to free markets an obstacle to preserving some coporatist forms. It was in fact Thatcher's new Environment Secretary who in 1979 formed th so-called "Group of Eight" to provide ministerial access to representatives of the construction industry. The group's membership included the trade unions, the design professions, and the two major peak associations in the housebuilding industry, the Building Employers Confederation and the Federation of Civil Engineering Contractors. Unlike earlier governments' consultative machinery, it excluded smaller builders and subcontractors -- an interesting move, given the current government's professed support for small business and economic competition.

Even in systems which have strongly favored housing allowances and subsidies to ownership at the expense of direct subsidies to production, we see a universal tendency for producer interests to organize into large-scale associations in order to bargain with the institutions of government. Admittedly, their focus under conditions of privatization seems slightly different: instead of seeking direct subsidies, they lobby for measures that will maximize consumer demand for housing. The locus of activity shifts accordingly to finance and tax policy. But they have not dissolved, nor should we expect them to.

Privatization and the Politics of Consumption

Do housing consumers, whose influence on postwar production programs was extremely limited, wield any greater influence in privatized systems? Historically, consumer associations have been conspicuously absent from the corporatist bargaining that has shaped housing policy. Accounts of the construction programs of several European nations reveal that in fact, policymakers frequently ignored consumer preferences in their rush to erase postwar shortages. The Swedish government continued to support high-rise housing even after public opinion clearly favored low-rise or single-family dwellings (Headey 1978:64, Nesslein 1982:242). The French government's long-term sponsorship of the large-scale, high-density projects known as *grands ensembles* showed a similar lack of concern for consumer tastes. Although there were already indications of consumers' dislike for these huge slab or tower apartment buildings in the 1960s, the government continued to support their construction throughout the 1970s. Should we conclude that in such cases public officials actively resisted pressure from consumer interests? Not necessarily. Dunleavy's study of British high-rise housing shows that even though high-rise housing was an extremely unpopular form of housing among the British working class, the tenants and prospective tenants most affected by the government's building program almost completely failed to protest or to try to influence the policies favored by public officials and the construction industry (Dunleavy 1981; see also Ash 1980).

Some observers have suggested that indeed we *can* expect to see increasing political activism on the part of those who consume government-subsidized goods and services. Castells, Szelenyi and other theorists proceed from the assumption that government in advanced capitalist systems must increasingly assume responsibility for supplying consumer goods and services that are unprofitable. Growing government intervention in such fields as health, education, transportation and housing leads to the emergence of a visible agent that may be held responsible for various distributive effects which consumers previously accepted as the natural and inevitable consequences of market forces. By intervening to supply public services, therefore, government politicizes service issues and invites a collective response, particularly from lower income groups which depend most heavily on collective services (Castells 1977). Other researchers studying middle and upper-middle income communities in Western postindustrial cities have similarly concluded that government must cater to consumer tastes or risk mobilizing service users into an organized political opposition (Ley and Mercer 1980). Following on Castells, a great deal has been written on the question of whether the cleavages arising in communities around consumption issues (particularly the fissure between consumers of collective services and consumers of private market services) are co-terminous with class cleavages. Castells appears to think that they are, and that class struggles can readily be linked to struggles over consumption issues. Others believe that production-based (class) cleavages are independent of consumption-based cleavages. Dunleavy (1979) argued that consumption sectors are only partially independent from consumption sectors; class influences one's access to different modes of consumption, for example, in housing and transportation), yet consumption sectors nonetheless tend to cross-cut class cleavages. Saunders (1984) thinks that the division between those who consume privatized as opposed to collective services (especially housing) is totally distinct from the question of class. It is neither the basis of one's class position nor an expression of class, yet it is just as important as class for understanding contemporary social stratification. Magri (1977) has argued for France that government promotion of owner occupation divides the working class into those oriented toward accession to ownership and those for whom ownership becomes ever more distant.

How should we assess the effects of privatization on the prospects for more political activism among consumers and perhaps even major party realignments? Saunders asserts that

> privatization of welfare provisions is intensifying this cleavage to the point where sectoral alignments in regard to consumption may

come to outweigh class alignments in respect of production, and that housing tenure remains the most important single aspect of such alignments (Saunders 1984:203).

The conclusion of much of the current commentary on consumption cleavages is that the differing material interests of renters and owners will manifest themselves in organized political acitivity, either through protests and single-issue campaigns, or via a realignment of political parties. Consumers, in short, will become a more potent political force.

Yet a great deal of what we know about political behavior calls such a vision of consumption politics into question, particularly given the privatization of housing policy. It has, of course, always been far more difficult to organize consumers than producers. Olson has offered an explanation for this widely-observed fact in his logic of collective action (Olson 1965). The advent of indirect subsidies in the form of housing allowances and tax expenditures makes it even less likely that housing consumers will organize around issues of housing policy. Entitlements of this kind are distributed individually to those in eligible categories. This structure of benefits atomizes recipients, discouraging the development of political solidarity or the organizational basis needed to acquire and wield political power. Nor can recipients of government subsidy in these forms be readily identified by others in the community. How would renters know which of their neighbors received housing allowances and what the size of those allowances might be? Nor is it easy to distinguish a homeowner benefiting from tax concessions from one who carries no mortgage and hence derives no tax benefits. In a government-owned housing project the tenants can easily identify one another and organize against their "landlord;" they see themselves, and are seen by outsiders, as a group sharing a common political interest. But strategies that rely on private market mechanisms take policy out of the realm of mass politics. They cannot as easily be openly debated as can direct expenditures. The recent experience of housing advocates in America's low-income communities is illustrative. Organizers find themselves more often negotiating with private investors than with political officials: "tax policy tools and market implementation strategies force neighborhood groups out of the political arena and into the economic marketplace" (Clarke 1984).

A related consequence of privatization is that the locus of conflict over housing policy shifts away from local governments, which in many nations have been among the important operators of social housing programs. Local officials have provided a target against which consumers could mobilize. And local governments have provided a forum in which people from non-producer groups could participate more easily than in the corporatist bargaining at the national level (Sharpe 1984). When national governments shift from production programs to housing allowances, they limit the role and the political liability of local governments for housing provision. The advantage to national policymakers is, of course, that entitlement programs are not dependent on local implementation. This can be especially important for conservative national governments, which may find it difficult to secure cooperation from localities that are dominated by opposition parties or coalitions. In implementing allowances or tax concessions, national politicians can act unilaterally. Ironically, it appears that the general shift to consumer subsidies may thus weaken consumers as a political force, further aggravating the imbalance between consumers and the producers who are so well-organized at the national level.

What about the prospect of national party realignments that might reflect the new consumption cleavages? Granted, there is scattered evidence from several nations that homeowners are more likely than renters to vote conservatively. For example, electoral studies in Sweden show that even within the same occupational groups, homeowners are somewhat less likely than renters to vote for the Social Democrats (Holmberg 1981). In the U.S., research has uncovered only a very modest association of homeownership with conservatizing political effects, both for working class and for all owners (Kingston 1984). But do we have here the makings of dramatic political realignments? Probably not, for two main reasons.

First, in order for votes to realign themselves on the basis of housing issues, there must be identifiable differences in the positions taken by different parties. But the move toward privatization, based chiefly on housing allowances and tax expenditures to promote homeownership, has attracted widespread agreement among parties of both the left and right. Rather than lose their traditional electoral base, parties of the left have endorsed programs which assign the major role to the private market. For example, electoral considerations have played an important role in changing the British Labour Party's stance toward homeownership (Harloe 1981, Kelley et al. 1985).

One might, however, take the position that it is not merely the party's position on housing issues that determines voter allegiance. Rather, housing can be seen as tied to a whole constellation of issues (including education, health and transportation) which separate the interests of voters who find themselves in different consumption sectors. But here one must recognize the possibility of cross-cutting cleavages that give rise to severe cross-pressures (Franklin and Page 1984). What about the voter who owns his own home, yet relies on public education and public transportation? The cross-pressures produced by voters' different positions vis-a-vis different consumer goods may very well lead to political stability rather than change. More likely than dramatic voter realignments is the prospect of increased tension within parties between the interests of private market consumers and those who depend on collective services.

Changing Policy Arenas

Up to this point I have argued that privatization brings about only modest changes in the organization and activities of the key players in the policy process. Housing producers continue to be represented in the halls of government, lobbying now for policies that maintain high levels of demand instead of production programs. Consumer groups continue to play a marginal role, poorly organized and excluded from the policy process; if anything, their influence declines under privatization. And political parties, though they may experience internal conflict between the advocates of private versus collective consumption, typically reshape their programme to accommodate to the desire for ownership in all classes.

Let us turn now to an aspect of housing policymaking that *does* change with privatization: the arena in which bargaining occurs. Privatization leads to a gradual migration of housing issues into the realm of finance and tax policy. Obviously, housing policy has never been made in isolation from wider policies of taxation and economic management. But in the current economic climate, tax and finance instruments have become the most important levers on housing expenditures. The reasons are two-fold, having to do with both the economic context and the nature of consumer subsidies.

Throughout the industrialized West there is concern in the 1980s about recapitalizing industries to make them more competitive in international markets. The globalization of the economy, increasing competition from low-wage countries, and high levels of unemployment have prompted policymakers to search for ways to channel investment capital to productive sectors of the economy. Debates on housing policy are focused increasingly on the competition for capital between housing and other more productive investments.

U.S. critics of housing policies charge that they have drawn savings and investment away from more productive uses and thereby jeopardized economic productivity (Tuccillo 1980, Sternlieb and Hughes 1980, Peterson 1980). Similarly, British economists in the late 1970s began to worry that the privileged position of housing finance had made it too attractive an alternative (Lansley 1979, Kilroy 1978). More recent evidence shows that homeowners are re-mortgaging their homes to finance other consumer purchases like automobiles, burdening even further the mortgage credit market (Kemeny and Thomas 1984). One particularly outspoken critic charged British building societies with directly contributing to Britain's industrial decline:

> Having wrecked industrial investment in the last decade they (the building societies) should be encouraged to find ways to direct their ten billion a year mortgage disbursement towards it in a massive rescue operation (Pawley 1983).

A comparative study of the U.S. and several West European countries has suggested that the nations giving the highest incentives for homeownership are those with the slowest-growing small business sector, because the lure of homeownership draws potential entreprenuers to put their capital into housing (Farmer and Barrell 1982). In several of these countries, economists are pressing government to restrain investments in housing.

Yet the adoption of privatization as a policy strategy has made it harder to control housing investments than it was in the past. This is not solely because responsibility for housing investment has shifted out of governmental hands and into the private capital markets. It is also because governments find it harder to restrain their own expenditures for housing. Funding for production programs could be limited by building targets set from year to year. When funding ran out, no new projects were subsidized. But outlays for housing allowances and tax concessions, distributed as entitlements to categories of eligible beneficiaries, are much harder to limit. They are excellent vehicles for encouraging consumption, but less appropriate for restraining it. This is to some extent an unforeseen result of privatization; in fact government policy favoring homeownership has often been perceived as a way of cutting back government support for housing (Lundqvist 1984). But of course governments have *not* reduced their support for housing, only transformed it from direct subsidy into tax expenditure.

Given the drawbacks of these major housing policy instruments as levers on housing investment, some governments are turning to the regulation of financial institutions as an avenue of influence. In all the advanced industrial countries governments exercise considerable control over the legal and institutional framework of financial markets and the differentiated channels through which credit circulates into the spheres of industrial development, housing finance, consumer debt. etc. Governments also regulate the amounts of capital flowing into these various channels by fixing interest rates, and sometimes even by direct allocations of credit.

Perhaps the strongest grip on the housing credit market is exercised by the French government, whose main vehicle for influencing the credit supply is the *Credit Foncier*, a private corporation owned by private shareholders, but run by senior executives who are appointed by the government, according to policies decided in agreement with the government (policies which limit the type, the cost, and the size of housing for which loans are made). The *Credit Foncier* makes subsidized loans to borrowers (either individual homeowners or builders) for up to 80 per cent of the house price, and also controls France's secondary mortgage market. Through its relationship with the *Credit Foncier*, the French government can limit the total amount out on loan without consulting the legislature, simply by mutual agreement of the Ministry of Finance, the *Credit Foncier*, and the Bank of France (DuClaud-Williams 1978:221).

As a point of comparison, we note that Britain has historically exercised much less direct control over that country's building societies, the principal providers of housing finance loans. Although they meet regularly together, government officials cannot compel these private institutions to hold interest rates, or to lend to specified types of borrowers for particular types of housing. Yet even without formal leverage over the societies, British officials have drawn them even closer to government in recent decades. Although they are perceived to be local institutions, the societies have become more concentrated and centralized, keeping their interest rates similar throughout the country through a central association which fits the definition of a peak association. Several times during the 1970s the government advanced large, low-interest loans to the societies in order to insure a continuous supply of mortgages at stable interest rates (Balchin 1985:228–229). The societies, in turn, have been responsive to certain governmental priorities, for example by agreeing to give favorable consideration to borrowers who are nominated by local housing authorities (Craig and Harrison 1984:83; see also Boddy 1981).

Like many countries, Britain shelters a "special circuit" of finance that directs a portion of the nation's savings to institutions specializing in mortgage lending. Examples are France's *épargne-logement* and West Germany's *Bausparkassen*, both of which are savings societies in which individuals who make deposits according to a specified schedule earn moderate interest and an entitlement to mortgage loans at interest rates below the regular market. Britain's building societies serve the same function, though they operate somewhat differently, paying depositors a more competitive rate of interest and not necessarily guaranteeing each depositor a mortgage loan. In all three cases the government subsidizes the scheme by foregoing all interest earned by depositors. In the U.S. the savings and loans banks (the so-called "thrift" institutions) which specialize in mortgage loans have been sheltered both by interest rate regulations and by generous tax concessions to all institutions having at least 82 per cent of their loans in mortgages. In all of these systems economic and political pressures are calling into question the sheltered nature of the housing finance system, as other sectors compete for capital (Rosen 1981).

The clearest evidence to date of this conflict is found in the U.S., where the government has since 1980 revolutionized the housing finance system, virtually eliminating the favored status of housing finance and subjecting it to the full market force of credit competition. The events precipitating this "revolution" were the spiraling inflation of the 1970s and the inability of thrift institutions to cope with that trend. Inflation had undermined their fundamental mode of operation, which was to take in deposits at current interest rates and lend them for long terms through fixed-interest mortgage loans. The thrifts' solvency depended on the assumption that short-term rates would remain lower than long-term rates. In the 1970s they did not, and many of the savings and loan societies were paying out high current interest rates while collecting much lower returns on their mortgage portfolios.

The Reagan administration used this occasion to promote legislation which essentially transformed the savings and loan associations from specialized mortgage institutions into regular commercial banks (Downs 1985). Various elements of this deregulation allowed the thrifts to attract more deposits by paying higher interest rates, to accept demand deposits (offering depositors the same access to their savings as commercial banks), and to invest more of their funds in the most profitable alternatives rather than restricting them to home loans. This latter provision signaled the end of the sheltered credit circuit for mortgage loans, and was opposed by the housebuilding lobby. The president of the National Association of Home Builders testified against it:

> The bill authorizes thrifts to make commerical loans, to invest in tangible personal property, and to expand the percentage of assets placed in non-residential real estate and consumer loans. Because it would divert thrift resources away from residential mortgage investment, NAHB is concerned about the overall effect on the availability of mortgage credit (Napolitano 1982).

Yet in the political arena of banking and financial regulation, the normally-powerful housebuilders did not prevail. Rather than dominating the debate on this legislation, so critical to their interests, they lost out to lobbyists for the U.S. League of Savings Associations and the National Association of Mutual Savings Banks, who emphasized the need for "broader and more flexible investment powers" to help their members "work their way back to profitability" (Green 1982). If the American case is any indication of broader trends in the advanced industrial nations, then the shift of corporate bargaining over housing investment, out of the traditional realm of housing policy and into the realm of tax policy and financial regulation, will increase the competition faced by producer groups. For these are realms in which virtually all major sectors of the economy are represented. And under current economic conditions housing producers are by no means assured of prevailing against competing claimants.

CONCLUSION

I have attempted to sketch in this paper some of the political consequences of the privatization that is a common feature of the housing policies of many western industrial nations. It is important that we understand these relationships, not only because of their impacts in the housing field, but because of the signs that privatization is under way in other policy spheres as well. Moreover, it is a policy trend that promises to alter our traditional notions of left and right on the political spectrum. Leftist ideologies have historically connoted government intervention into the economy. The right, on the other hand, is usually associated with free enterprise unfettered by public control. The left favors a positive role for government while the right leaves the economy to be shaped by market forces. But privatized policy instruments (such as housing allowances and tax expenditures) supply a means for government to subsidize certain sectors of the economy without exercising direct control. Both socialists and free marketeers can therefore support them.

To date more attention has been paid to the implications of privatization for mass politics and political realignments than for the everyday conduct of government. In this paper I have begun to explore the latter question, asking in particular whether privatization erodes the corporatist arrangements which grew out of postwar production programs. My general conclusion is that it *does* alter those arrangements, though not for the reasons usually cited. It is not the case, as some neo-liberal proponents would argue, that privatization eliminates the need for institutionalized bargaining between government and representatives of the housebuilding industry. Even in political systems where housing policy has been strongly privatized (for example, the U.S. and West Germany), we still see well-organized producer groups active at the national level. Nor does privatization promise to introduce consumer influence into a bargaining process that has typically excluded consumers. Although it may enhance the power of *individual* consumers in the housing market, it does not improve their prospects for exercising *collective* influence on housing programs.

Privatization does alter corporatist arrangements somewhat by diluting governmental control over housing production, because the indirect instruments that are characteristic of privatized systems (housing allowances and tax expenditures) do not offer the same leverage as production subsidies. Yet, as we have seen, policymakers can to some extent compensate for this loss of control by using their regulatory powers over financial institutions to influence capital flows into the housing market.

The important difference between the new and old policy arenas is that bargaining between government and producer groups becomes less compartmentalized as it moves into the realm of tax policy and financial regulation. In classical corporatist models, negotiation over policy proceeds between agencies of government and hierarchically-organized, functionally defined sectors which divide the polity into vertical units of interest aggregation. In the new politics of housing, however, producer groups find themselves increasingly in competition with other claimants on capital. It is this inter-sectoral competition which is inconsistent with traditional corporatist models. And it is this competition, more than any manifestation of mass politics, that will determine the level of resources devoted to housing in the decade ahead.

REFERENCES

Achtenberg, E., and P. Marcuse (1983) "Towards the Decommodification of Housing: A Political Analysis and a Progressive Program", pp. 202–231 in Hartman, C. (ed.), *America's Housing Crisis*. London: Routledge & Kegan Paul.

Ash, P. (1980) "The Rise and Fall of High-Rise Housing in England", in Ungerson, C., and V. Karn (eds.), *The Consumer Experience of Housing: Cross-National Perspectives*. Aldershot: Gower.

Balchin, P. (1985) *Housing Policy: An Introduction*. London: Croom Helm.

Bandyopadhyay, P. (1984) "The State, Private Capital and Housing in the Paris Region", *Science and Society* 48: 161–191.

Castells, M. (1977) *The Urban Question: A Marxist Approach*. Cambridge, Mass.: MIT Press.

Cawson, A. (1982) *Corporatism and Welfare*. London: Heinemann Educational Books.

(1985) "Varieties of Corporatism: The Importance of Meso-level Interest Mediation", pp. 1–21 in Cawson, A. (ed.), *Organized Interests and the State*. Beverly Hills: Sage Publications.

Checkoway, B. (1980) "Large Builders, Federal Housing Programs, and Postwar Suburbanization", *International Journal of Urban and Regional Research* 4: 21–45.

Clarke, S. (1984) "Neighborhood Policy Options", *Journal of the American Planning Association* 50: 493–501.

Craig, P., and M.L. Harrison (1984) "Corporatism and Housing Policy: the Best Possible Political Shell?", pp. 75–91 in Harrison, M.L. (ed.), *Corporatism and the Welfare State*. Aldershot: Gower.

Dickens, P., and M. Goodwin (1981) *Consciousness, Corporatism and the Local State*. Working Paper 26, Urban and Regional Studies, University of Sussex.

Dolbeare, C. (1985) *Federal Housing Assistance: Who Needs It? Who Gets It?* Washington, D.C., National League of Cities.

Donnison, D. (1967) *The Government of Housing*. Baltimore: Penguin.

(1984) "The Progressive Potential of Privatisation", pp. 45–57 in LeGrand, J., and R. Robinson (eds.), *Privatisation and the Welfare State*. London: Geroge Allen & Unwin.

Downs, A. (1985) *The Revolution in Real Estate Finance*. Washington, D.C., The Brookings Institution.

DuClaud-Williams, R. (1978) *The Politics of Housing in Britain and France*. London: Heinemann Educational Books.

Dunleavy, P. (1979) "The Urban Basis of Political Alignment: Social Class, Domestic Property Ownership, and State Intervention in Consumption Process", *British Journal of Political Science* 9: 409–443.

(1981) *The Politics of Mass Housing in Britain 1945–1975. A Study of Corporate Power and Professional Influence in the Welfare State*. Oxford: Clarendon Press.

Eisinger, P. (1982) "French Urban Housing and the Mixed Economy: The Privatization of the Public Sector", *Annals of the American Academy of Political and Social Sciences* 459: 134–147.

Farmer, M., and R.T. Barrell (1982) "Enterpreneurship and Government Policy: The Case of the Housing Market", pp. 709–734 in Rist, R. (ed.), *Policy Studies Review Annual*. Beverly Hills: Sage Publications.

Forrest, R., and A. Murie (1983) "Residualization and Council Housing: Aspects of the Changing Social Relations of Housing Tenure", *Journal of Social Policy* 12: 453–468.

Franklin, M., and E. Page (1984) "A Critique of the Consumption Cleavage Approach in British Voting Studies", *Political Studies* 22: 521–536.

Grant, W., and W. Streeck (1985) "Large Firms and the Representation of Business Interests in the UK and West German Construction Industry", pp. 145–173 in Cawson, A. (ed.), *Organized Interests and the State*. Beverly Hills: Sage Publications.

Green, R. (1982) "Statement", *Hearings: The Depository Institutions Amendments of 1982*. U.S. Congress Committee on Banking, Finance and Urban Affairs, Subcommittee on Financial Institutions Supervision, Regulation and Insurance. Washington, D.C., pp. 435–437.

Harloe, M. (1981) "The Recommodification of Housing", pp. 17–50 in Harloe, M., and Lebas, E. (eds.), *City, Class and Capital*. London: Edward Arnold.

Harloe, M., and C. Paris (1984) "The Decollectivization of Consumption", pp. 70–98 in E. Szelenyi (ed.), *Cities in Recession*. Beverly Hills: Sage Productions.

Harrison, M.L. (1984) "Themes and Objectives", pp. 1–16 in Harrison, M.L. (ed.), *Corporatism and the Welfare State*. Aldershot: Gower.

Headey, B. (1978) *Housing Policy in the Developed Economy*. New York: St. Martin's Press.

Heclo, H., and H. Madsen (1986) *Policy and Politics in Sweden*. Philadelphia: Temple University Press.

Heidenheimer, A., Heclo, H., and C. Adams (1983) *Comparative Public Policy: The Politics of Social Choice in Europe and America*. New York: St. Martin's Press.

Howenstine, E.J. (1986) *Housing Vouchers: An International Analysis*. New Brunswick: Rutgers University, Center for Urban Policy Research.

Kelley, J., McAllister, I., and A. Mughan (1985) "The Decline of Class Revisited: Class and Party in England 1964–1979", *American Political Science Review* 79: 719–737.

Kemeny, J., and A. Thomas (1984) "Capital Leakages from Owner-Occupied Housing", *Policy and Politics* 12: 13–30.

Kilroy, B. (1978) *Housing Finance: Organic Reform?* London: LEFTA.

Kingston, P. et al. (1984) "The Politics of Homeownership", *American Politics Quarterly* 12: 131–150.

Lansley, S. (1979) *Housing and Public Policy*. London: Croom Helm.

Lehmbruch, G. (1979) "Consociational Democracy, Class Conflict and the New Corporatism", pp. 53–62 in Schmitter, P., and G. Lembruch (eds.), *Trends Toward Corporatist Intermediation*. Beverly Hills: Sage Publications.

Ley, D., and J. Mercer (1980) "Locational Conflict and the Politics of Consumption", *Economic Geography* 56: 89–109.

Lilley, W. (1973) "The Homebuilders' Lobby", pp. 30–48 in Pynoos, J. et al. (eds.), *Housing Urban America*. Chicago: Aldine Publishing Co.

Lundqvist, L.J. (1984) "Housing Policy and Alternative Housing Tenures: Some Scandinavian Examples", *Policy and Politics* 12: 1–12.

McLeay, E.M. (1984) "Housing as a Political Issue: A Comparative Study", *Comparative Politics* 17: 85–106.

Magri, S. (1977) *Logement et Reproduction de l'Exploitation*. Paris: Centre de Sociologie Urbaine.

Marcuse, P. (1982) "Determinants of State Housing Policies: West Germany and the U.S.", pp. 83–115 in Fainstein, N., and S. Fainstein (eds.), *Urban Policy Under Capitalism*. Beverly Hills: Sage Publications.

Martin, R.M. (1983) "Pluralism and the New Corporatism", *Political Studies* 31: 86–102.

Merrett, S. (1979) *State Housing in Britain*. London: Routledge & Kegan Paul.

Napolitano, R. (1982) "Statement", *Hearings: The Depository Institutions Amendments of 1982*. U.S. Congress, Committee on Banking, Finance and Urban Affairs, Subcommittee on Financial Institutions Supervision, Regulation and Insurance, Washington, D.C., pp. 369–371.

Nesslein, T. (1982) "The Swedish Housing Model' An Assessment", *Urban Studies* 19: 235–246.

Olson, M. (1965) *The Logic of Collective Action*. Cambridge, Mass.: Harvard University Press.

Pawley, M. (1983) "Reform", *Roof* 8: 27–28.

Pearsall, J. (1984) "France", pp. 9–54 in Wynn, M. (ed.), *Housing in Europe*. London: Croom Helm.

Petersen, G. (1980) "Federal Tax Policy and the Shaping of Urban Development", pp. 399–425 in Solomon, A. (ed.), *The Prospective City*. Cambridge, Mass.: MIT Press.

Priemus, H. (ed.) (1983) *Who Will Pay the Housing Bill in the 80s?* Delft: Delft University Press.

Rosen, K. (1981) *A Comparison of European Housing Finance Systems*. Berkeley: University of California, Center for Real Estate and Urban Economics, Working Paper 81–37

Salisbury, R. (1979) "Why Corporatism in America?", pp. 213–230 in Schmitter, P., and G. Lehmbruch (eds.), *Trends Toward Corporatist Intermediation*. Beverly Hills: Sage Publications.

Saunders, P. (1979) *Urban Politics: A Sociological Interpretation*. London: Hutchinson.

-- "Beyond Housing Classes", *International Journal of Urban and Regional Research* 8: 202–225.

Sharpe, L.J. (1984) "Functional Allocation in the Welfare State", *Local Government Studies* 10.

Sternlieb, G., and J. Hughes (1980) "The Post-Shelter Society", pp. 93–102 in Sternlieb, G. et al. (eds.), *America's Housing: Prospects and Problems*. New Brunswick: Rutgers University, Center for Urban Policy Research.

Tuccillo, J. (1980) *Housing and Investment in an Inflationary World*. Washington, D.C., The Urban Institute.

Van Weesep, J. (1984) "Intervention in the Netherlands: Urban Housing Policy and Market Response", *Urban Affairs Quarterly* 19: 329–353.

The Relation of Politics to the Instruments of Housing Policy

156-85

U.S., U.K

9320

Nathan H. Schwartz, Department of
Political Science, University of
Louisville, USA

INTRODUCTION

When many programs compete for limited public funds, when increasing
taxation is seen as a danger to already stagnant economies, and when the
basis of the welfare state is under question, housing policies are bound to
be criticized and likely to be cut back. It is easy to see such developments
as the inevitable result of simple causes: fiscal strain and conservatism
leading to the pruning of programs. This simple approach is appealing, but
does not explain why, even in this period, some programs grow while
others are cut. The simple approach also fails to provide insight into what
elements govern the success and failure of housing policy outside the
specific fiscal and political conditions of the present.

This paper aims to place the politics of housing policy in a framework
that will help us understand the configuration of current housing policy in
Great Britain and the United States as well as the interaction between
policy and politics that will shape future housing policy. Emphasis is
placed on the instruments of action: the state institutions in which policy
is made and implemented, and the relation of those institutions to the tools
used to implement housing policy. Elements of the analysis are developed
through a critique of theories of public policy proposed by Theodore J.
Lowi and Lester Salamon. The approach is then applied to elements of
American and British housing policy.

Arenas of Power

One basic approach for the study of public policy is Theodore Lowi's
"arenas of power" (Lowi, 1964, 1970, 1972). Lowi's four-fold typology
of policy starts from the assumption that (1964:688):

> The types of relationships to be found among people are determined
> by their expectations -- by what they hope to achieve or get from

relating to others... In politics, expectations are determined by governmental outputs or policies... Therefore, a political relationship is determined by the type of policy at stake, so that for every type of policy there is likely to be a distinctive type of political relationship.

For Lowi, the defining characteristic of policy (government outputs) is "in terms of their impact or expected impact on the society" (Lowi, 1964: 689).

Lowi argues that each type of policy is found in its own "arena of power," a unique political subsystem, characterized by its own "political structure, political process, elites, and group relations" (Lowi, 1964: 689). Lowi's approach is very important because he identifies syndromes, or ideal types, of the political conditions that surround each type of policy. The idea of the "arena of power" should allow us better to understand the birth, development, and death of policies.

Developing a typology of American public policy, Lowi defined four basic types of policy each with its own arena of politics: distributive policy, regulatory policy, redistributive policy, and constituent policy. For use in comparative analysis, it is not clear that these specific types of policy are of great utility, but the approach, which emphasizes that policy takes place in distinctive arenas, is of importance.

A major problem with Lowi's typology is the assumption that every policy has one type of impact, which in turn defines the kind of politics around that policy. In fact, policies can have multiple impacts. A housing policy which has the effect of shifting resources to equalize the position of individuals (in Lowi's terms "redistributive") may also simultaneously benefit the construction industry (in Lowi's terms "distributive").

Lowi tries to eliminate the issue of multiple impacts by stressing the criterion of time, arguing that the short-term impact is the most important (1964: 690): "politics works in the short run." This would seem to eliminate the problem of multiple impacts, one only needs identify the short-term impact. But this use of "short-run politics" to determine the classification of policy hobbles Lowi's theory by introducing an element of circularity into his argument. Lowi argues that policy, defined in terms of its impact on society, is associated with particular forms of politics. But using short-run politics to define policy results in the politics predicting the politics.

Once provision is made for multiple impacts (in terms of Lowi's typology), then the assumption that every kind of policy is accompanied by only one kind of politics becomes suspect. Evidence for this view is provided by the case of the U.S. Farmers Home Administration in which "redistributive" housing policies are made in a "distributive" arena of politics (Schwartz, 1985).

Lowi's theory can provide insights into policy if we avoid his assumption that each type of politics must be directly associated with a particular form of policy. Assuming with Lowi that there are arenas in the policy process differentiated by the form of their politics, it is reasonable then to assume that many of the policies dealt with in that arena will be particularly suited to that form of politics. For example, distributive policies, those which, by definition, are easily distributed and whose existence does not appear to threaten other policies, would seem to be most likely to survive in an arena of iron triangles and logrolling, where policies are passed as the result of backroom deals without much conflict. On the other hand, those redistributive policies which engender much conflict cannot be dealt with in a distributive arena, which cannot resolve major conflicts. In other words, each arena can be seen as having its own calculus, or rules of the game, which make some particular form of policy likely, but not inevitable. A policy with a particular impact (distributive, redistributive, etc.) may be able to survive in a different arena than indicated by its type because the policy in question has not evoked the kind of response that would place it in a different arena.

The Tools of Government Action

Opposed to Theodore Lowi's contention that the key to understanding policy is understanding the arena in which it is made, Lester Salamon has written in his discussion of implementation research (1981: 256):

> rather than focusing on individual programs, as is now done, or even collections of programs grouped according to major "purpose," as is frequently proposed, the suggestion here is that we should concentrate instead on the generic tools of government action, on the "techniques" of social intervention that come to be used, in varying combinations, in particular public programs.

The techniques that Salamon calls the tools of government action include devices like loans, loan guarantees, social regulation, insurance, government corporations, and tax incentives. The importance of these tools to Salamon is that they represent government sharing its authority and discretion with other governmental and non-governmental entities. Not unlike Lowi, he observes that "those who exercise authority on the Federal government's behalf in these programs frequently enjoy a substantial degree of autonomy from Federal control" (Salamon, 1981: 260).

For Salamon, each of the tools has its own political economy which affects the efficacy of government action and the politics of the policy. In examining these tools, he identifies a set of dimensions by which the tools can be analyzed. These include "directness-indirectness" ("the extent of reliance on nonfederal actors"), "automatic-administered" (the amount of administrative decision-making involved), "cash versus in-kind" (the form of benefits), "visibility-invisibility" (how much of the action is visible in the budget'), "design standards versus performance standards" (the approach used to encourage program efficiency) (Salamon, 1981: 266–272). His conclusion about implementation is what he calls "the public management paradox" (Salamon, 1981: 272):

> the types of instruments that are the easiest to implement may be the hardest to enact; conversely, the forms that are most likely to be enacted are also the most difficult to carry out.

Salamon's paradox complements Scharpf, Reissert, and Schnabel's (1978) analysis of policy implementation in the Federal Republic of Germany, where they find that the tools chosen to implement fiscal policy are often inappropriate and that politics makes it difficult to use the appropriate policy instruments to obtain desired consequences.

While Salamon's emphasis on tools provides some insights, some of the hypotheses he derives from the approach are not supported by the cases he draws from housing policy. For example, he proposes as a formal hypothesis that: "the more direct the form of government action, the more likely it is to encounter political opposition" (Salamon, 1981: 268). This is derived from his notion that:

> the price of political acquiescence in the establishment of a federal role... is frequently the acceptance by the federal government of a tool of action that cuts... third parties into a meaningful piece of the federal action (Salamon, 1981: 267–268).

Such is not the case of the Farmers Home Administration, in which a major loan program is directly administered by the federal government, contrary to what Salamon considers to be an American ideology in which "the protection of the private sector from governmental intervention and the preservation of state and local autonomy are viewed as political values in their own right" (1981: 268).

Similar sorts of problems crop up in Salamon's hypothesis that:

> the more automatic the tool of government action, the less certain the achievement of program purposes, the greater the leakage of program benefits, and the more problematic the generation of needed political support (1981: 269).

Yet there is a housing policy in both the U.S. and Great Britain that is automatically administered, the mortgage interest deduction, which requires no governmental approval in order for an individual to take advantage of it. Contrary to Salamon's prediction, the mortgage interest deduction has much political support. Virtually every tax reform plan, while railing against deductions, retains this one deduction, for many elected officials would not survive politically if they opposed the deduction.

The fundamental flaw in Salamon's approach is the failure to recognize that policy affects several different arenas: the impact of the policy tool and its salient dimensions differ according to whether one is examining its impact on the relevant legislative bodies, the executive, or the publics affected. The political economy of each of these arenas is different; the analysis of the effect of the tool must take these differences into account. For example, in the U.S., the "visibility" of the method of budgeting a given tool is very important to both the Congress and the Executive in their fights over the budget, but is of precious little direct interest to those individuals and groups affected by the policy. Some of Salamon's hypotheses ring false because he is assuming that the salient dimensions of a tool of governmental action remain the same in the entire policy process. In short, the distinctive elements of the different arenas making, implementing, and affected by policy must be considered in judging the effect of any particular tool.

Tools and Arenas in the Analysis of Housing Policy

I argue that elements of Lowi's "arenas of power" and of Salamon's "tools of policy" can be used to forge an approach to examining policy that overcomes the problems of each. Lowi's "arenas of power" approach is powerful in that it signals important configurations of politics that are most clearly identified with certain types of policy. Salamon's "tools of policy" approach helps us understand the different dimensions of the tools of government action and their political and administrative implications.

The key to overcoming the difficulties and utilizing the strengths of these approaches is to recognize that policy is formulated and implemented in diverse policy arenas, with the tools chosen to implement policy having different political implications in the different arenas. Thus, the analysis of the dynamics of policy should include identification of the different arenas of policy: where the politics around the policy take place, where policy decisions are made, and where policy is implemented. Secondly, the analysis must identify how the tools chosen to implement policy work in each of the arenas. Third, it is necessary to ascertain the relationships between the different arenas involved in a policy: their role in the policy and their ability to influence or dominate the other arenas.

UNITED STATES: DIFFERENT ARENAS OF POLICY

In examining the case of housing policy in the United States, we find that different parts of housing policy are implemented in distinctly different arenas, that there are also distinct differences in the kinds of policy tools used to implement the policy, and that the kinds of politics around the policies at the national level are also very different. Three types of American housing policy are examined here: policies providing direct subsidies for rental housing (predominantly in urban areas); programs that aid owner-occupiers; and policies subsidizing home purchase in rural areas funded by the Farmers Home Administration (FmHA). In each of these policy areas we find different implementing authorities, different tools of policy used to implement the policy, and different politics at the national level around the policies.

Subsidized Housing

A distinction is usually drawn between "subsidized housing" and other forms of housing, such as owner-occupied or privately-owned rental housing. However, in the U.S. as well as in Britain, virtually every form of housing receives subsidies, with owner-occupiers in both countries receiving richer subsidies than other individuals. While "subsidized housing" is not the only housing to receive substantial government aid, the term "subsidized housing" will be used here to denote programs of housing aid not connected with home-ownership and largely oriented toward urban areas. These forms stand in contrast to home-ownership (subsidized in the U.S. largely through the mortgage interest deduction in income tax) and the Farmers Home Administration which provides subsidies for owner-occupiers and for the construction of rental units.

In the local arena where housing subsidies are delivered, in demographic terms, those receiving housing subsidies are not likely to be a potent political force in most areas. For example, public housing in the United States accounts for only 1.6% of total housing units, compared to British public housing (council housing) which accounts for 31% of all housing (U.S. Department of Commerce, 1982: 751, 760; Government Statistical Office, 1983:114). Simply in terms of numbers, public housing is not a major source of housing in most communities. In terms of population distribution, owner-occupiers (representing 65.6%) of all units, and those renting from private owners (representing 32% of all units) are much more likely to be politically powerful in advocating their interests in the United States.

But demographics are not alone an adequate measure of political influence; the concerns of groups of potential suppliers or those who feel there is a problem that needs addressing may be able to create or maintain a policy. One such potential support for subsidized housing is local government. For local government in the U.S., public housing is much less important politically than council housing is in Great Britain. In addition, while local government may have a role in determining eligibility for public housing, Section 8 units (privately-owned units subsidized by the federal government), and for approving construction of certain types of subsidized housing, housing policy doesn't seem in a general way to have become a focus for political activity -- in line with the much smaller role of government in providing housing than in Great Britain. In addition, working against its role as a potential institutional center for housing, local government in the U.S. has little direct role in providing aid and encouragement for home ownership in comparison to the British case.

In addition, the connection of local government to central government seems much weaker in the U.S. than in Britain. First of all, the role of party in policy-making in the U.S. is much weaker than in Great Britain. It is not clear that local parties carry much clout with national parties on issues of local governance and, even if local governments have influence over the national parties, it is not clear that the national parties have much influence over national policy. In terms of their influence over specific Congressmen, it is not clear that local governments have been very effective in influencing their activity either. While Congress has not gone along with all of President Reagan's proposals for budget cutting, nevertheless they accepted major cuts in the subsidized housing programs. It may be that the relatively small size of these programs meant that cities put other issues first in the attempts to fight Reagan social-budget cutting, but there is still doubt about the role of local governments as a clear and effective institutional center for policy-making. The suggestion is that there are very real limits on the ability of local government to affect national policy.

In the arena of national legislative activity, there also appears to be a paucity of effective support for subsidized housing. National interest groups that have had an incentive to support subsidized housing in the United States include advocacy groups for the poor, housing-finance institutions, and the housing construction industry. In fact, the initiation and expansion of subsidized housing programs in the United States often seemed motivated not simply out of concern for the needs of the poor, but by the needs of the housing finance and construction industries when they were in periods of recession or depression (Schwartz, 1984:150–151).

Interviews with staff members of housing advocacy interest groups and staff from both parties of Congressional housing committees during 1984 and 1985 produced very similar views about the relative influence of these different groups on current housing policy decisions in the Congress. None of those interviewed felt that the advocacy groups for the poor had been able, by themselves, to influence Congress or the administration on issues of subsidized housing.

Those interviewed also argued that the home-builders lobby (primarily the National Association of Home Builders) was no longer supporting the building of public housing as a way of boosting the industry. Their concern had turned to the effect of federal spending on the mortgage interest rate, which affects non-governmental demand for housing. The position taken by the home-builders was seen by those interviewed as supporting budget cuts that might reduce the federal deficit, with the hope that there would result lower mortgage interest rates and an increase in demand for private sector housing. In other words, the home builders were perceived as deciding that a trade-off existed between subsidized housing and private market housing and deciding to go with private home-building.

Basic trends in U.S. housing policy may well reinforce this lack of interest in subsidized housing on the part of the construction industry. American subsidies for low-income housing are increasingly oriented toward subsidizing individuals and not providing direct subsidies for new units of housing. Thus, funding subsidized housing only benefits the construction industry when new housing is cost competitive with existing housing, which is rarely the case. The Reagan housing voucher plan, which provides direct cash subsidies to renters, furthers this trend, providing no special subsidies necessary for new construction, based on the assumption that there is already sufficient housing available. In a situation where the normal operation of housing programs does not benefit the construction industry, industry interest in those programs may well remain small.

But these programs are also rendered more vulnerable by the nature of the tools used to implement them. In a period when budgetary concerns dominate much of the action of Congress, as well as relations between Congress and the President, the budgetary tools can render a program more or less susceptible to budget cuts. In Salamon's typology, the relative dimension is "visibility-invisibility," or how much of the program is visible in the budget (Salamon, 1981:270–271). The implication is that the more visible the program, in budgetary terms, the more likely it is to suffer cuts. As will become obvious in the analysis of other American housing policies (see below), "subsidized housing" programs have the greatest degree of budget visibility. Subsidized housing funding must be approved each year as part of the federal budget, not hidden through special financing arrangements (as FmHA programs have been) or cemented into the tax code (as the mortgage-interest tax deduction). Not only do subsidized housing programs require yearly approval, but every request for additional units of subsidy requires that the entire projected cost of that unit of subsidy over its lifetime be included in the budget request. So, not only is the funding visible, it also appears very expensive.

The lack of effective support for subsidized housing, the use of tools of policy that leave housing policy very susceptible to budget cuts, and great concern about the size of the U.S. federal budget have given the President a great deal of power. Under Ronald Reagan, the arena of executive politics has had great success in determining housing policy, especially the budgetary aspects.

For example, Reagan has been able to get massive cuts in subsidized housing aid. That is not to say that there wasn't considerable variation before Reagan. For example, while the fiscal year 1977 appropriation was sufficient for an estimated 373,000 units to be added to the subsidized housing stock of the United States, by the end of Jimmy Carter's administration, the problem of fiscal constraints had led that Administration to request only 260,000 additional units (Fiscal Year 1982). Nevertheless, the cuts under Reagan have been massive and sustained. When Reagan took office, the Carter budget proposal for approximately 260,000 units for fiscal year 1982 was pending. The Reagan administration proposed cutting this back to 175,000 units; a Congress eager to please cut this figure back even more to approximately 142,000 units.

On the surface, the 1983 budget, the first budget originating with the Reagan administration, called for a slight increase over the 1982 budget to 219,000 units of subsidized housing. However, as is not the case with the Carter budgets, this number considerably overstates the actual number of units that would be added to the stock of subsidized housing. After subtracting the number of units that were simply units under one program converted to another program, as well as subtracting the cancellations proposed for units approved in earlier years but which had not yet been constructed, this budget called for an actual decrease in the number of subsidized units available (Schwartz, 1984b: 158). Similar budgetary magic took place in the 1984 requests where the budget called for the funding of 90,000 additional units; after subtracting the conversions of existing units of subsidized housing from one program to another, the actual number of new units being added to the stock of subsidized housing was only 63,000 units (Schwartz, 1983: 19–20).

In addition to cutting the number of subsidized housing units added to the housing stock, Reagan has sought to shift more of the cost of subsidized housing to the recipients. In its first year in office, the Reagan administration gained Congressional approval to raise from 25% to 30% the proportion of income that the recipients of housing subsidies were expected to pay as rent. But the executive arena has not totally dominated policy. In their Fiscal Year 1983 budget, the Reagan administration proposed adding the cash value of food stamps received by a family to the calculation of their total income, thus raising the amount they would pay as part of their 30% of income contribution to the cost of housing. Analysts at the Urban Institute have estimated that the rise in rent to 30% of income plus the addition of food stamps to the calculation of income would result in a reduction of 44% of the benefits received by those in public housing (Struyk, Tuccillo, and Zias, 1982:411). This time, however, the Congress was not as willing to adopt every Administration proposal and refused to go along with these changes.

In addition, concerns with controlling the federal budget deficit have led to the adoption of measures that also have the effect of cutting housing programs. The Reagan administration's concern with the particular budgetary implications of housing subsidies was clear in the Fiscal 1983 Budget, which identified two particular items of concern to those who write budgets. The first is that all the programs "involved long-term subsidy commitments that result in uncontrollable budget outlay increases for many years" (OMB, 1982c: 104). In other words, most housing subsidy programs commit the government to subsidize a housing unit in some manner for fifteen to forty years. The second budgetary defect noted was that since the "tenant's rent contributions are capped by law, any unanticipated cost increases are borne solely by the Federal Government" (OMB, 1982c: 104).

The response to these concerns with budgeting can be seen in the new housing voucher program. First, to eliminate the long term commitment (which appears in the budget the year the commitment is made), the period of subsidy guarantee has been reduced to five years. While reducing the initial budgetary commitment, the voucher program doesn't reduce the actual outlays per year for each family receiving subsidy. The voucher program does create an almost invisble cut in the number of subsidized units. As subsidies expire on particular units, the approval of seemingly "new" subsidies becomes only the renewal of old subsidies, not additions to the total. In this case, reducing the subsidy period to five years greatly increases the number of subsidies that can be seen simply as renewals, rather than as additions to the total. The budgetary legacy of this action will be to require approval in the future of many more units per year simply to keep the number of families receiving subsidy the same.

But another legacy of current policy is a trend toward deinstitutionalization: an increasing reliance on markets rather than governments to provide housing services. In the United States, the movement away from government as the direct provider of housing started with the 1959 Housing Act, which provided federal loans to non-profit groups to provide housing for the elderly and handicapped. The 1968 Housing and Urban Development Act furthered the trend with its Section 236 program, providing subsidies to reduce interest rates on mortgages for non-profit groups building low-income housing. But then housing policy moved away from funding institutions specializing in housing to using market mechanisms as the base for housing policy. The major housing program of the nineteen-seventies, the Section 8 program of the 1974 Housing and Community Development Act provided subsidies to landlords in the private sector to provide housing to those in need. The Reagan administration's "housing voucher" program (a limited version of which was adopted in 1984), in which those deemed eligible for housing subsidies would receive a cash grant for housing, assumes that housing will be found in the general housing market.

The political implications of the trend toward deinstitutionalization may indicate a bleak future for subsidized housing. The tools used in these deinstitutionalized policies correspond to the forms that Lester Salamon has termed "automatic." Salamon has defined this type of "automatic" implementation mechanism as "one that utilizes existing structures and relationships (e.g., the tax structure or the price system) and requires a minimum of administrative decision-making" (1981: 268). Housing policy increasingly becomes removed from the sphere of direct government activity (even though in areas like the mortgage interest deduction, the cost to government may continue to rise). The political result of this deinstitutionalization may be to weaken political activity around housing issues. As Salamon (1981: 269) has hypothesized:

> The more automatic the tool of government action, the less certain the achievement of program purposes, the greater the leakage of program benefits, and the more problematic the generation of needed political support.

Especially for those who are not already well organized, the clear institutional presence of the state may serve to provide a focus for political activity; without that organizational focus, such activity may be seriously reduced. In terms of implementation, there is no clear political arena in which the advocates or recipients can operate, short of national politics. Without an arena of implementation in which to operate, it is difficult to see conditions under which groups of tenants or landlords are likely to organize sufficient strength to represent their interests in the arenas of national politics.

Home ownership

In the United States, the most important forms of aid to owner-occupation are implemented through the tax code in a manner that Salamon describes as automatic. In that sense, like subsidized housing, there is no clear political arena, short of the Congressional or Presidential arenas, in which implementation takes place. However, in this case, proponents of owner-occupation are well-placed to affect politics in those arenas. The political base of support for owner-occupation is quite clear: in the U.S. 65.5% of housing is owner-occupied (U.S. Department of Commerce, 1982: 751,

760). The size of the owner-occupier sector makes it unlikely that policies worsening its position would be adopted -- one takes on majorities only in extraordinary times. In addition, the owner-occupier sector has the institutional resources to look after itself in the arenas of national policy-making. The institutional interest of housing finance institutions and home-builders in encouraging home ownership, as well as the desire of Congress to avoid alienating the affections of a majority of households, makes cutbacks in support to owner-occupiers unlikely.

The primary subsidy to home-owners in the United States is the mortgage interest deduction from personal income tax which allows the home owner to deduct from his/her taxable income interest payments made on the mortgage. There is no limit on the size of this deduction. Thus, the richer the citizen, the greater the potential subsidy, both because the deduction constitutes relief from a higher marginal rate of tax, as well as the fact that interest payments may be higher for more expensive housing.

The importance of the mortgage interest deduction in national politics is its "invisibility" (Salamon's term) in the annual federal budget. It is a tax expenditure, a subsidy provided by exempting recipients from tax. As such, its cost is in funds not collected rather than funds spent by government, thus not requiring annual approval as part of the budget. It is "off-budget," thus better sheltered from budget cutting than "on-budget" subsidized housing. It is a program that grows by itself, not requiring legislative or executive affirmation.

The combination of strong political support and the invisibility of the tool used to implement the subsidies to home-ownership are visible in the size of the mortgage interest deduction. According to government calculations, the cost of the mortgage interest deduction is considerably higher than the amount spent on "subsidized" housing and is growing at a much faster rate. In 1977, the cost of subsidized housing to the federal government was $2.968 billion, and had grown by 1984 to $9.467 billion, an increase of 219% (OMB, 1982a: 9–53; 1985a: 5–115). The loss to the U.S. Treasury of the mortgage interest deduction was $5.435 billion in 1977, growing to $22.735 billion by 1984, an increase of 318% (OMB, 1982b: 130; 1985b: G–44). So in 1984, the size of the home-owner subsidy was 2.4 times as great as the subsidy to "subsidized housing," while its cost was increasing 45 percent faster than the cost of "subsidized housing."

At the same time, it is difficult to imagine any political force capable of dislodging the mortgage interest deduction. The shared interests of builders, construction workers, banks, and much of the middle and upper classes, plus a widely shared ideology of the benefit of home-ownership, makes it difficult to conceive of an elected executive or legislature willing to take on the issue. The invisibility of the subsidy allows the issue to be avoided; unlike "on-budget" (visible) items, the size of the subsidy does not have to be publicly confronted in the arenas where decisions about the subsidy are made. For proponents of the mortgage interest deduction, no politics is good politics.

The Farmers Home Administration (FmHA)

The Farmers Home Administration (FmHA) is the agricultural credit and rural development arm of the U.S. Department of Agriculture. In 1949, the FmHA began to assume a direct role in the provision of rural housing. Over time, this role in housing has come to include making housing loans to low- and moderate-income rural residents, supplementing housing loans with interest subsidies, providing loans for housing repairs, and subsidizing rental and self-help housing programs (FmHA, 1985: 1–16).

The lion's share of FmHA activity has taken place in its loan programs. The Section 502 and 504 programs, which provide direct loans for home-ownership and home repair respectively, account for the greatest share of FmHA housing program costs from their inception to date. Out of a total of $45 billion in housing grants and loans provided by the FmHA housing programs through 1984, the Section 502 and 504 programs account for $34.5 billion, or 77% (FmHA, 1985: 21). These programs have provided a total of 1,850,136 loans for housing.

Two elements of these FmHA loan programs stand in contrast to the housing programs administered by the Department of Housing and Urban Development (HUD). The first is that the bulk of the FmHA activity has been the *direct* provision of loans for housing; the FmHA acts directly as banker. In contrast, in HUD (U.S. Department of Housing and Urban Development) loan programs the government has acted as guarantor of loans made by others, rather than directly as banker. Secondly, the FmHA makes these loans directly through its own network of almost 2,000 county offices serving virtually every rural county in the country. In most HUD programs, other units of government or private organizations directly implement the program with HUD acting on program applications higher up the paper chain. In Salamon's terms, the FmHA programs represent "direct" administration, in contrast to HUD programs where the federal government acts primarily through intermediaries.

In the face of the decimation of federal aid for subsidized housing, the FmHA has done very well, particularly in comparison to the HUD housing programs (HAC, 1985; for information on HUD cuts also see: Hartman, 1982; Schwartz, 1984b; Struyk, Tuccillo, and Zais, 1982). In the period from 1981 to 1985, the HUD programs have been cut back approximately 58%, while the FmHA cuts have only amounted to 13% (HAC, 1985: 7,

22). Another way of looking at the relative position of these housing programs comes from examining the number of units actually receiving an aid commitment in any particular year. (These figures may not be directly related to expenditure figures because of changes in the mix and cost of the different housing subsidy programs.) Using 1980 as the baseline, it is still apparent that FmHA programs have fared better than HUD programs, dropping only 17% as compared to the 52% drop in HUD programs (HAC, 1985: 23). If we go back to the last two years entirely under Carter administration budgets (1979 and 1980), there was already a substantial shrinkage in the number of HUD unit reservations, while the decline in FmHA units was much smaller (HAC, 1985: 23), an indication that the FmHA programs have generally been less vulnerable to budget cuts than the HUD programs.

Looking at how the tools of policy operate in multiple arenas in the domain of FmHA policy, there appear to be three different arenas, or settings, that are important: the arena of implementation outside Washington, that is, the operation of the FmHA programs in rural areas; the arena of agricultural politics in the Congress; and the arena of executive politics, the attempt of the President to shape policy.

In the arena of implementation, the rural areas affected by FmHA housing programs, the most salient dimensions of the tools of the FmHA housing policy appear to be the provision of credit *and* the direct administration of the programs by the FmHA. In many rural areas there is a shortage of private credit available for housing finance (HAC, 1981: 1). Given the shortage of other forms of credit as well as the relative poverty of many rural areas, these loan programs have created the dependence of home-builders and low- and moderate-income families on the FmHA (Schwartz, 1985). This dependency has the potential for translating into support of the program. The direct administration of the program has also created a clear focus for such support; to support the program is to support the FmHA. What is also important in this arena is that there is no evident organized group opposing the program; there seems to be little concern on the part of rural financial institutions with the Federal government's major role in providing rural housing finance (Schwartz, 1985). In this situation, the program builds a clear constituency focused on the national program, with all the active participants feeling they have a great deal to lose and little to gain from radical cuts in the program.

The second arena of policy is the relevant Congressional arena, focused around the Agriculture Subcommittee of the House Appropriations Committee, which is very skilled in defending the FmHA in Congress. Providing interest-group support to the FmHA are a set of housing advocacy groups, but most important is the powerful National Association of Homebuilders

(NAHB). NAHB support of the FmHA reflects the dependence of many rural homebuilders on FmHA finance. Interestingly, the NAHB has not recently supported the urban subsidized programs (for reasons discussed elsewhere in this paper). So, in contrast to urban housing programs, the FmHA is the recipient of much interest group support.

In this Congressional arena, the most significant elements of the tools used to implement FmHA policy would seem to be the use of "invisible," off-budget, financing techniques, which allow the subsystem to protect the program against some of the winds of budgetary exigencies. The FmHA funds much of its housing loan activity through an "off-budget" mechanism. The FmHA is allowed by law to create securities called Certificates of Beneficial Ownership (CBOs) that are backed by the mortgages for which the FmHA has provided loans. These CBOs are then "sold" to the Federal Financing Bank (FFB). Under current budgeting practises, the FmHA is allowed to credit these against its total outlays, thus reducing the amount of its total outlays (U.S. Senate, 1983: 372). But these transactions with the FFB are also not included in the calculation of the unified Federal budget, hence the invisibility of this part of FmHA outlays in the federal budget. A President or Congress worried about the size of the budget gets no help by cutting these FmHA programs because the cuts will not show up in the budget figures. The size of these transactions is important relative to the FmHA housing program budget: in 1984, FFB outlays to purchase CBOs from the FmHA were virtually the same amount as the new loans obligated by the FmHA (OMB, 1985a: page 6–14; 1985c: page I–E59).

Salamon's analysis of the tools of policy makes clear how such "invisible" tools may render such a program less susceptible to attack than a more visible tool, like some form of "on-budget" financing. The success of the FmHA in protecting its budget provides support for Salamon's hypothesis that the "less visible a tool of government action is in the regular budget process, the less subject it will be to overall management and control" (Salamon, 1981: 270). One basis for the survival of the FmHA's housing programs in a period of a general reduction in domestic expenditure is, therefore, the tool chosen to budget the program.

But another important factor which has made this arena function effectively in protecting the FmHA housing programs has been its relation to the arena of implementation, the rural areas served by the FmHA. The rural interests' relation to the congressional subsystem with regard to the FmHA is largely one of support. The subsystem is not faced with the internal conflict between supporters and opponents of the programs, which safeguards the policy, because the subsystem is protected from the kinds of conflict that it cannot handle and that lead to issues being considered in different, more hostile arenas within the Congress.

The third arena of policy with regard to this issue has been the executive. Since coming to office, the Reagan administration has attempted to make major cuts in the FmHA housing programs. Up to the Fiscal Year 1986 budget, the administration had failed to curtail those programs, perhaps because of the "invisibility" of the budgeting for FmHA programs. Arguably, the Reagan administration's attack on other social programs has succeeded largely as part of a budget-cutting strategy; it is hard to make that strategy work on "off-budget" items. In addition, the configuration of the other two arenas makes attacks on the FmHA less likely to succeed than similar attacks on other programs. In the rural arena, the Administration has no clear allies: the banks are not active on the issue and the home-builders, who oppose large subsidy programs for urban housing, strongly support the program. These factors, in turn, strengthen the ability of an already cohesive congressional policy arena to keep the issue from getting into other arenas within Congress where the program might have less support.

The attempt of the administration in the 1986 budget to cut back the FmHA housing programs is illustrative of the themes discussed here. Overtly, the budget called for a temporary moratorium on new FmHA housing loans, with the programs to be transferred to the Department of Housing and Urban Development. Overtly, this would have changed the focus of the constituency, putting the FmHA programs into a much larger and conflictual setting within the general housing policy arena, and would have changed the congressional arena from the powerful agriculture subsystem to the committees dealing with urban housing issues (who have been much less successful in defending their program turf). Even more devastating, the tools used in the program would be the same as those used in the existing HUD programs, which are very visible in the budget and hence more easily attacked by the executive. Congress and involved interest groups fought off these changes -- just as they had fought off earlier Reagan challenges to the FmHA.

A greater threat to FmHA programs was another proposed Fiscal Year 1986 change: the proposal to put the Federal Financing Bank "on-budget." Putting the FFB on the budget would have the effect of putting all the FmHA transactions with the FFB "on budget," which would make the FmHA programs more vulnerable to budget cuts. This change was considered likely to be adopted because it was made a general budget issue by the Administration; in a year when the Congress is preoccupied with the deficit, those interviewed suggested such a general measure would be very difficult to resist. Potentially, the FmHA would find itself subject to the same budgetary pressure as other social programs because the Administration may have found an effective "end-run" around the Congressional arena to change the policy tools that affect the FmHA.

It is not clear that the Administration has succeeded in its end run. The budget resolution adopted in mid-summer of 1985 called for the FmHA programs to take cuts of 30–40% and for an end to off-budget financing through the Federal Finance Bank. However, the budget resolution called for the FmHA to replace its selling of mortgage-based securities to the FFB with mortgage-based securities sold to private sector financial institutions. The effect of this maneuver as one lobbyist interviewed suggested, "was to put the FmHA on-budget just long enough to put it off-budget in a different way." So the FmHA may have survived the attack with cuts occurring only during the change from one off-budget mechanism to another.

GREAT BRITAIN: TWO ARENAS OF POLICY

The British case stands in contrast to the U.S. case in which different housing policies are implemented and formulated by different sets of institutions. In the British case, with the exception of the mortgage interest deduction, most housing policies are implemented by local government, with basic decisions about finance and the form of policy being made by the national state. Central government provides the finance and basic guidelines for the creation and administration of subsidized housing; local government builds and administers council housing, approves grants to "housing associations," sells council housing to tenants, hands out improvement grants to home-owners, and in some cases directly provides mortgage money for those wishing to become owner-occupiers (Malpas and Murie, 1982:46–48).

In applying the idea of policy arenas to the British case, two kinds of arenas appear: the national arena and the local arenas. The "national arena of policy" includes: the components of the national state such as the executive, parliament, the political parties, and other bodies that attempt to influence the national state on issues like housing, including the associations of local authorities and other interest groups active in the area. In the American case, there was a distinction drawn between the arena in which the executive and the legislature operated, an appropriate distinction given the constitutional independence of each. At the end of the day, policy requires some kind of agreement between the legislature and the executive, but up until that point the politics encountered by each can be quite different. In the British case, the executive and the legislature are intertwined, with party a key factor in their connection. As opposed to the American case, it is not often that one finds the executive and the legislature going in different directions.

The "local arenas of policy" not only refers to local government, but also to the political forces active around local government. This is not to say all local arenas are alike. While the mix of aid may differ, both Labour- and Tory-controlled local government councils are likely to be active on the issue; Labour councils are more likely to be active in the provision of council housing, but both provide improvement grants and other aids to owner-occupiers as well as approving government grants to housing associations. Accompanying the major role of local authorities in providing subsidized housing, the politics of housing are also very important at the local level. It is important to remember that it is not only council housing that is controlled by local governments, but also the approvals of funding for the voluntary housing associations, the non-governmental agencies providing housing, as well as various direct grants for owner-occupiers. So in institutional and political terms, local governments are a focus for housing policy. Thus, the key issue for explaining the development of housing policy in Great Britain is determining whether this concentration of policy and politics in the local arenas influences national decisions about housing policy.

Separate from the general pattern of British housing policy, where public policy is made in the national arena and implemented in local arenas, is tax relief on mortgage payments. The configuration of tools and arenas involved in this policy looks very much like the arrangement of tools and arenas of the mortgage-interest deduction in the United States: invisible in terms of the budget, administered automatically, and receiving great political support. The implication of this provision for overall British policy will be discussed in the concluding section of the discussion of British housing policy.

The Dominance of the Executive

Current trends in British housing policy indicate the dominance of the national arena (especially the executive) in policy-making. This dominance is perhaps clearest in the Conservative government's ability to change the shape of British housing policy to reflect a preference for home ownership and a downgrading of council housing. For example, while James Callaghan's 1977 budget called for 1.263 billion pounds to be made available for local authorities to construct new housing, Mrs. Thatcher's budget for 1984–5 called for only half that amount, .650 billion pounds, for the same purpose (Cmnd. 9143–II:50). The effect of these budget cuts can be seen in the ability of the subsidized housing program to meet the needs for such housing. The 1977 consultation paper, "The Housing Policy Review," presented by the last Labour government included estimates of how many units of housing would have to be provided by the public sector in order to meet the projected needs for such housing. These projections assumed that such needs would decline, for example, from 161,000 units in 1976 to 122,500 units in 1981. But the effect of the budget cuts has been a massive shortfall relative to those needs projections. For example, in 1977, under the Labour government, 180,000 units of council housing and housing association housing were started, a "surplus" of 19,100 units over what the Green paper had projected. In 1978, still under Labour, cuts in the housing budget meant that only 110,000 units were begun, a deficit from projected needs of 49,100 units. But by 1981, well into Mrs. Thatcher's first term, when the 1977 Green paper had projected needs for 122,500 units (a reduction of 37,500 units from the 1978 level), funds were available for starting only 40,200 units, a shortfall relative to the need projections of 82,300 units (cited in Environment Committee, 1983:19; Government Statistical Service, 1983:112). Thus, Mrs. Thatcher's government has made substantial cuts in funding of council housing and association housing. Rhodes (1984:279) has reported that "the clampdown on capital expenditure for new council housing looks set to re-create a gross housing shortage in the United Kingdom... by the mid-1980s."

In addition to the mortgage interest deduction to encourage home-ownership, the British government provides two other aids to home-ownership -- both of which have grown under the Thatcher government. One takes the form of "renovation grants," which are direct grants covering 50% to 90% of the costs for improvement of existing housing, repairs, and provision of standard amenities (bath, water, etc.) (Government Statistical Service, 1983: 200). These grants are available to both individual home-owners and local governments with funding divided roughly between the two. Under the Thatcher administration, the amount of money available in this category has jumped considerably: in 1977–78 (under the previous Labour government) it was 440 million pounds, under the Thatcher government in 1982–83 it had jumped 168% to 1.18 billion pounds (Cmnd. 8789, 1983: 33–34).

The other way in which the British government aids home ownership (beyond the mortgage interest deduction) is by offering council house occupants the right to buy the unit that they occupy, a policy pushed by the Thatcher government. Despite some local government resistance to such sales, the policy was ultimately upheld by the courts, and much council housing has been sold. In the period from May 1979 to August 1983, 525,000 families had purchased their council housing and another 150,000 requests to purchase were awaiting action. To make the purchase of these units attractive, the government has made these council houses available for substantially less than their full valuation; it has been estimated that the discount from full valuation is 43% (*Sunday Times*, 14 August 1983:2). The policy of selling the property at a substantial discount has also come in for much attack from critics, including some Conservative members of Parliament who have suggested that in the long run the policy will cost government more than it will save, while potentially worsening the housing situation of the elderly, large families, the disabled, and ethnic minorities (Environment Committee, 1981b: lxvi–lxvii). In addition, there appear to be limits on how many units will actually be purchased; there are many council house tenants who, while wishing to own their own housing, have no desire to own the council house they reside in (*Times*, June 29, 1983:2).

The Relation Between Central and Local Government

In general, the character of recent center-local relations seems to minimize the influence of local policy arenas over national policy-making, but it is oversimplifying that relationship to ignore significant connections that do give the local arenas important forms of influence over national policy-making. Starting in the seventies and furthered by the Thatcher government, central government has radically extended its powers over local government finance (Ashford, 1984; Goldsmith and Newton, 1984; Rhodes, 1984). These powers used by the Thatcher government to control local finance include: requiring central government approval of capital expenditures by local government; setting cash limits on central government aid to local governments; and the Local Government Planning and Land Act of 1980 which gave the central government the seeming ability to determine the appropriate levels of spending by each local authority and to penalize severely any that exceeded these levels (Rhodes, 1984: 270–71).

The extension of such control has been seen as detrimental to local government. R.A.W. Rhodes (1984: 283) has argued that when central government's approach to dealing with local government finance is based on a strategy of control, "the outcome will be unintended consequences, recalcitrance, instability, ambiguity and confusion: in short, the *policy mess* that has become the defining characteristic of British central-local relations." Douglas Ashford (1984: 111) has attributed part of the problem to a lack of connection between central and local governments:

> there is no clear institutional link between levels of government that, on the one hand, keeps central politicians honest and, on the other hand, enables local politicians to influence decision-making at higher levels.

Ashford (1984: 105) argues that British central government policy toward the finance of local government suffers from an orientation based on national party conflict and that the result is to leave local governments at the whim of central government without the corporate interests of local government as a whole being adequately represented within the system.

However, care must be taken in extending the analyses offered by Ashford and Rhodes. They do not seem to be useful if used as the basis for the conclusion that local governments (and the other constituents of the local policy arenas) do not have a voice in national policy making. What Ashford and Rhodes are suggesting is that there is no single institution representing local government with a clear and constitutionally powerful voice to affect national policy-making. Instead, what is apparent is that there are a host of different institutional connections between local and central policy arenas that provide the local arenas with a chorus of voices. None of these institutional connections bestows decisive influence on the local arenas, and only rarely do all the elements of the local arenas seek similar goals. In addition, local influence varies depending on the issue and the specific connection used to exercise influence; nevertheless, that local influence exists.

One of the important links between the local and national policy arenas is party organization. To varying degrees, it is clear that through the channel of party organization, governments listen to their local partisans. Gyford and James (1983: 87) point to the important role of local government sections within the major parties, and of the prominent place of doctrines of local government within the smaller parties, as indicators of the general importance of the local to the national parties. Indicating the importance of local partisans to the government of the day is the finding that local government officials are appointed to important national government positions (Gyford and James, 1983: 130).

A third indicator of the importance of the party connection is that on occasions, national government has backed off certain positions when the national party has lined up behind the affected local authority. In general, local government and party officials (especially in the Conservative Party) are not keen to embarrass a national government of their own party (Gyford and James, 1983: 161–165, 196), but this is not always the case. In 1975 the Labour-controlled South Yorkshire County Council came into conflict with the national Labour government over the issue of public transit fares. Ultimately the national government settled on a compromise which relieved it of subsidizing the (low) fares which the council had implemented, but without the County Council being forced to change its policy and raise fares (the County being willing to subsidize the fares out of local taxes). Gyford and James (1983: 138–147) consider that the ultimate position taken by the government was the result of Labour Party pressure put on the government. Hence the connection through the political party between national and local arenas can be an important avenue of local influence.

Another important institutional connection providing the local arena with influence on national policy-making comes from the influence of local government and local parties on parliamentary activity. Even given the strength of a Prime Minister like Mrs. Thatcher, who possesses a solid majority in Parliament, there is the possibility, or threat, of a backbenchers' rebellion threatening the government's majority. This situation occurred when the Thatcher government, as part of its attempt to control local government spending, attempted to enact legislation requiring local authorities to hold a referendum before levying additional taxes to overcome reductions in the central government grant to local government (Rhodes, 1984: 270–271). According to Gyford and James (1983: 203), the power of local Conservative government leaders was manifest in their ability:

> to persuade nearly forty Conservative MPs to make known their hostility to the rates referendums proposal, thereby removing the 'environmental constraint' of a guaranteed government majority and enabling discussions to take place on alternative legislative proposals.

Despite the strong intentions of the Thatcher government, Conservative local governments were able to exercise influence over central government policy-making. While this connection is clearly in evidence where there is commonality in party affiliation, there is also good evidence that Members of Parliament are often willing to plead the case of their local authority to the government regardless of party differences (Schwartz, 1984a: 219–220).

Another case demonstrating Parliament's ability to force changes in executive decisions was the Thatcher government's attempt to shift more of the cost of council (public) housing to those receiving benefits. In January 1984, Mrs. Thatcher's government sought to reduce housing aid by almost 230 million pounds. Commenting on this proposal, *The Economist* (21 Jan. 1984: 49), hardly known as a champion of the welfare state, characterized the proposal as "bashing the poor," arguing that the "burden of the proposed saving – 230 million pounds a year – was laid unfairly and squarely on Britain's poorest," the incentives for low-paid workers to go on the welfare dole increased as well because of the way the cuts were to be implemented. Later the government, in the face of a backbench revolt on the issue, reduced the cuts to 185 million pounds (*The Economist*, 11 Feb. 1984: 54–55) -- still a major reduction, but indicating there are some limits to executive decisions in these areas.

Constituting another connection between local and central policy arenas are the associations representing the different kinds of local authorities: the Association of County Councils (ACC), the Association of District Councils (ADC), and the Association of Metropolitan Authorities (AMA). While these organizations are often in conflict because of different political affiliations, Rhodes has characterized them as the "national community" of local government because of their great contact with each other and their many shared activites (Rhodes, 1984: 263). Rhodes (1984: 263) has also argued that there are three policy areas in which this "national community" is prominent: "alterations to the structure and functions of local government, negotiations over central grant and decisions on pay increases for local government employees." While the Thatcher government has not been interested in a process of negotiating the central government grant to local governments, it is also clear that it takes the associations seriously. For example, it appears that the government made a set of technical amendments to the 1980 Local Government Planning and Land Bill in order to gain the support of the Conservative-controlled ACC so as to gain approval at the point when the act was being considered by the House of Lords (Gyford and James, 1983: 164; Rhodes, 1984: 279). Not unlike the connections discussed before, local authority associations are another avenue of significant (although not decisive) influence used by the local policy arenas.

In addition, with regard to many of the issues of local policy such as housing (or finance), national governments and their local partisans often share a general ideological perspective. For example, years before the election of the Thatcher government, a number of Conservative-controlled local authorities began selling council housing -- their actions building broad Conservative party support for such activity culminating in the 1980 Housing Act (Gyford and James, 1983: 130). Such a shared position may act as a constraint on central government policy-making. The example of council housing sales indicates an even more active role for local government; what constitutes appropriate policy for national government may be set, in part, by the previous action of local governments which defines and builds political support around particular policies.

Local Arenas and the Politics of Policy

What is clear from the preceding analysis is that there are many channels through which local arenas can exercise some measure of influence on national policy. However, at the same time, this does not mean that the local arenas of policy have been able to establish a clear role in the national policy arena. In part, as noted earlier, the influence of local arenas is limited by the lack of a clear constitutional role for local government (or any of the other constituents of the local arena). Even if clear policy positions on housing policy emerged from the local arenas, it is not clear that they would become part of the national debate.

Whether based in a deficit of power or the lack of a clear vision, the inability of local arenas to exercise a decisive influence on national policy making is reflected in the incoherence of the views about local government held in the national arena. Gyford and James (1983: 206–207) have suggested that there are three distinctly different views of local government held within the national parties and that these views cut across party boundaries, suggesting that rarely can we assume continuity of view within any single party. In addition, shifting coalitions within the parties make it difficult to assume a clear continuity of party policy toward local government (Gyford and James, 1983: 204–205). Thus, even within individual parties, partisans from the local arena have failed to put forth a view of local government likely to guide government decisions.

That lack of a clear vision of local government within the national parties has several implications. One is that this incoherence may serve to enhance the influence of those local voices within the parties; the concerns of those from local government become important because those individuals are important as potential supporters in intra-party conflict. But on the other hand, the lack of a consistent or clear view of local government may enhance the ability of the executive to control the formulation of policy, unconstrained by clear party position.

Short of having a constitutional role in national policy-making, the local arena needs to consolidate sufficient political support to be able to impress on national policy-makers, through the various channels discussed earlier, that local views must be taken into account. Of course, these positions must be sufficiently clear that they are not garbled in transmission. In addition, while not implying that only one view emerges from all of the local arenas, the input through any one channel (such as a party) must be unambiguous enough that the local arena position is taken as having substantial political support.

The fact that most housing policies are implemented by local government at least provides an organizational focus for the creation and support of housing policies. But working to reinforce national arena dominance of the local arena are the tools used to implement policy within the local arena. The housing policies implemented at the local level do not contribute to unifying policy concerns, but fragment them. Different programs are implemented with different tools, the differences in tools serving to create barriers to the building of political support behind housing policy. To the degree that the differences in tools create difficulties in building support, the local arena's ability to affect national decisions is reduced.

The possibilities of fragmentation for housing policy can be seen in the different ways that the locally-implemented policies link citizens to local and central government. The differences in how these programs link citizens to the state may well predict different concerns and interests with housing policy that are otherwise difficult to bring together. For example, council-housing tenants, who are affected by local government decisions about general management issues (including allocation, maintenance, and rent policies) as well as national policies dealing with subsidy levels, may be potentially supportive of political action at the national and local level. On the other hand, tenants in privately-owned rental properties who receive rent rebates may be politically moved by issues around the changes in subsidy levels and eligibility (nationally determined). Owner-occupiers may be very concerned with local policy toward allocating improvement grants, but may well lose interest upon receiving one. Similarly, council tenants interested in buying their council house may lose interest in these policies after obtaining a mortgage for their unit. In short, the issues that gain the attention of people seem highly dependent on their housing status and varies from status to status. It is hard to see a current issue that could bring together support from all these groups. Without that support, the local arena, despite all its connections to the national arena of policy, may not be able to push its concerns to the fore.

Owner Occupation

In size alone, the power of owner-occupation is clear in Great Britain. As in the United States, owner-occupiers (including those people who are paying off mortgages on the house they reside in) constitute the largest housing sector, comprising 56% of all housing units (compared to 65.5% in the U.S.), compared to 31% in the publicly-owned sector, and only 13% rented from private landlords (Government Statistical Office, 1983: 114).

The figures for Britain show an emphasis on aid to the owner-occupier sector similar to that in the U.S., despite a much larger subsidized sector. Britain grants home-owners mortgage deductions like those in the U.S., except that "mortgages on second homes are now specifically excluded, and there is an upper limit of 25,000 pounds beyond which tax relief on mortgage interest payment is not allowed" (Murie, Niner and Watson, 1976: 172). The costs of these deductions (and the other aids to home-owners discussed above) are also substantial. During the Thatcher administration, the relative position of subsidies to "subsidized housing" and those to owner-occupiers has reversed -- aid to owner-occupiers becoming larger than aid to those in subsidized housing. For example, in 1979–80, general subsidies to public sector tenants and rent rebates to renters came to a total of 1.915 billion pounds, 174% more than the 1.100 billion pounds of mortgage tax relief. By 1981/82 the balance was estimated to have switched in favor of mortgage tax relief, coming to an estimated 1.3 billion pounds, as compared to 1.28 billion for general subsidies to public sector tenants plus rent rebates (Environment Committee, 1981a: xii).

As in the U.S. case, the mortgage interest deduction does not directly involve the administrative activity of any housing agency of government.

In terms of its relation to the institutions of housing policy, the mortgage interest deduction certainly does not seem to involve home-owners in any concerns shared with those in other forms of housing. In that sense, the lack of shared institutions reinforces the political fragmentation of housing policy that already characterizes policies implemented in the local arena. However, while there is little similarity in the implementation of "subsidized housing" and the mortgage interest deduction in the United States, there are some similarities in the British case. Aside from tax relief of mortgage interest, many British home-owners receive aid from local government (in forms such as improvement grants). This aid is implemented in the same local arena as most other forms of housing subsidies. The sharing of this arena at least makes possible the linking of the concerns of some home-owners to those of recipients of other housing subsidies.

CONCLUSION

To understand the configuration of housing policy and politics, this paper has taken an approach based on an analysis of both the arenas of politics in which policy is made and implemented, and the effect of the specific tools chosen to implement policy. Both the arenas and the tools of policy appear necessary to understand the present configuration and the likely future of housing policy.

Housing policy in Great Britain and the United States presents us with two very different configurations of arenas and tools. In the U.S. case, the analysis shows that different policies tend to take place in different arenas, with the tools of policy reinforcing a differential susceptibility to program change. "Subsidized housing" policies, moving toward market approaches (such as Section 8 and the housing voucher programs) may lead to the situation where there is no political arena of implementation. This form of housing policy also deprives subsidized housing of any supportive interest groups (such as the home-builders) sufficiently strong to influence Congressional policy decisions. In addition to the lack of an arena of implementation to focus support and the lack of strong institutional support, the use of highly visible budgeting forms leaves these subsidized programs very susceptible to cuts. Recently, this weakness has meant that the executive has been able to dominate budgetary politics around subsidized housing (although somewhat less successfully to alter the forms of policy).

In the U.S., the use of tax-based "automatic" subsidies to owner-occupation in the tax code also results in arena-less implementation. However, in this case, the institutional forces behind policy (including financial institutions, home-builders, and a very high level of political support) are more than strong enough to maintain support in national policy arenas. That support, plus the invisibility of the mortgage-interest deduction in the budget process, has rendered the policy invulnerable, even in periods of massive budget cutting.

Farmers Home Administration housing represents a third configuration of tools and arenas. Starting with direct implementation by the federal government, the program has stimulated interest group support which is reflected in strong Congressional support. Because the program has been cloaked in the invisibility of an off-budget financing mechanism, it has avoided most of the budget-cutting that has decimated other housing and social welfare programs. However, a change to a more visible form of budgeting could render its Congressional and interest group support insufficient for protection from the intrusion of the executive.

In the British case, with the exception of the mortgage interest deduction afforded owner-occupiers, most housing policy is implemented by local government, with policy formulation dominated by national government. Thus, there is a clear arena in which the politics around housing may be focused. However, the very different tools used to implement those policies work against unifying and concentrating the issues so that the local arenas of policy cannot routinely become a decisive influence in national policy. In the absence of clear local influence, the executive dominates policy-making. Innovation is possible in the system, but change depends largely on the initiative of the executive. For concerns originating in the local arena to gain significance in the national arenas where policy decisions are made, it will be necessary for political support to be aggregated to a much greater degree than currently exists. Thus, locally-based initiatives may be effective only where the issue chosen cuts across the set of different programs implemented by local government. In that case, the various channels linking local and central government may prove effective in imposing the local view on national policy-making.

Neither Lowi's "arenas of power" or Salamon's "tools of policy" alone can explain the relation between politics and housing policy. Advancing beyond a simple combination of the two approaches, accepting that policy takes place in multiple arenas and that the tools of policy have a different significance in each arena, provides a useful vantage point from which to explain the configuration and development of housing politics and policy.

REFERENCES

Ashford, D.E. (1984) "At the Pleasure of Parliament: The Politics of Local Reform in Britain", pp. 102–125 in D.T. Studlar and J. Waltman (eds.), *Dilemmas of Change in British Politics*. Jackson, Mississippi: University Press of Mississippi.

CMND. 8789–II (1983) *The Government's Expenditure Plans: 1983–84 to 1985–86: Volume Two*. London: H.M.S.O.

CMND. 9143–II (1984) *The Government's Expenditure Plans: 1984–85 to 1986–87: Volume Two*. London: H.M.S.O.

Environment Committee (1981a) House of Commons (United Kingdom). *DOE's Housing Policies: Enquiry into Government's Expenditure Plans 1981/82 to 1983/84 and the Updating of the Committee's First Report for the Session 1979/80* (HC 383 i–ii). London: H.M.S.O.

--- (1981b) *Council House Sales: Volume 1* (HC 366–I). London: H.M.S.O.

--- (1983) *Session 1982–83: Department of the Environment's Winter Supplementary Estimates 1982–83: Minutes of Evidence* (170–i). London: H.M.S.O.

FmHA (Farmers Home Administration) (1985) *A Brief History of the Farmers Home Administration*. Washington, D.C.: Farmers Home Administration. U.S. Department of Agriculture.

Fraser, D. (1973) *The Evolution of the British Welfare State*. London: Macmillan.

Goldsmith, M., and K. Newton (1984) "Central-Local Government Relations: The Irresistible Rise of Centralized Power", pp. 216–233 in Hugh Berrington (ed.), *Change in British Politics*. London: Frank Cass.

Government Statistical Service (1983) (United Kingdom). *Social Trends No 13: 1983 Edition*. London: H.M.S.O.

Gyford, J. (1976) *Local Politics in Britain*. London: Croom Helm.

Gyford, J., and M. James (1983) *National Parties and Local Politics*. London: George Allen & Unwin.

HAC (Housing Assistance Council) (1981) *Where Credit is Due: the Rural Credit Gap and the Farmers Home Administration*. Washington, D.C.: Housing Assistance Council.

--- (1985) *Terminating Options: An Analysis of the Administration's Proposed Fiscal 1986 Rural and Indian Housing Budget*. Washington, D.C.: Housing Assistance Council.

Hartman, C. (1982) "Housing", pp. 141–161 in A. Gartner, C. Greer, and F. Riessman (eds.), *What Reagan is Doing to Us*. New York: Perennial Library.

Lowi, T.J. (1964) "American Business, Public Policy, Case Studies, and Political Theory", *World Politics*, 16: 667–715.

--- (1970) "Decision-making vs. Policy-making: Toward an Antidote for Technocracy", *Public Administration Review*, 30: 314–325.

--- (1972) "Four Systems of Policy, Politics and Choice", *Public Administration Review*, 32: 298–310.

--- (1979) *The End of Liberalism*. 2d edition. New York: Norton.

Malpass, P., and A. Murie (1982) *Housing Policy and Practice*. London: Macmillan.

McAllister, I. (1984) "Housing Tenure and Party Choice in Australia, Britain and the United States", *British Journal of Political Science*, 14: 509–522.

Murie, A., P. Niner, and C. Watson (1976) *Housing Policy and the Housing System*. London: George Allen & Unwin.

OMB (Office of Management and Budget) (1982a) Executive Office of the President (United States). *Budget of the United States Government: Fiscal Year 1983*. Washington, D.C.: Government Printing Office.

--- (1982b) *Budget of the United States Government: Fiscal Year 1983: Appendix*. Washington, D.C.: Government Printing Office.

--- (1982c) *Major Themes and Additional Budget Details: Fiscal Year 1983*. Washington, D.C.: Government Printing Office.

--- (1985a) *Budget of the United States Government: Fiscal Year 1986*. Washington, D.C.: Government Printing Office.

--- (1985b) *Special Analyses: Budget of the United States Government: Fiscal Year 1986*. Washington, D.C.: Government Printing Office.

--- (1985c) *Budget of the United States, 1986 -- Appendix*. Washington, D.C.: Government Printing Office.

Rex, J., and R. Moore (1967) *Race, Community, and Conflict: A Study of Sparkbrook*. London: Oxford University.

Richards, P.G. (1978) *The Reformed Local Government System: Revised Third Edition*. London: George Allen & Unwin.

Rhodes, R.A.W. (1984) "Continuity and Change in British Central-Local Relations: 'The Conservative Threat', 1979–83", *British Journal of Political Science*, 14: 261–283.

Salamon, L.M. (1981) "Rethinking Public Management: Third-Party Government and the Changing Forms of Government Action", *Public Policy*, 29: 255–275.

Scharpf, F., B. Reissert and F. Schnabel (1978) "Policy Effectiveness and Conflict Avoidance in Intergovernmental Policy Formation", pp. 57–112 in K. Hanf and F.W. Scharpf, *Interorganizational Policy Making: Limits to Coordination and Central Control*. London: Sage.

Schwartz, N.H. (1983) "Reagan's Housing Policies", Birmingham, Alabama: Southern Political Science Association Meetings, mimeo.

--- (1984a) "Race and the Allocation of Public Housing in Great Britain: The Autonomy of the Local State", *Comparative Politics*, 16: 205–222.

--- (1984b) "Reagan's Housing Policies", pp. 149–164 in A. Champagne and E.J. Harpham (eds.), *The Attack on the Welfare State*. Prospect Heights, I11.: Waveland Press.

--- (1985) "The Farmers Home Administration: Social Politics in the Pork Barrel", New Orleans, Louisiana: Annual Meetings of the American Political Science Association, mimeo.

Struyk, R.J., N. Mayer, and J.A. Tuccillo (1983) *Federal Housing Policy at President Reagan's Midterm*. Washington, D.C.: Urban Institute Press.

Struyk, R.J., J.A. Tuccillo, and J.P. Zais (1982) "Housing and Community Development", pp. 393–417 in J.L. Palmer and I.V. Sawhill (eds.), *The Reagan Experiment*. Washington, D.C.: The Urban Institute Press.

U.S. Department of Commerce (1982) Bureau of the Census. *Statistical Abstract of the United States: 1982–83*. Washington, D.C.: Government Printing Office.

U.S. Senate (1983) Committee on Banking, Housing, and Urban Affairs, Subcommittee on Rural Housing and Development. *Hearing to Consider the Future of the Federal Role in Rural Housing and the Principal Agency Responsible for Those Programs, the Farmers Home Administration, March 23, 1983 (S. Hrg. 98–155)*. Washington, D.C.: G.P.O.

Housing and Social Research

Introduction

Jim Kemeny, The National Swedish
Institute for Building Research

The sociology of housing has been undergoing enormous changes since the
mid-1970s. Two developments in particular stand out. First, there has
been a growing awareness among researchers of the importance of getting
away from the dominance of abstracted empiricist perspectives in which
tabulations are churned out in a seemingly endless stream but with little
awareness of the theoretical framework which underlies them or any real
attempt to conceptualise. Equally important, there has been a rapid
growth in comparative housing research — not merely juxtapositional
research, in which one country is described and juxtaposed to the next
country description, nor even general international descriptive research
which characterised much of the early literature. Rather, there has increasingly been comparative research which is clearly focussed and with
countries carefully chosen to reflect underlying structural similarities or
differences.

The Sociology Keynote Addresses were chosen to reflect these developments. The first address, given by *Michael Harloe,* was a paper prepared by
him jointly with *Maartje Martens.* Harloe and Martens have previously
been highly critical of much traditional comparative housing research and
in this paper they develop elements of this theme and by way of illustration they examine some recent trends in Europe and the USA in terms of
the provision of housing. This paper breaks considerable new ground in
seeking to identify the main trends in housing innovations which are still
in the process of emerging after a period of severe cut-backs in housing
provision. Their discussion is based on extensive research carried out over
many years into comparative housing markets.

Marino Folin's paper also takes a "provision of housing" perspective but
focusses instead more on housing policy. Folin traces the history of housing

policies in a number of european countries and the way in which the overall mix of different policies related to changing political and social circumstances.

Peter Marcure's paper deals with the concepts of oppression and liberation in the context of housing. This is a novel treatment which casts new light on the social significance of housing. Marcuse points out the multifarious ways in which housing can both oppress and liberate, including its sexist and racist dimensions. This address was particularly notable for the way in which it dealt with the ways in which housing impinges on the individual in everyday life and contributes to the forming of character and behaviour both in broad economic, social and political terms and in terms of status and social position.

Finally, *Ivan Tosics'* paper deals with the specific problems of housing and housing policy in Hungary, as an example of the general situation which heavily state-controlled housing has resulted in. Tosics points to the fact that state involvement in housing has produced its own forms of social inequalities and argues for more market-oriented policies from an essentially socialist viewpoint, as a means of correcting very gross inequalities. This paper exemplifies the great strides being made in Eastern European housing sociology in recent years, and points to the very different conditions which pertain there in comparison with capitalist societies.

If the above sociology contributions were to be characterised, the following observations might be made. First, the clear tendency to move away from analyses of the ways in which housing policy affects housing consumption which has been a hallmark of recent developments in housing sociology is very apparent from the papers. Both Harloe/Martens and Folin explicitly take a perspective which is firmly founded in the analysis of the provision of housing. Second, there are signs that there has been increasing disillusionment with established forms of housing provision. Harloe and Martens explore new directions in this sense, and Tosics, in the Hungarian context also does so but in a rather different manner. Finally, Marcuse's paper reflects a growing trend in the sociology of housing which is still embryonic but very much a growth-point. This concerns the increasing emphasis upon the individual and personal control over housing. Harloe and Martens paper also touches on this theme when they indicate that some of the innovations now being tried are based on consumer engagement in the production of housing, rather than as passive recipients, and draw more on the populist traditions of self-help than either State or Market solutions.

Innovation in Housing Markets and Policies

Michael Harloe, Department of Sociology,
University of Essex, U.K. and
Maartje Martens, Department of Sociology,
University of Essex, U.K.

W. Europe

9320

THE SIGNIFICANCE OF CONTEMPORARY HOUSING INNOVATIONS

In the past 25 years there has been an enormous improvement in the quality and quantity of data collection and social research concerning housing. Most of this work has taken place at the national level, although there is a growing interest in cross national, comparative work. Much housing research is carried out or supported by governments, private sector organisations and others – such as pressure groups – whose main concern is with current events and distributional aspects of the development of housing markets and policies. A good deal of the more academic research has been carried out in a rather similar manner – i.e. on distributional aspects of housing provision, with limited reference to their links with other features of provision, let alone to the broader socio-economic, political and historical context in which housing is located.

In another paper (Harloe and Martens 1984) we have provided a detailed critique of such studies, especially those involving cross national comparisons. We shall not repeat this critique here but it is necessary to summarise two of the main conclusions of our earlier paper. These are that;

1. useful policy oriented or theoretically productive cross national housing research needs to provide a *detailed* yet *broad* examination of housing policies and markets; explore interrelationships within the housing 'system' and also the ways in which housing provision is moulded by the wider national, and increasingly international, societal context.

2. even the more sophisticated academic studies often suffer from a reluctance to explore the historically determined political, economic and ideological determinants of the forms in which housing is provided – the *social relations of housing provision*. Such studies have concentrated in a narrow and misleading way on examining housing policies alone, by examining the

state's performance within the limits set by itself and without criticising the terms and categories within which national housing policy debates are conducted.

This critique of much existing comparative housing research (and nationally based work) helped to guide a series of cross national studies of capitalist housing provision in Western Europe (Britain, France, the Netherlands, West Germany and Denmark) and the USA which we have carried out over the past few years (e.g. Harloe 1981, 1985; Martens 1985; Harloe and Martens 1984, 1985; Ball, Martens and Harloe, 1986). In developing an understanding of both general and nationally specific features of trends in housing markets and policies we have carried out historically based studies of the following matters;

i. the broad social, economic and political characteristics of different societies and how these have helped to define their housing markets and policies;

ii. nationally specific structures of housing provision, including forms of state support;

iii. factors 'internal' to housing markets, such as the effects of demand and supply mechanisms on the cost and availability of housing during the different phases of the conomic cycle.

One major conclusion of our research is that during the post war era some profound shifts in the nature of capitalist housing provision have taken place. Of course many of these changes have been widely recognised by other housing researchers, particularly where distributional aspects and changes in the relative importance of the major tenures are concerned. However, the underlying mechanisms of these changes have been much less adequately researched and there is certainly no general or widely held consensus on what they are.

In purely descriptive terms there is a good deal of recognition that the following shifts in the role and nature of major tenures have been occurring;

1. the decline of private rented housing as the houser of most of the urban working class and significant sectors of the middle class too (see Harloe 1985). Instead this tenure increasingly accomodates only those low income groups who do not have the economic or political power to obtain access to other tenures. At the other end of the spectrum there are still limited sub markets for middle and upper income households, especially in large cities and in areas of rapid population growth;

2. a decline since the late 1960s — mid 1970s in the production of social rented housing and an erosion of political support for this tenure. Many better off tenants have moved to owner occupation and some sections of this tenure have become 'residual' housing for a 'marginalised' population

— in short a population which is now surplus to the requirements of national economies. In some areas physical deterioration of the stock and social conflict are rapidly increasing (see Prak and Priemus 1985, Harloe 1987).

3. a growth of owner occupation, enormously encouraged by subsidies and by the terms on which alternative forms of accomodation are available (cost, quality, availability etc.) (see Martens 1985). This trend has been supported by a coalition of consumer and producer groups and political parties which has become the most powerful influence on national housing policies. It has also been sustained by the perceived value of home owner-ship as a hedge against inflation and by an ideology which asserts that homeownership is a natural instinct of the human species. The reality is somewhat different. Apart from the persistence of rural, low income and low quality owner occupation in a number of countries, there is con-siderable evidence, especially in countries where 60–70% of the stock is now owner occupied, of poorer households being forced into this tenure and living in very insecure and inadequate conditions (see, for example, Karn, Kemeny and Williams 1985).

Over the past decades there has been a transition from one form of the commodity production and market distribution of housing to another — from renting to owner occupation. In relatively few countries, mainly in Western Europe, this pattern has been modified by the existence of a considerable stock of social rented housing. However, this housing is rarely seen (as it was for some years in the heyday of post war social democracy) as *the* major alternative for the majority of the population to private rented housing. Without discussing the details here, there are various reasons why most larger scale housing capital now prefers to be involved in the production of owner occupied rather than rented housing. But there were certain other economic/institutional preconditions for the emergence of mass owner occupation (note these are *preconditions* not determinants — political, social and ideological factors have also been important). These include the need to organise the finance required to purchase a house so that loan repayments could be sustained by a substantial proportion of households and for these households to have a sufficient level and stability of income to afford home ownership.

In many countries it was not until the post war boom of the fifties and sixties that the economic preconditions of full employment, economic growth and hence rising real incomes for large sections of the population made mass owner occupation a possibility. It was in this climate too that large scale finance and construction capital saw the opportunities for prof-itable investment in owner occupied housing, aided by governments which underwrote the development of long term private mortgage finance, which legislated for protected circuits of housing finance, which promoted private housing development by planning regulations and infrastructural investments, and which provided subsidies for homebuyers. In general, state housing policies have been increasingly biased towards owner occupation. The roots of this phenomenon need much more research — political development has, cross nationally, been very uneven and the promotion of home ownership by all political parties — common to most English speaking advanced capitalist societies — has been slower to develop elsewhere (and may now be diminishing in some cases) (see Martens 1985). But, insofar as political attitudes have fed off popular demands, these demands have in turn been heightened by the growing inequality in the terms upon which the various forms of housing have been made available to the population. In physical, financial and ideological/social terms, the perceived (if not always the actual) benefits of home ownership rather than rental housing have grown in the past decades. And these terms have been set by the interaction of the state, the economy and the agencies which produce and finance housing — rather than, as some economists suggest, by individual consumer choice or, as many housing policy analysts imply, by a state which acts in the 'public interest'.

So in the post war era new patterns of housing provision developed, varying in detail from country to country according to specific historical legacies and contemporary circumstances, but with strong common features too. For many years these arrangements could be regarded as highly successful. The expansion of private, owner occupied housing became the vehicle for a wider growth of consumer goods and profits. The quantity and quality of housing increased, so overall housing conditions steadily improved. Policies which opened up these improved conditions to the mass of the population were electoral winners. By the seventies the conventional wisdom was that *the* housing problem had been solved. Remaining problems, although severe in some cases, were limited and localised — geographically or in terms of the sections of the population or the parts of the stock involved. The success of the postwar private housebuilding boom encouraged the shift in housing policies, which for a few years after the war had involved massive direct intervention in housing provision (social housing, production controls, controls on private renting and housing allocation etc.), towards ever greater reliance on and support for private markets.

However, a continuation of this pattern depended on the maintenance of the social, and particularly the economic, conditions which made it possible. Since the late seventies these conditions have changed. There has been the deepest recession in fifty years. Industrial output and incomes have stagnated or even declined, unemployment has accelerated to levels undreamt of a decade ago and the future prospects and security of those who remain in employment are much less certain than hitherto. Public spending has been constrained, and even when it has not been cut, expenditure patterns have often changed as the relief of unemployment, spending on law and order, defence and so on have taken higher priorities than housing. Such trends have been accompanied, as well as reinforced, by a shift in political ideology. This is seen most clearly in countries where the New Right has come to power, committed to rolling back the welfare state, 'setting the market free', endorsing income inequality and so on. But even in countries where more socially progressive politics survived, housing spending has been under pressure and other priorities, such as industrial investment have become more important.

These changes have had a profound effect on housing markets, weakening — although to an extent not yet wholly clear — the structures of provision established during the boom years. The most immediate indicators of these effects include:

1. depressed levels of new construction and of investment generally in housing.
2. a reversal of the post war trend of improving housing conditions — both with respect to condition and occupancy.
3. increasing problems of affordability, extending beyond those low income groups for whom this is a perennial difficulty.
4. arising from these, increased problems of accessibility of housing.

A major topic for further research is the extent to which such trends are indicators of a large scale break down of established structures of housing provision. An immediate problem is the limits of the available data. In some cases, for example regarding stock condition, official surveys only reveal aggregate trends. In other cases, for example regarding accessibility, reliable information is hard to obtain (and governments may be reluctant to collect such information). Even when some information is available, it may not throw much light on distributional issues — for example which socio-economic groups, types of household or geographical areas are particularly affected by reduced construction output, growing disrepair etc.

However, the collection of such empirical material only provides limited information about the ways in which changes are taking place. It reveals much less about the reasons why such changes are occurring and the factors which are likely to determine their further development. To begin answering such questions we have to examine the changing social relations of housing provision, not just collect information about the consequences of these changes. Social relations imply the existence of social actors. In housing we can identify a range of social actors, including various types of households (defined by class, demographic structure, income level etc.)

and of institutions or organisations (defined by status — e.g. public/private — by function — e.g. financial, development, landlord). The central research task then becomes the study of the ways in which these actors are responding and adapting to the sharply changing economic and political context of the past few years, and to the responses of other actors and, consequently, how the established forms of housing provision are being reshaped.

Of course adaption is a constant feature of housing markets and policies — there are always incremental adjustments to changing conditions. Our concern here is with changes which may have more radical implications for housing provision, which indicate that new or substantially modified structures are emerging. It must be admitted that often the distinction between radical and incremental changes is far from clear in practice. Such differences become more evident with the benefit of hindsight. However, it is not acceptable for housing researchers who are studying the changes now taking place to *assume* that these are no more than adjustments at the margin, any more than one should *assume* the converse. The issue is one for empirical research, not *a priori* reasoning. Nevertheless, given the links which we have traced between the historical development of housing provision and the broader socio-economic and political context *and* the major changes which have recently occurred in this context, the *hypothesis* that major changes in structures of housing provision will follow is a reasonable starting point for research. And there is, in fact, some empirical evidence of break down in existing structures of housing provision and of newly emergent patterns. In the last part of this paper we shall review, in a cross national context, a few of the more important features of these new patterns.

Of course, there are still many households which remain well housed and for whom problems such as increasing housing costs are of minor importance — requiring limited adjustment in household budgets or future housing expectations for example. A similar point applies to those agencies involved in housing markets and policies. But the full significance of the changes now occurring in housing provision has yet to be seen. However, it is by examining *innovation* in housing provision, by discovering how these innovations relate to the growing problems faced by some households and institutions, that the hypothesis that we are now in a period of major change in capitalist housing provision can begin to be tested.

THE STUDY OF INNOVATIONS: SOME KEY ISSUES

There are several problems about the nature and study of innovations which, in the course of our research, it has become important to clarify. The first concerns the way in which innovations are evaluated. Discussion of innovation is often accompanied by an implicit or explicit assumption that social innovation is a beneficial process — or that research into innovations ought to be mainly concerned with such benefits. But innovations may have positive and/or negative consequences for those affected by them. While it may be politically more acceptable to concentrate on positive consequences, this would be one sided and misleading. Our research is particularly concerned with the impact of housing market and policy changes on consumers — especially those who are often excluded from access to mainstream housing provision. One suggestion has been that we can distinguish between positive and negative innovations in respect to consumers. However, this division seems to create more problems than it solves. For example, certain innovations benefit some consumers at the expense of others.

A second issue concerns what is to be regarded as innovatory. Obviously a new housing tenure, mortgage instrument or subsidy policy is an innovation. But only to classify such developments as innovatory would be far too restrictive. It would surely be accepted that the major growth of state subsidised social rental housing in Western Europe after 1945 was an innovation. It marked a new level of state involvement in housing, with important consequences for other agencies and consumers. Yet social rented housing did not originate then, it simply developed on a scale hitherto unknown. Likewise today the 'doubling up' of low income households in accomodation, as a solution (of sorts) to a lack of access to low income housing, is not, in the narrow sense, an innovation. In fact it is one of the classic responses to housing problems, as many nineteenth century housing studies show. But the (so far scattered) evidence that doubling up is increasing, after decades in which it declined, is an indicator of a radical change in accessibility/affordability for some groups and should therefore be studied.

Therefore, a study of innovatory developments must cover a broad area. It should encompass not only wholly new developments but also major changes in existing aspects of housing markets and policies. It should include, for example, sharply changing trends in indicators of housing stress/inadequacy/affordability, radical changes in the nature and functioning of existing housing institutions and housing policies and in the forms and terms of the housing choices that are available to specific households, as well as in the types of households constrained to accept particular forms of accomodation. In fact there are no precise limits to what should and should not be included in a study of housing innovations. The point of the research is not to examine innovations as individual, self contained phenomena but rather to focus on a wide variety of changes which, taken together, may indicate that a substantial restructuring of the forms of capitalist housing provision is occurring and to analyse the nature of these new forms.

The final, and most important, consideration follows from this last point and concerns the meaning or significance of innovations. We have suggested that the study of innovations is important because of what it may tell us about broader changes in the social relations of housing provision. But most innovations are small scale at first. The type of evaluative material that usually describes such innovations (especially if produced by those who wish to promote them) frequently fails to go beyond the level of description and very limited analysis to consider the wider significance of what is being studied (how a new mortgage instrument works, for example, but not whether it is an indicator or consequence of potentially broad ranging changes in mortgage provision or is of minimal applicability and marginal importance).

Therefore, there is a need to move beyond a descriptive, narrowly conceived analysis of innovations to assess their social meaning. A paper by Tarozzi *et al.* (1986) has usefully discussed some of the issues which then arise, although their substantive concern was not housing but the rise of new social movements in Italian cities. The following points partially derive from their discussion;

1. social science investigations of innovatory developments which use concepts based on 'common sense' meanings and classifications shared by 'average' members of society are unduly restricted. This is because these are *new* developments, so the common sense concepts and frames of reference available to explicate them may as yet be only weakly developed.

2. this implies severe limitations on the extent to which innovations can be studied and their social significance evaluated when relying solely on the standard methods of quantitative social science. Such work is limited by its concentration on those phenomena which can be quantified with available concepts (usually based on accepted, common sense meanings) and by the types of research instruments used. Such points are of course commonly made in critiques of empiricist methodology. But the problem is greater in the case of innovations whose potential social significance is, as yet, unclear. Social survey research may, for example, show the existence of developments which are no more than minor, or, perhaps, temporary deviants from a norm. But these developments may, alternatively, be the first signs of major changes. While such research can identify new trends, it is rarely able to explore their broader significance. One consequence, as Tarozzi *et al.* state, is that social science which limits itself to a narrow empiricism has often failed to recognise that major social changes may be imminent — for example the outbreak of social protest and conflict on an intense and widespread scale in the sixties was quite contrary to the expectations of many social scientists at the start of that decade.

3. this has a variety of implications for research methodology. When quantitative methods are used, the categories for analysis and the information collected should not exclude, as marginal and socially irrevelant, developments which may be of minor significance quantitatively. Of course, some quantitative work can be essential — for example, to identify new trends and provide some measures of their immediate impact. But research into innovations which is limited to measurement and quantification (plus the various standard tests of 'significance' etc.) is inadequate.

4. such research must be accompanied by qualitative work which examines the relations between innovatory developments and the wider social structures in which they are located. It should answer questions such as whether a specific innovation is a response to the breakdown of major aspects of existing social relations and whether it has the potentiality for being more than a limited/transitory/ineffective response to such a break down. Answering such questions requires research which is not limited by an assumption that the main task is to discover what is already typical or of major quantitative significance. Rather it requires research which examines the reasons for innovatory developments and the constraints and opportunities which will determine whether or not such innovations are more widely diffused. Such research must combine supposedly 'hard' methods (such as the collection and analysis of data) with less restrictive approaches (such as semi-structured interviewing of 'key' informants, documentary research and so on) and should reverse normal practices by paying more attention to 'minority' rather than to 'majority' phenomena. It also requires research which, because it is concerned to locate innovation in its broader social context, traces the links between developments specific to housing markets and policies and those occurring in areas which are conventionally regarded as beyond the concerns of housing research.

Our own research is using a combination of these methods to explore the nature and significance of contemporary innovations in housing markets and policies in several Western European countries and the USA. Cross national research can (due to limitations of time and resources and researchers' own ethnocentricity) be very superficial. But it also has major advantages. At a rather general level similar problems are arising in capitalist housing provision and similar choices and constraints face policy makers in many countries. Comparative analysis can provide a clearer understanding of the principal links between, for example, changes in the national and international economy and housing markets. Innovations which are a response to similar problems arising in a number of different countries are a high priority for more detailed examination with a view to assessing their broader and longer term significance for future patterns of housing provision. At the same time, whilst there are certain common problems and broad choices available in different countries, the detailed nature of these problems and choices, and of innovatory responses to them, varies considerably. As we have argued in an earlier paper, general *trends* in capitalist housing provision can be identified (Harloe and Martens 1984). But at the same time there are important variations in the detailed nature, extent etc. of such trends. These are the consequences of specific, nationally based structures and histories of housing provision and we cannot hope to understand the dynamics of the development of these trends if we ignore this fact. So while cross national research is invaluable in *helping* to identify potentially major innovations as well as the factors which give rise to them, we cannot answer the key questions raised above concerning their social significance without careful and detailed exploration of the distinctive national contexts in which they arise.

In the third part of this paper we present some of the preliminary findings of our research. At this stage we can only indicate some of the most important common problems and general categories of innovative response which, because they are occurring in several countries, may well be significant for future patterns of capitalist housing provision.

SOME ASPECTS OF INNOVATON IN HOUSING PROVISION

In the first part of this paper we stated that to understand developments in housing provision, it is insufficient to focus on state policies and their distributional effects. As we shall see, the study of innovations underlines the point, because many of the new developments occur outside the sphere of state policies. This is not totally surprising considering that many national governments aim to withdraw from their direct involvement in housing markets and to promote the role of private institutions.

Current developments in housing markets indicate that much change is occurring, not just across different countries, but also across locations within each country. Assumptions about there being a growing role for private housing and hence a declining role for government intervention are too simplistic. Actual developments are much more complex and contradictory. The following description of innovatory areas in housing provision is not comprehensive, but can be seen as a way of approaching the complexities and contradictions of current trends.

An additional problem of analysing current changes in housing markets is that we are looking at different countries and each has distinct structures of housing provision. So what are new developments in one country may be part of the traditional structures of provision in another. In this paper, it will, however, not be possible to describe the separate national housing systems in detail (see Ball, Harloe & Martens, forthcoming, for a more comprehensive account).

In what follows, three different levels of innovation will be described. Changes in the institutions and agencies traditionally involved in housing provision will be dealt with first, and the new circumstances to which they have to adapt noted. Second, we discuss changing relations between these institutions. Finally, and only briefly, we examine some of the ways in which ideological and political concepts relating to traditional forms of housing provision are changing. Our research on innovatory developments in housing markets and policies focusses on West Germany, Denmark and the USA, but also some mention will be made of trends in Britain, Denmark and France.

Institutional Changes and Transitions in Housing Services

Trends in Investment. There has been a secular decline in housebuilding rates since the late 1960s/early 1970s. The decline has, however, been punctuated by short boom periods. Overall investment in housing continued to grow during the 1970s due to substantial levels of house price inflation during certain periods (usually coinciding with housebuilding booms) and an increase in investment in the existing housing stock. The latter concerns maintenance and improvement investments, but also an increase in housing stock transactions. In an era of inflation, owners of both rented and owner occupied housing aimed to capitalise on house price increases, raising the level of investment that new owners needed to make. So, despite the decline in housebuilding rates, housing market activities and investment continued to increase.

Both housebuilders and housing finance institutions, particularly the bigger ones, expanded their businesses during housing market booms. Housing finance institutions in particular profited from the growth in housing stock transactions by providing funds for housebuyers. The main problem for traditional mortgage lenders during the 1970s was increased competition from other financial institutions. Commercial banks had started to develop market shares in the profitable business of housing loans. Competition for funds also intensified, but this mainly affected specialised mortgage lenders who derive funds from personal savings, the traditionally dominant type of housing finance circuit in English speaking countries.

Business prospects of housebuilding firms depend directly on new construction and investments in housing improvement. The industry was already forced into major adjustments during the 1970s in response to a substantial contraction of new orders. A restructuring of the housebuilding industry has taken place as investments have become more cyclical and builders were forced to adjust production processes to sharply fluctuating building rates. Furthermore, housing improvement activities have become more important and require different production techniques and labour relations (Ball, forthcoming).

Low rates of inflation and high real interest rates in the 1980s created new problems for housing market participants. In the early part of the decade, interest rates were at peak levels and a slump in housing investment was apparent in all western economies. Private housing markets are still stagnant in some countries, for instance the Netherlands, or in certain regions, such as areas in the USA, which are particularly affected by crises in the agricultural and energy sectors. But in most cases, private housing markets recovered when nominal interest rates declined and the world economy improved. The current housing market boom is, however, likely to be short-lived when taking account of the basic cause of the long term decline in housebuilding, which is the growing inaffordability of new housing, not just for poorer households, but increasingly also for middle income households.

Reducing the Cost of New Housing. Innovatory developments in this context concern attempts to reduce entry costs to new housing. Land and construction costs increased substantially during the 1970s in part because of rises in the quality, size and equipment of new housing. Rising interest rates and higher mortgage to income ratios, in addition, further reduced the affordability of new housing.

Attempts to reduce land costs in the 1980s include the promotion of higher building densities and the introduction of land lease schemes by local authorities. The latter may reduce land cost by spreading its repayment over a longer time period and charging lower rates of interest. It is only a major issue where municipal land leasing was never common, as for example in West Germany. (Whereas in Amsterdam, for instance, municipal land ownership and leasing has dominated urban extensions since the late 1900's.) New developments also include state subsidies to reduce land costs. In some areas in the USA, local authorities provide cheap land for low income housing, or reduce real estate taxes for such projects. In the Netherlands, special subsidies have been made available to reduce the land costs of new housebuilding. Finally, costs can be reduced when in mixed projects, private market housing cross subsidies low income housing, or when there are cross subsidies between housing developments in separate areas. Such schemes are, however, currently quite rare, as they assume a thriving private housebuilding market or policy instruments which can attract or force builders to participate in such schemes. They seem to be most developed, so far, in the USA.

A major element in policies which aim to reduce construction costs is (apart from various ways of depressing construction industry wages) a reduction in the quality, equipment and size of new housing. Such innovations are aided by central and local government policies aimed at deregulating housing and building standards. Public support can further be given by providing research and development resources to study the most efficient ways of reducing building costs. The issue of lowering the price of new housing is of particular relevance to West Germany, where new house prices are higher than in any of the other countries which we surveyed (around £85,000 for a terrace (row) house in a large town or £100,000 for a detached house in a small town in 1983, compared to an average price of £31,000 for new housing in Britain in the same year) (Martens 1985). But substantial savings have also been made in the Netherlands, where building costs always have been under very stringent public control.

There are, however, physical and psychological limits to the extent to which housing quality and standards can be reduced. Children's bed rooms of 5 sqm, kitchens without natural light and ventilation, steep stairs, thinner partition walls are only a few examples which lead one to question this new trend. A reduction of private space for each member of the household can inhibit personal development and is generally recognised as a major cause of stress.

Another significant trend in reducing the costs of new housing is the introduction of self help in housebuilding. In West Germany, like France and other Mediterranean countries, there has been a long tradition of self building by individual households. In these countries, self building or commissioned housebuilding remained a dominant form of owner occupied housing provision throughout the postwar period. The prevalence of self building is reflected by high down-payment contributions by West German households. Until around the mid 1970s, about half the costs of new housing were contributed by the household in the form of own savings and labour. Since then, mortgage/house price ratios went up and reduced the necessary self help contributions. But with high costs of building and borrowing in the 1980s, self help is again encouraged.

In the Netherlands self help projects are now being tried experimentally, since there is no tradition in this sphere. Experiments are collective and usually concern terrace (row) houses which are built at the same time for a known group of clients who can put forward their specific wishes with respect to the design of the units. Local authorities play a major role in developing these projects. Some experiments are based on the principle of dividing the 'shell' from the 'infill' processes of housebuilding. Self help contributions can concern both phases, but in principle, the shell is delivered to the clients when it is water and wind tight and linked to the local services. The scheme is usually referred to as 'Open Building' (cf Lukez

1986). But generally, self help contributions per housing unit in the Netherlands amount to less than in West Germany, about 250 hours, compared
to estimates of over 1200 hours in the neighbouring country (Schäfer,
1985).

Self help in the forms described above does reduce housing costs and
enable households to fulfill specific living arrangements, but some critical
notes should be added. Such self building is oriented to the lower end of
the owner occupied housing market and does not cater for the housing
needs of the poor, unless substantial subsidies are made available. Experiences with urban homesteading in the USA, which was aimed at low income
households, have not proved very successful, since most of the poor lack
the skills and resources necessary to organise the building process. Self
building is also not neccessarily efficient. In West Germany it mainly
concerns detached housing, which is not the most economic form of
landuse. But more generally, self building prolongs completion times. In
the case of individual self building, possible economies of scale are lost.
Furthermore, self builders are rarely skilled in all the trades that are required. Despite self building, mortgage costs remain high and require a
basis of steady earnings for the household concerned. Self building can
also be criticised for the time claims it puts on households, especially
when it is built at that stage of the family lifecycle when young children
also need to be taken care of. This causes not only extra stress on the
members of a household (in West Germany it is referred to as 'housebuilding syndrome'), but it also reinforces traditional family roles, with
father spending every evening and weekend at the building site, and
mother looking after the kids. It has also been suggested that self building
practices may reinforce class differences in cases where support from
friends or relatives is imperative. The form by which support is given may
involve financial donations when it concerns the middle class, whereas a
'helping hand' is given by those with less resources (Blöss 1986).

Many of these criticisms can be overcome if self building is based on
cooperation and solidarity, rather than relying on relatives of the individual
households concerned. It has been proved in the past that on this basis
better land-use plans can be designed, and that self building can be more
efficient, when use is made of a range of skills and of economies of scale
and that less reactionary attitudes occur with respect to women when
child care is taken on collectively. Collective forms of self building do require central coordination. In the experiments we have come across, such
services are often provided by local authorities, but also by architects or
planners, or the collective of (future) occupants.

Finally, there are innovations which aim to reduce the costs of access
to new housing. These concern new instruments which reduce the initial

mortgage costs for housebuyers or limit the effect of fluctuating interest rates on housing expenses. Although some of these new instruments may have encouraged new entrants into home ownership, the overall fall in nominal interest rates from about 1983 onwards has been more significant.

Innovations which aim to reduce the costs of housebuilding and the costs of housing loans may be insufficient to prevent a new down-turn in housing markets. New developments in these areas will continue, but as we argued above, there are physical and psychological limits to the extent to which housing standards and quality can be reduced and self help can be introduced. Also, mortgage finance institutions are restricted by the costs and other conditions attached to the funds they attract and by the type of loans they can offer to borrowers. There are other problems now affecting housing markets. Where the innovations described above dealt mainly with reducing initial entry costs to housing sectors, current low rates of inflation and high real interest rates *maintain* housing costs at high levels. The following section will describe in more detail the effects for social rented and owner occupied housing.

Changes in Social Housing Provision. Cuts in subsidies to social housing were in effect in all the countries which we are concerned with for much of the 1970s. In combination with steadily rising building costs, social housing built during the last decade became increasingly only affordable for middle income households, or for those who had (most of) their housing costs met by social security housing allowance payments. (This is different in Britain where the costs of new housing are pooled with those of the existing housing stock, but where rent increases under the Thatcher government in the 1980s have had a similar effect.) Adding greatly to the problems of the social housing sector is the widespread adoption of degressive subsidy schemes, as these are based on a gradual decline in government subsidies corresponding to annual rent increases and therefore assume continuously rising incomes. Earnings are now rising much slower than the assumptions contained in the degressive schemes, especially when these were introduced in the 1970s. Thus rents in the social housing stock built ten years ago are now, in some cases, even more expensive than the rents of currently new built housing (which are generally smaller and less well equipped, but also built with less subsidy). Some newer parts of the social housing stock have become difficult to let.

Tensions between governments, which aim to enforce continuous rent increases in order to reduce public spending on housing, and tenants are growing. Tenant's protests are in some cases joined by social housing land-lords who would also like lower rents in order to reduce stock vacancies. But in the Netherlands, for instance, such attempts have been frustrated by the direct intervention of the central government. In Denmark stock vacancies increased substantially during the 1980s following decisions by many local authorities to end payments of supplementary housing allowances. A growth in vacancies and rent areas, together with problem of physical decay of parts of the social housing stock, caused financial crises for many of the social landlords (Harloe, forthcoming).

Rent increases in social housing are an inevitable consequence of policies to reduce housing subsidies, irrespective of the way such cuts are implemented. But additional funds are now also needed for investments in maintenance and improvement or for making difficult to let estates more attractive and safer places to live. The issue of the rapid deterioration of the large parts of the social housing stock which was built in the 1960s and 1970s is now receiving widespread attention. With rising management costs of social housing and state subsidies reducing, social landlords are forced to look for cost saving policies. Opting for good economic management and reliable, rent paying, tenants, social housing landlords increasingly resist government policies aimed at limiting social housing to lower income tenants. Alternatively, they try to limit such marginalisation processes to the least desirable parts of the social housing stock. Both in France and Denmark, discriminatory allocation policies in social housing are aided by some local governments, who try to prevent the entry of low income or welfare dependent households to their area (Harloe ibid). New investments in maintenance and modernisation of the social housing stock are often aimed at improving the social image of the sector and attracting middle income households.

One way of raising funds for new investments in social housing (and increasingly encouraged by government policies) is to realise capital assets by selling properties. Such policies have, so far, been most developed in Britain, where the 'right to buy' provision for sitting council tenants in the 1980 Housing Act has already allowed the sale of over 700,000 council houses. But since the number of annual sales under the scheme has tailed off, a new privatisation scheme was introduced with the Housing and Planning Act (1987). The new act makes provision for local authorities to sell whole estates to the private sector. In the USA, public housing authorities have also been encouraged to sell large parts of their stock, but the effect has been much more limited, due to the lack of housing alternatives for the very poor tenants already living in the sector. In the Netherlands and Denmark, the issue of selling social housing is now on the political agenda. But in West Germany, a large proportion of social housing is privatised automatically when subsidised housing loans are fully repaid by the landlords, which is after about 25 to 30 years. This mainly concerns social housing which was provided by private developers. The West German government has now allowed an early repayment of these loans and it is expected that by 1995 the social rented housing sector will be reduced by half. The privatisation, so far, mainly concerns the cheaper social housing stock, built in the 1950s/early 1960s, which is also owned by private landlords. But also the 'Neue Heimat', West Germany's biggest social housing corporation, is selling substantial parts of its stock to meet losses in speculative ventures made elsewhere. The policies of the 'Neue Heimat' and the scale of their sales may be for the moment quite exceptional, but as elsewhere, pressures to sell major parts of the social housing stock are increasing.

Another major innovatory development in social housing is the introduction of decentralised housing services and tenant management schemes. Neither of them are necessarily cost saving exercises, at least, not unless significant self help contributions by tenants are involved. Decentralised management schemes are also introduced with the aim of democratising the bureaucratic management structures of housing corporations, claiming that decentralised management structures can respond better to tenants needs. There are, however, still many problems to solve, such as the degree of financial autonomy of tenant management and who has tenancy allocation responsibilities. Self help management schemes, in addition, require special training programmes for tenants, but are also subject to a similar critique as was mentioned for self building earlier in this paper. Self management brings a lot of responsibilities and work upon tenants and only tends to be taken on as a last resort to maintain or obtain low cost housing. But because tenant management is still in its experimental stages, the issues raised here can only be speculative and no real assessment can yet be made about possible longer term consequences of tenant management for social housing and its tenants.

Changes in Owner Occupied Housing Provision. Owner occupied housing sectors are affected by the currently low rates of inflation and high real interest rates in a different way. The recent *relative* recovery of owner occupied housing markets may have been encouraged by the fall in nominal interest rates, as the initial costs of home ownership may *seem* much lower than in the early 1980s. But in fact they are higher in *real* terms. If the current low rates of wage inflation and high real interest rates continue, the real burden of housing costs for owner occupiers will erode much slower than in the 1970s, when rates of inflation were very high. The number of households defaulting on mortgage payments has already increased substantially in recent years. This indicates that there are many households who have bought homes that are only just within their financial means and who cannot cope with adverse changes in their employment or income situations, or in their costs of borrowing. Furthermore, the down-market expansion of individual homeownership is slowing down, due to the high real interest rates and insecure income and employment prospects for many households. Unlike the 1970s, the long term decline in housebuilding rates is now less likely to be compensated for by an increase in market transactions in existing properties or by substantial rates of house price inflation.

Specialised housing finance institutions are trying to diversify their investment portfolios, partially in response to the prospect of contracting housing market activities. Increased competition from other financial institutions for both mortgage lending and funds have only added to their wish to diversify. Unlike their competitors, specialised mortgage lenders have few other investment outlets during downturns in housing markets. And, as they became used to expansion, temporary squeezes in profit margins, or even losses, were not seen as acceptable, even to non-profit mortgage lenders. In most countries, major specialised mortgage finance institutions are now being deregulated and allowed to diversify their sources of funds and types of investments. One exception is the Danish government, which prevents such a move with the argument that specialisation is more efficient in providing readily available and relatively cheap loans for housing. In some countries, institutional changes in mortgage lending have also come about through major failures and bancrupties in the sector, followed by the take-over of housing finance institutions by commercial banks or insurance companies.

So in most countries specialised circuits of mortgage lending are disappearing and with them the special privileges, usually tax advantages, which maintained these specialised circuits. The trend is part of a general growth in the competition in financial markets, nationally and increasingly also internationally, and of the development towards the domination of financial markets by relatively few large financial conglomerates. Government policies allowing for the integration of mortgage finance circuits in international capital markets may be seen as symptomatic of a weakening of the high political commitment to private housing (although this will rarely be admitted in public). Deregulation of housing finance institutions implies that the housing sector has to compete directly with other economic sectors for funds. A sufficient inflow of funds to housing will thus increasingly depend on its rate of return compared to other investment areas. The future cost of housing loans will become less predictable and depend more on the general state of financial markets (Ball & Martens, forthcoming).

Part of the deregulation trend is that mortgage lenders, as indeed other financial institutions, take on the provision of new housing services as well as providing long term housing loans. The division between traditionally seperately operating housing market participants, such as builders, land-lords, lenders or estate agents, is slowly disappearing. Larger financial institutions, including mortgage lenders, now seem to have integrated many of these agencies within their firms, via mergers, take-overs, or by setting up new subsidiaries.

Changes in the Relations Between Housing Agencies

Changes are not only occurring in the way participants in the housing market operate and the types of services they offer, but also in the relations between them.

With current developments in housing markets and policies, housing stress is increasing, particularly for lower income households. Housing costs are going up and the availability of low cost housing is reducing rapidly, due to rent policies, policies to privatise social rented housing and gentrification processes. Developments such as the growth in homeless households are indications of a current shortage of cheap housing. The number of households in need of low cost housing is also growing fast as a result of the current economic recession, with higher rates of unemployment, and demographic and social developments, as for instance, the growth of elderly households, single parent families and the more general increase in one and two person households.

With central governments trying to reduce their direct responsibility for low income housing provision, the role of local authorities, who are directly confronted with growing housing needs, is becoming more pronounced. But despite growing local housing problems, fewer funds are being made available to local councils. The decentralisation of responsibilities for housing to local authorities can take different forms. It can be implicit, as for instance in the USA or West Germany, where the federal government has stopped making funds available to social housebuilding and leaves it to the states and local authorities to meet the funding gap. Decentralisation can also be carefully orchestrated, as is happening in France or the Netherlands. In the latter case the tasks and responsibilities of local and provincial governments are defined precisely, as well as the spending items that are covered by the budgets made available. Local authorities can still prioritise new investments, but too many contending needs have to be met by budgets that are too small. So, as local housing responsibilities increase, local financial autonomy is reduced by central government actions.

With limited finances to meet local housing needs local authorities have to look for resources elsewhere. These can involve control over local housing markets or cooperation with the private sector. Examples of measures to control local housing markets include, amongst others, tenancy allocation policies and measures to prevent the sale of rented housing to owner occupiers. In most countries social housing is managed by private, limited profit, housing corporations, so municipalities do not automatically have allocation rights. In West Germany allocation rights can be linked to municipal land lease contracts or social landlords can be 'persuaded' via subsidy payments to take families from the council waiting lists. Since 1982, local authorities can also force allocation policies upon social housing landlords in certain areas with high housing stress. The implementation of this measure, however, still causes many problems.

Local allocation powers over both social and private housing sectors have existed for most of the post war period in the Netherlands, at least for areas with major housing problems. But these powers have become less effective in recent years, partially because housing allowances are linked to rent (as well as income) maxima. A growing part of the housing stock is therefore becoming unaffordable for most households who are on the council waiting lists. There is now a new act in preparation, which will restrict tenancy allocation powers for municipalities further, as it is based on the principle that the interests of private landlords (which includes housing corporations) may only be affected by the local authority in extreme circumstances.

So the attempts of local councils to control access to the housing stock can be frustrated by central government intervention. Similar developments are occuring where local authorities aim to prevent gentrification or the sale of rented housing to owner occupiers, since most central governments are keen to promote the expansion of individual homeownership. A good example here is the failed local resistance to centrally implemented council house sales in Britain. But there are also a few examples where, in the case of sales of social housing, tenants prevent privatisation. For example in West Germany, some local authorities or states have been encouraged to take over parts of the housing stock of the Neue Heimat housing corporation (see above). In the state of Hessen a special development agency has been founded by the Red/Green government coalition, the "Stiftung Nachbarschäftliche Träger", which deals with purchases of housing properties from the private housing market. One condition linked the scheme is that tenants manage the properties themselves. Amongst the cases where tenant management has been introduced, is the purchase of a major estate (around 1000 dwellings) from the Neue Heimat.

With more responsibilities, but less money and power, the housing policies of local authorities are shifting towards a growing support for the private sector. There are experiments to bring together voluntary and community groups, landlords, builders and financial institutions for new housebuilding or urban redevelopment programmes. In such projects, local or state authorities can offer expertise in the form of planners and architects, they may be able to offer land cheaply, guarantee housing loans or provide special tax relief schemes. Especially in the USA, a considerable number of lower income housing developments have been set up under such conditions. But with limited public funding, these projects tend to benefit middle to moderate income households, rather than the poorer ones. Speculative housebuilders and building societies in Britain are keen to take over the ownership of some council housing estates for rehabilitation and sale to owner occupiers, and local authorities are increasingly prepared to accept such offers, particularly where they concern estates with high vacancy rates. The new Housing and Planning Act encourages this trend and increases the powers of local authorities to evict tenants for this purpose.

Private sector housing institutions are generally looking for new housing investment opportunities and the privatisation of assets linked to the social housing stock is one of them. The new partnerships that are currently developed between builders, financial institutions, public authorities and others, are also important in this context, both in rehabilitation programmes, and in new building (for example the earlier mentioned "Open Building" scheme in the Netherlands). Builders and financial institutions tended to operate within their own spheres of specialisation in the past, but increased competition and contracting housing markets have encouraged them to diversify or to seek forms of cooperation to guarantee new business. Local authorities, prevented by a lack funds and government legislation from developing adequate low income housing programmes, are increasingly forced to support private sector initiatives. Sometimes certain conditions are imposed in exchange for public support, for example regarding allocation rights or anti speculation conditions. But generally, the new housing solutions offer most benefit to middle income households (and the private housing sector), not those on low incomes.

Changing Housing Ideologies

Many of the traditional ideological and political concepts linked to housing provision now seem to be in transformation. This reflects the changes in housing markets and policies described above. Ideological concepts began to shift during the 1970s, particularly in response to a growing critique, from left and right, of the bureaucratic and paternalistic structures of social housing (and the 'welfare state' generally). Decentralisation of management structures, democratisation and tenant participation then became major issues. These concepts are still important, but are no longer limited to the social housing sector. Concepts of self help and self reliance are now enthusiastically promoted by right wing critics of the welfare state and include private sector housing policies.

The introduction of concepts such as self help, partially reflects the unwillingness of governments to provide for low income housing needs and the desire to transfer responsibilities for dealing with these needs to the private sector and to individual households. A growing emphasis on self help also reflects new attitudes amongst the middle class, which is now also faced with growing housing costs and difficulties in access to desired forms of housing. Housing solutions amongst these groups now increasingly include collective efforts to meet housing needs, for instance in the form of setting up shared ownership housing coops. This trend is also closely followed by private developers and financial institutions, who consider introducing consumer participation as a means by which to open new housing markets.

So, together with the current privatisation trends in housing provision, issues like consumer participation, decentralisation or self help are now being rapidly taken up by the middle class, politicians and the private housing sector. The value of these concepts are more ambiguous for lower income households. Often their financial means and other resourses are too limited to take on such projects voluntarilly. Many low income tenants desire better housing services, but not necessarily by taking on management roles themselves.

Parallel to the increased stress which is being placed on self reliance, there is an increasingly negative attitude towards state support for low income housing needs. There is a clear move towards a residualised conception of the 'welfare state' and an increasing degree of stigmatisation of those in need of state support. Low income tenants living in substantial parts of the social housing sectors are blamed for their dependance on public subsidies, even though it is by now generally known that most public housing subsidies flow into private sector developments.

In conclusion, current innovatory developments in housing provision respond to a wide range of changing circumstances and conflicting interests. But its focus seems to be on a down-market expansion of private housing markets for middle income households. Private agencies linked to housing provision, such as builders or financial institutions, are looking for ways to expand investments, despite a contracting housing market, and, next to strategies to diversify investment powers, increasingly seek cooperation from public authorities to do so. Housing policies and ideologies only seem to support the trend, Access to housing is (also amongst the left) increasingly regarded as an affordability problem, rather than a problem which is also related to the defects of the mechanisms of the private market provision of housing. Low income housing subsidies are increasingly only targeted at special need households or special projects, which are often only taken on after intensive campaigning by residents. Yet, despite the fact that there is little cause for optimism in current innovatory developments in housing markets, the creativity which is presented in many of the projects may well encourage the development of more substantial and longer term solutions for low income housing provision in the future.

ACKNOWLEDGEMENTS

The research reported on in this paper consists of three separate but linked streams of work. The first concerns a wide range of housing innovations and is being carried out in West Germany, the Netherlands and the USA. Consultants to this project are Peter Marcuse, Chester Hartman and Norma Chaplain (USA), Jos Smeets and Helga Fassbinder (Netherlands) and Ruth Becker and Klaus Novy (West Germany). This research is funded by the Joseph Rowntree Memorial Trust. The other two projects concern the narrower topic of developments in mortgage finance in the above countries plus Britain and Denmark. We are working in collaboration with Michael Ball on these projects which have been funded by the Anglo-German Foundation for the Study of Industrial Society and the Economic and Social Research Council (UK). Earlier work also drawn on in this paper was funded by the Leverhulme Trust. We gratefully acknowledge the support and assistance of all these individuals and organisations.

REFERENCES

Ball, M. (forthcoming) "The international restructuring of housing construction", in Ball, M., M. Harloe, and M. Martens, *Housing and Social Change*. Beckenham: Croom Helm.

Ball, M., M. Harloe, and M. Martens *Housing and Social Change*. Beckenham: Croom Helm.

Ball, M., M. Martens, and M. Harloe (1986) *Mortgage Finance and Owner Occupation in Britain and West Germany (Progress in Planning)*, vol 26, pt 3). Oxford: Pergamon Press.

Ball, M., and M. Martens, (forthcoming) *As Safe as Houses? The International Mortgage Finance Revolution*. Brighton: Wheatsheaf.

Blöss, T. (1986) "Housing plots as highly segregated family efforts towards individual ownership", paper presented at the International Research Conference on Housing Policy, Gävle. June 10–13.

Harloe, M. (1981) "The recommodification of housing" pp. 17–50 in Harloe, M., and E. Lebas (eds.), *City, Class and Capital*. London: Arnold and New York: Holmes and Meier.

(1985) *Private Rented Housing in the United States and Europe.* Beckenham: Croom Helm and New York: St Martins Press.

(1987) "The declining fortunes of social rented housing in Europe" in Clapham, D., and J. English (eds.), *Public Housing: Current Trends and Future Developments.* Beckenham: Croom Helm.

(forthcoming) "The changing role of social rented housing" in Ball, M., M. Harloe, and M. Martens, *Housing and Social Change.* Beckenham: Croom Helm.

Harloe, M., and M. Martens (1984) "Comparative housing research", *Journal of Social Policy* 13(2): 255–77.

(1985) "The restructuring of housing provision in Britain and the Netherlands", *Environment & Planning A* 17: 1063–87.

Karn, V., J. Kemeny, and P. Williams (1985) *Home Ownership in the Inner City: Salvation or Despair?* London: Gower.

Lukez, P. (1986) *New Concepts in Housing Support in the Netherlands.* Cambridge, MA: Network USA.

Martens, M. (1985) "Owner-occupation in Europe: post-war developments and current dilemmas", *Environment & Planning A* 17: 605–24.

Prak, M., and H. Priemus (eds.) (1985) *Post-war Public Housing in Trouble.* Delft: Delft University Press.

Schäfer, H. (1985) *Wohnungsversorgung durch Selbstbau, Selbsthilfe beim Eigenheimbau, Soziale Voraussetzungen und ihre Wohnungspolitische Bedeutung.* Darmstadt: Verlag für Wissenschaftliche Publikationen.

Tarozzi, A., P. Faccidi, and S. Poreu (1986) "Approaches to the study of processes of social revolt", *International Journal of Urban and Regional Research* 10(2): 154–61.

Housing Policies
in West European Countries:
The Beginning

214 - 31

Marino Folin, Architectural University of
Venice, Italy

W, Europe
9320

INTRODUCTION

Around the late 1970s and early 1980s several authors focussed their attention on the changes in the housing policies adopted in West European countries during the 1970s. These changes became apparent both in comparative studies (Donnison and Ungerson 1982; Harloe 1980, 1985; Folin 1982; Heidenheimer et al. 1975; UN 1983) and in examinations of the housing policies of individual countries (Merrett 1979; Marcuse 1982; Duclaud-Williams 1978). The changes were also extensively discussed during international conferences such as those in Venice in 1980, Hamburg in 1981 and in Frankfurt in 1984[1].

Their main features, which were common to several countries albeit in varying forms and degrees of intensity, may be summarized as follows: a) a definite fall in subsidies or public loan facilities in support of new public or social rented accomodation; b) increased state support for home ownership through tax reliefs or mortgage facilities; c) measures to deregulate rents or to regulate them in such a way as to ensure an absolute and relative increase; d) measures to deregulate fundamental "factors" of housing production such as land and finance capital; e) extensive recourse to allowances or other personal cash subsidies intended to cover a proportion of housing costs.

The visible signs of these changes included: drop in the number of dwellings completed for the purpose of letting as social/local authority subsidized rented accomodation; cuts of capital expenditure of the state on housing; the marked increase in state expenditure on personal subsidies and grants or a fall in state revenue as a result of increased mortgage interest tax reliefs to encourage home ownership.

Various terms were used to describe those changes as a whole: "recommodification" (Harloe 1981); "recapitalization" (Miller 1978), etc. The phenomenon was seen as part of a wider process marking the end of the welfare state, a return to market forces and the defeat of Keynesian policies. In this context, the situation was interpreted in terms of a *crisis* in the field of house-building and housing policies (Venice 1980, Hamburg 1982, etc.)

During the first half of the 1980s the processes noted above were in part confirmed, though there were also some signs of faltering and in a few cases trends were temporarily reversed. There has been a continuing fall in the number of new dwellings being completed yearly in every country in Europe despite a marked increase in investments. The decline of public or social rented accomodation has continued, though the fall has been less dramatic than in the past: in some countries the number of social dwellings yearly completed seems to have levelled out at the low-point reached at the end of the 1970s; in Holland there has been a period of considerable growth in investments in this sector, suggesting that the trends identified are not so uniform as had been assumed. There has been no significant increase (indeed, if anything there has been a decrease) in the private housing built for the market, despite the support given to this sector in every country.

I have already suggested that the interpretations given to the changes which have occurred in housing policies, attractive though they may be deal only with some aspects of the question and do not provide satisfactory overall explanations (Folin 1981, 85). These changes have not taken place suddenly: their origins lie way back in time (UN-ECE 1954; UN-ECE 1966). As has recently been stated with reference to the case of Britain, rather than the end of state intervention, what we are witnessing is a change in the forms of state intervention (Ball 1984; Forrest and Murie 1986).

I believe that consideration of the crisis in housing policies should take their origins into account: the present situation may, at least in part, be implicit in the shapes the policies took when first formulated. What follows therefore is a study of those origins.

HOUSING POLICY AS STATE INTERVENTION IN THE FORMS OF HOUSING PROVISION

Before going on to examine the various forms housing policies have taken in Europe and how they started, we must define our term *"housing policy"*.

According to Donnison & Ungerson (1982: 13), "Housing policy is any sustained course of action designed to affect housing conditions". And with reference to "action", they distinguish between "aims" and "instruments", which "will change as time goes by".

Why should the state in its various forms, central peripheral and local, act in such a way? It is important to answer this question if we are to understand the extent of such action.

According to Lansley, "The fundamental case for state intervention in housing is that market forces alone would provide neither an adequate housing stock nor its fair distribution" (1979:21). Hence state intervention as a response to "market failure", which corresponds exactly to the motivation for state intervention as a "duty", which we find at the origins of political economy[2].

Lansley's definition contains, however, an important qualification as far as state intervention in housing is concerned; he defines the housing situation as including the concepts of the *quantity* of "adequate" dwellings and their "fair" *distribution*[3].

So housing policy is seen as a response to a social problem — but what exactly are the contents of such a policy? What is the nature of "extreme social usefulness", to use Smith's terminology, for the sake of which the State should intervene? Numerous theoretical interpretations have been put forward, with the functionalist or consensus approach at one extreme and the theory of conflict at the other (Murie & Malpass 1982:3 ff.).

Housing is not only a social problem however: in the U.N.'s first document on the housing problem drafted after the Second World War, housing is seen as "a strictly economic problem" (Myrdal in UN-ECE 1949:IV) in two senses. The first is that: "The successful accomplishment of many of the tasks which governments are trying to carry out [...] depends in large measure on the availability of housing accommodation for the workers who must man essential industries and agriculture". The second is that: "the building industry can play a large part in mitigating [...] economic depression" (Myrdal op.cit.).

There are therefore at least three different qualifying phrases that can accompany the term "housing policy" and explain its extent or specific field of application: "*social* policy of housing", "*economic* policy of housing" and "political *economics* of housing".

What terms should we use to describe the various housing policies which have been adopted over the years? How should we distinguish between the policies followed in different countries? The approach generally adopted has been to suggest broad classifications or types of policy. A given housing policy "model" is therefore usually described by refering both to the qualifying adjectival phrase, which specifies the policy in question, and also to the instruments used and the position of the public authorities involved in the action.

Thus, for example, in referring to the "roles" or "patterns of responsibility" of the State, Donnison identified three broad models or types of housing policy practised in Western European countries since the Second World War (Donnison & Ungerson 1982: 62–92): *"first objectives and second thoughts", "social housing policy"* and *"comprehensive policies".* Following a different theoretical approach. Headey sees three distinct "types" of housing policy in those adopted in the United States, Great Britain and Sweden: "stimulating private enterprise", "the development of a socialist market" and "the welfare approach to housing".

The limits of this way of proceeding by classes and types have already been noted (Harloe and Martens 1984).

The approach I am suggesting differs from those summarized briefly above. The hypothesis from which I start is that any state action "aiming to change housing conditions" is, irrespective of the specific qualifying adjectives that accompany the action – and hence irrespective of the instruments adopted – an action which lies *within* the existing forms of housing production. It is therefore an action which *presupposes* and *reproduces* certain forms rather than others. Thus, no attempt can be made to analyse policies without these forms of production being recognized.

The definition of the term "forms of production" which I have adopted derives from a concept of the production process as a valorization, i.e. a process of increasing or reducing available capital. It may be described as a system of relations between distinct rationalities, commanded by a promoter whose aim is to increase value of available capital. The rationalities in question are those of the actors involved in the development process and result from the relation of ownership which each exerts over the main "factors" of production: land, finance capital, means of production and labour force. Further discussion of the main forms of production can be found in Topalov (1982), Cardoso and Short (1983). For discussion of the different rationalities that operate in the production – valorization process, see Topalov (1974) and, from a quite different theoretical point of view, J. Harvey (1981).

Housing policies may therefore be described as direct or indirect state action on forms of housing production within the system of relations which defines them.

THE FORMS OF HOUSING POLICIES IN
WEST EUROPEAN COUNTRIES

If we examine the housing policies practised in Europe after both the First and the Second World War we can recognize three main forms:

a) financial aid, tax exemptions or other special treatment offered by central and/or local government to:

a.1.) public or private promoters producing housing destined to remain their own property and to be let at rentals which were restricted or controlled in some way. Financial aid took various forms (lump sum grants or interest relief facilities, state loans at reduced interest rates, guarantees) and was offered to various extents over the years. Financial aid was also made available to a variety of promoters and in different ways at different times and in different countries (financial assistance for all forms of promotion, on condition that the dwellings produced were let as "social housing"; assistance to particular promoters – public or public utility bodies – in that they had a statutory obligation to produce "social housing").

In France the promoters chosen as recipients of aid were public or private agencies for the production of HLM, while the financial instrument adopted was that of low interest loans and lump sum grants. In Germany it was private individuals, housing developers and non-profit-making organizations who received aid as long as they produced "social housing" at controlled rents and here the instrument chosen was state loans (second mortgages); in Great Britain it was the local authorities and, on a far smaller scale, the housing associations, who received annual government subsidies for every dwelling built; in Holland the promoters were the local authorities and non-profit-making organizations and the instruments used were state loans and annual subsidies.

This aid achieved a dual effect: 1) control over the end product (through regulations concerning size, building methods and dwelling types, on fulfilment of which the granting of aid was made conditional); from this point of view the presence of such a policy was probably much more effective than any other kind of town planning control in determining the overall shape and nature of towns and also in ensuring certain quantities and qualitatives standards of housing; 2) the selection of the end-users of the housing thus promoted according to income class or whether or not the subject was an employee; from this point of view, such policies were an integral part of the more general income policies adopted after the War.

a.2) private promoters of dwellings destined to remain the property of the promoter and to be placed on the rented accommodation market. This form of support, entirely absent in Great Britain, was present to a limited extent in the other countries (Harloe, 1985), and took forms similar to those seen above, though the funding involved was not so extensive.

a.3) private promoters of dwellings destined for their own use.

b. rent control and other forms of protection for the tenant: these tended to regulate relationships between tenant and landlord irrespective of the specific form of production of the dwelling. These interventions concerned rented dwellings and the existing housing stock (after a certain date)

c)   cash subsidies, credit or tax benefits directed at the end-user, the tenant in the case of the subsidies, the owner in the case of the credit or tax benefits.

In case a), the housing policies were directed at the promoter; in this way government aimed to regulate the quality, the cost and end-user of the dwellings being produced; in case b), the policies were intended to regulate relations between owner (of a dwelling in the form of a fixed capital asset) and user (of a dwelling in the form of use value) within the existing housing stock, assumed as a given entity, irrespective therefore of its production; in case c), the policies were directed at the end-user, with the intention of giving him the opportunity of access to a dwelling (either as owner or as tenant), in the context of total freedom for the producer or owner of the dwelling.

... AND THEIR FORMING

These different forms of housing policy each have their own rationality, in the sense that they followed paths that were more or less conditioned by the nature of the original economic plus historical context. They can be practised completely independently from each other (although they may affect each other and will in any case combine to create the housing system and also its problems) or they may occur in integrated, interdependent forms. They have different beginnings; different political motivations influenced their conception and later developments. We must now look briefly at these beginnings.

Support for the promotion of 'social housing'. State intervention historically follows upon the establishment of forms of cost-price promotion. It consists initially in the acknowledgement of these forms and in the allocation of privileges to those promoters who operate through them.

In Germany, the law which acknowledges the existence of "public utility companies" (gemeinnützige Baugenossenschaften) and regulate their actions dates from 1868.

It comes twenty years after the constitution of the first company of this kind, the "Berlin Baugesellschaft"[4] in Berlin, and it incorporates some of the company's constitutional principles; a later law, passed in 1889[5], introduced the principle of limited responsibility for such companies and remained on the statute books until 1930, when it was replaced by a new law. The law governing the activities of "Gemeinnützge" until 1930 therefore dated from 1889; and it was this period that saw the growth in numbers and size of this companies, while their activity, in terms of dwellings completed, reached its height in the years 1924–1930.

In the same year as the law on "gemeinnützige" was passed, the law which lay at the basis of the Welfare State in Germany was also approved by Parliament. On 22nd June 1889, the law ensuring cover against sickness and old age entered the statute books and came into operation on 1st January 1891. As well as instituting a state pension and health insurance scheme, the law also contained several decisive measures encouraging insurance companies to invest part of their funds in the form of loans to public utility companies, to local authorities or to employers intending to create "sound" dwellings for their employees. For the first time a channel for institutional financing of low-cost housing[6] had been created.

The 1889 law marks the beginning of state intervention by derived and indirect means in the field of housing. The first law to deal with the whole question of direct state intervention in Prussia was approved on 13th August 1895. It was important for several reasons. For the first time in the history of Germany a state fund was created by an issue of Government Bonds specifically for the purpose of improving housing conditions both for industrial workers and for low-paid clerical staff employed by the various state administrations; secondly, the law established the two basic forms of direct state intervention in housing: the various administrations could now either arrange directly for the building of houses for their eimployees or they could make loans to public utility companies to enable them to build housing for state employees[7]: for the first time these public utility companies were acknowledged as privileged instruments of state intervention in housing production, although for the time being the beneficiaries were to be only particular categories of workers. The law also defined the *conditions* governing state intervention, the *rules* it had to follow, the *actors* through which intervention was to be effected, the ultimate *beneficiaries* of such action and the *forms* it could take. Many of the principles embodied in the law's treatment of these sub-headings eventually became a permanent forming influence on the machinery of state intervention.

Finally another cornerstone was the decree issued jointly by the Ministries of Trade and Industry, of the Interior, of Religion, Medicine and Education of the State of Prussia on 19th March 1901. This decree extended State recognition to all the various forms of public intervention in favour of such members of the population in general as were in need that had hitherto been practised by the main cities of Germany on the basis of their respective independence. It starts by acknowledging that only a "legislative initiative of a general nature" (*umfassendes gesetzliches*

Vorgehen) can bring about the elimination of the serious "unseemlinesses" (*Misstande*) to be found in the "housing conditions of the poorer classes (*Wohnwesen der minder bemittelten Bevolkerungsklassen*). Meanwhile the local authorities were strongly urged to take all necessary measures in their areas insofar as "the present legislative situation" (*gegenwartingen Stande der Gesetzgebung*) allowed them to, to ensure the "construction of small, cheap and sound dwellings" (*der Herstellung gesunder (...) billiger, kleiner Wohnungen*).

The measures that may be taken and that are reviewed by the decree are: 1) to arrange for the building of houses for local authority employees, as envisaged by the 1895 Law and its later amendments; 2) to promote the building of more "kleiner, gesunder und preiswerther" houses where housing conditions require them, giving "as much support as possible" to non-profit-making organizations and cooperative societies. In cases where the local authority considers it necessary, the same support may be extended to private firms who had undertaken to build suitable houses for letting at low rents.

The machinery described in the 1901 decree was applied extensively during the period of the Weimar Republic between 1924 and 1932, after the brief experiment of the "Beihilfen", in the period known as the "Hauszinssteuerära" (DBB, 85)[8].

In the case of France, the earliest "Société des cité ouvrières de Paris" was founded in 1849, with the aim of building 12 blocks of flats for workers, one in each *quartier* of the city (the only one actually to be built was in Rue Rochechouart). Part of the share capital came from Napoleon III (Guerrand, 1967). Once again therefore, the enlightened aristocracy were to be found amongst the promoters of initiatives of this kind[9]. In 1867 (24th July), the law governing the establishment of non-profit-making organizations was passed (ILO 1930, 230): dividends were limited to 4%; in 1889 George Picot and Jules Sigfried founded the "Société française des Habitations à bon marchè" and a few years later (1st August 1893), the new law concerning non-profit-making organizations and cooperative societes was passed (ILO ibid).

In 1894 (30th November) the first law to deal explicitly with "habitations à bon marchè" was passed, known as the Sigried law by the name of the minister who promoted it. The law governed the establishment of "Société d'habitations à bon marchè", private companies which had to be approved by the Ministry of Labour; these companies were exempted from various taxes and public credit institutions (Caisse des Depots et Consignations) and savings banks were authorized to set aside part of their reserve funds for use as loans or for the purchase of shares issued to finance the companies (Ferrand, in Congrès Internationl, 1911:940).

A precondition of state intervention therefore, as in the case of Germany, was the existence of companies to promote housing to be let at rents calculated on the bases of cost price plus a limited rate of interest. The Loi Sigfried remained the base of all subsequent legislation on the subject. In 1906 (12th April) the Loi Strauss made Comités de Patronage compulsory and extended the opportunities for credit and subsidies (Ferrand in Congrès International, 1911) open to HBM companies by authorizing local authorities too to use their funds in this way; as contemporary commentators do not fail to point out, the doctrine behind the law may be summarized in the two following principles: 1) local authorities must not themselves either build or administer such housing [and here lies the difference from Great Britain]; 2) it is legitimate to enact measures capable of helping *private initiatives* (by means of tax advantages and financial aid from the state) so long such measures *"do not constitute competition and therefore do not act to reduce free initiative"* (Dufourmantelle in Congrès International, 1911: 103) (my italics). The desire to avoid the creation of an alternative to the market and to observe the rules of the game is absolutely clear.

With the law of 23rd December 1912 an important innovation was introduced enabling local authorities to promote the construction of cheap housing, both directly and through the establishment of "Offices Publiques d'Habitations à Bon Marché"[10]. The local authorities were not, however, allowed to administer the dwellings thus built, which had to be handed over to the Offices Publiques for this purpose.

The principle of state subsidy was first introduced with the law of March 31st 1919 (Bovier Lapierre 1923: 1067). The subsidies envisaged were intended for: local authorities, the Offices Publiques HBM, the Sociétés HBM, charitable institutions, hospices and Caisses d'Epargne; the subsidy was granted only for the building of cheap housing for letting to large families (as defined by the previous legislation); the amount of the subsidy, which took the form of lump sum grant, just as it did in the same period in Holland and in Germany with the "Beihilfen", could be up to two third of the cost of construction.

The principle of a grant subsidy to cover a certain part of the building costs was soon replaced, with the law of 5th December 1922, by low interest state loans, which were distributed through the Caisse de Depots et Consignations and the Caisse Nationale de Retraites. The law redefined the intended beneficiaries of the HBM as "persons of small means and workers mainly supported by their wages", the intended recipients of low interest loans[11] and the conditions on which such loans could be granted.

With the Loi Loucheur (13th July 1928), the system created through previous legislation was used to launch a housing program on a huge scale. The machinery for state intervention so far assembled was not changed in the least. The financial support of the state was granted on more liberal terms[12] and the production of cheap housing was extended and distinctions introduced so as to reach wider sections of the population, with the introduction of two new types of dwelling that could qualify for aid, though on different conditions: "Habitations à Loyer Moderé and Logements à Confort Réduit". With the law of 27th July 1934, state financial support took its definitive form: Offices Publiques and HBM companies could raise the necessary finance directly, and the state would continue to pay the difference between the market rate of interest and 2%. The machinery built between 1834 and 1934 constitutes the base of all subsequent intervention by the state with respect to social housing.

Holland. The first law to allow local authorities to expropriate land for housing purposes dates from 1851[13], and the first building program to be promoted by Amsterdam City Council dates from 1873 (Conseil des Habitations à Amsterdam, 1913), following a report on housing conditions prepared by a specifically appointed Council committee. The method used by the Council was to channel its efforts through philantropic associations, in this case the "Amsterdamsche Vereeniging tot et bouwen van arbeiderswoningen". The policy was described in practical terms in a report drawn up by the Council in 1913: "It was assumed that such houses would yield a sufficient revenue to cover expenses of management, give a fair interest on capital invested, and gradually pay off the cost of the enterprise. It was therefore agreed that the city should furnish the land and advance a large part of the money needed, in return for which the ownership of the buildings should finally revert to it. For its part the association should [...] construct and manage the buildings and from the rents after meeting current expenses and taking fair profit upon such capital as it might have invested, should gradually pay off the cost of the enterprise [...]". In the opinion of some" [the rent] is so high that the poorer classes cannot rent these dwellings "(Conseil des Habitations à Amsterdam 1913; US Department of Labor-Bureau of Labor Statistics 1915:385).

1901 saw the passing of the Woningwet, which was greeted as a revolutionary law right from its first appearance, even by outside observers (US Department of Labor-Bureau of Labor Statistics 1915). In contrast to what occurred in other countries this was a comprehensive law. As well as detailing the duties and powers of the local authorities in terms of deciding on housing requirements, checking housing conditions and planning land use it also established the form of state intervention to be used to produce healthy dwellings for the working classes. The principle was the one tried out by the city of Amsterdam 30 years before, except that this time it was the state which would provide the finance. The machinery envisaged is so described by ILO (1924: 244): "The state made itself grant loans to the local authorities or to public utility societies through the local authorities. The money is advanced on mortgage rapayable in 50 years by equal annual instalments, the interest being fixed at the rate corresponding to the market quotation for state debentures on the Amsterdam exchange. The local authority is responsible for the payment of interest and instalments on the loan, so there is no financial risk for the state. The government was prepared to grant a loan up to 100 per cent of the total building costs. In addition to loans annual subsidies may be granted if an economic rent cannot be obtained, for example, if there is an extraordinary addition to working expenses or if the occupants are of very poor classes."

The law fixed forms of state support, actors and conditions: until late '60s it has been the basis of state intervention on housing in Holland.

State support for owner occupation. Policies promoting the practice of home ownership, either in the form of a promoter providing a house for its own use, or of purchase on the housing market, did not follow policies created to support the cost-price letting of housing; the former did not originate as a reaction to the latter, as an alternative or negation of them. On the contrary, they originated at the same time, if not before. Support for home ownership lies at the roots of housing policies. In France as in Italy intense debate accompanied the launching of the first law in favour of cheap housing, especially as regards the promoters who were to be the beneficiaries of the provisions of the law and the fact that dwellings built in this way could be sold. Though the Loi Sigried in 1894 did not provide support for owner occupation, the Loi Ribot of 10th April 1908 was specifically framed to "enable less fortunate people to purchase a small field or garden or individual house" (Doufourmantelle, in Congrès International des Habitations à Bon Marchè 1911: 293). In the Prussia of Frederick II, building land was given free to workers of state mines so that they could build their own house and from 1842 onwards it was possible for state employees to obtain grants or interest free loans for home building or buying; the 1895 law provided for the construction of dwellings for renting and, at the same time, gave to the employees in certain sectors of the civil service (mines, railways, building) the possibility to obtain loans for home ownership; later, this was extended to other sections of the population. Amongst the earliest measures taken straight after the war by the Weimar Republic, beside those for the miners and for rented housing, are those encouraging home ownership, such as the "Heimstätten Gesetz", a law promoting homesteads with features similar to those of the "Klein-gärten" and the "Kleinsiedlungen", which were extensively promoted during the Nazi period. Even where, as in Holland, private non commercial building associations were clearly appointed as the subjects of promotion, the local authorities had the power "to loan an individual a sufficient sum to build, enlarge or repair a house for himself" (US Department of Labor-Bureau of Labor Statistics 1915:383). In Sweden, the first measures taken in the name of a housing policy were directed towards home ownership: 1904 saw the funding of the "Public Home Ownership Loan Fund", the aim of which was "to enable low-income families to become home owners in rural districts" the dwelling being either a house with a cultivable plot of land or a small farm" (Svensson 1938:154). The fund created in 1934 for tenant protection (arrendelånefond) aimed to enable the low-income part of the population to have access to rented housing with right of redemption (Svensson 1938:156–57).

The lines separating one form of promotion from another are sometimes indistinct: the laws recognizing the statutes of non-commercial companies attribute the same standing to cooperative societies (which build for their own members) and to philanthropic societies which construct housing for renting. Similar, finally, are sometime the forms taken by state interven-tion in favour of promoters for their own use, and promoters of rented housing, varying the extent of the intervention in favour of one or the other, its size and practical method of application. At the very beginning there is an interweaving of the various forms of housing policy: innova-tions introduced to encourage one form of promotion are subsequently used to encourage others.

Rent control. At the outset and in its most radical form, this involved the freezing of rents on a certain date. In this particular form rent control damaged the interests of the owners in that their capital investment could not increase in value in time, *relative* to other capital values, when the rate of inflation was rising. Such measures involved a political decision to change the relative capital values of already existing assets and limited the powers of owners over what belonged to them. They were resorted to, as exceptional measures, in exceptional circumstances, catastrophes such as wars, epidemics, earthquakes or economic crises. They made their first appearance with the First World War: in France in 1914[14], in Great Britain in 1915 and, between 1916 and 1917, in all the other countries of Europe[15]. The years following the introduction of these measures are more or less difficult years of attempts gradually to return to normality, a process which was much more complicated and took much longer than initially expected; from this point of view, the events following the First and Second World Wars are similar in many ways. Originating as an independent measure concerning the provision of housing, directed at the owner and not at the investor — although it did nevertheless influence the decisions of the investor — rent control increasingly became an instrument for governing sale prices and thus of control over production. It started as a temporary suspension of the market and ended up as a form of control over the market. The search was for a unified market governed by a finally achieved balance between prices and costs, between fair rents and fair profits. But this smooth return to the market was implicit in the extraordinary nature of the measures initially taken. Any form of market regulation that sets out to fix rent levels and to control their movement in time — which is not therefore simply a definition of the rules governing negotiation between tenant and landlord — will find itself having to cope with the problem of how to bring the rents of newly built dwellings into line with those of already existing dwellings; and all this finally is made more complicated by the existence of at least two regimes governing newly built dwellings: cost-price rents and uncontrolled rents.

CONCLUSIONS

It is possible to describe the history of housing policy, and also to see the difference between the various European countries, in terms of *support* given to certain forms of housing provision rather than others, in terms of *methods* used and of the *place* state intervention takes within the internal mechanisms and in the system of relationships between the subjects involved.

What we call housing policy is in fact a whole set of policies which are often in conflict one with another: each of them originated at a different time; they were taken up and pursued for different reasons; different circumstances explain the length of time and the extent to which they were adopted.

The quantitative housing policies tried out straight after the war evolved from being post-war emergency policies to become an integral part of wider, general growth policies; this was part of the Keynesian policies of full employment and income control (Myrdal, 1949; Kalecki, 1948) practised in several European countries after the Second World War: certain forms of state intervention devised around the turn of the century have been therefore and adapted variously used within Keynesian types of growth policy.

The difficulty presented by the simple reproduction of social housing policies from the 1970s onwards, their so-called crisis, would seem in a certain sense to be implicit: in their initial form (in the sense of a crisis in production for cost-price letting); in the reasoning that prompted them (in the sense of a crisis in Keynesian policies based on support directed at demand); in the changes undergone by employment (with the gradual reduction in factory waged jobs: in the sense of a crisis of the social classes to whom the policies were adressed).

NOTES

1) "La casa e la sinistra in Europa", Venezia, march 1980: "Krise der Wohnungspolitik", Hochschule für Bildende Kunste. Hamburg 30th november–1st october 1981: "Wohnungspolitik zwischen Staat und Markt", Albertus Magnus Kolleg, Konigstein Frankfurt 25th–28th october 1984.

2) "The third and last *duty* of the sovereign or the republic is to create and conserve those public institutions and public works that, *extremely useful though they may be to a large society*, could not possibly yield enough *profit* to offset the expenditure of an individual or a small number of individuals" (Smith 1973,714, my italics).

3) "The aims of housing policy underlying government intervention are to ensure an adequate supply of housing of some minimum quality, at a cost that lower income groups can afford; and to ensure equity in housing provision between tenures and between households in each tenure, in order to produce a genuinely fair choice in housing" (Lansley 1979, 34).

4) After the 1868 law it became the "berliner Gemeinnütziger Baugesellschaft". The company statutes were approved on 28.10.1948; the first general shareholders meeting was held on 16.01. 1849 and in the following month Huber, who, through his writings had been one of the main inspirers of the movement, was made company chairman; on 27.03.1849 the foundation of the company's first house was laid at 28, Ritterstrasse; se Geist and Kurvers, 1980.

5) According to K. Novy and G. Uhlig, this law marks the passage to the second phase of the cooperative movement, helped also by the new channels of funding opened by the policies of the various states. "Bauwelt" 24/9/1982.

6) The law was revised in 1899 and the opportunities for insurance companies to make loans for the building of housing for workers were considerably increased. For ways in which funds were channelled, see Department of Labor, cit. p. 185–191. As regards the importance of this law in connection with the development of public utility companies and the construction of workers' housing in general, see also E.E. Wood, Housing Progress in Western Europe, London 1923, p. 170 ff. Wood rightly emphasized the influence exerted on the promulgation of the law by contemporary legislation in Belgium.

7) Amongst the conditions to be met before a public utility company could have access to loans from the fund was one which stated that "Applications for loans are to be considered only from those building associations whose membership is largely made up of workmen employed in Prussian government establishment or of Prussian Government employees (*Beamte*) of the lowest and intermediate salary grades." (U.S. Dept. of Labor, 1915, 202).

8) 1924/14/2: "Dritten Steuernotverordnung" – the third federal decree concerning emergency taxation. This instituted "a tax on existing urban real estate property and took the form of a special tax on increase in value or of an increase in ordinary taxes on real estate assets. A part of the revenue from this tax was used for the building of housing; it was distributed as extremely low-interest second-degree loans to those who agreed to build housing for letting at building-cost price". For comment on this experiment and the problems it posed, see Fleshmann 1936.

9) Similarly, in Great Britain, the first law to give local authorities definite powers to provide shelter for the working classes, the lodging Houses Act of 1851, was drafted and sponsored by Lord Shaftesbury.

10) Created by decree at the request of one or more local authorities or of the Conseil Général. Their purpose was "aménager, construir et gérer des immeubles d'habitations à bon marché [...] creer des Cites-jardins et des jardins ouvriers"; their funding was base on endowments from the local authorities or the Conseil Général, donations, loans from city or departmental administration; their composition was made of 18 members, 2/3 nominated by the prefect and the others by the municipal council.

11) Municipal authorities, Offices Publiques HBM, Sociétés HBM, (for the construction or purchase of low rent housing or for the conversion of existing dwellings for this purpose) and building societies (which provided loans to enable home ownership).

[12] By removing income thresholds beyond which it was impossible to have access to low-rent housing, by reducing interest rates on state loans to 2% (after they had been raised to 3.5%), by raising the proportion of costs covered to 80%. 90% in the case of municipal or departmental authority guarantees; in part the funds continued to come from the Caisse de Depots and the Caisse Nationale des Retraites and in part the promoters were authorised to apply for special loans, interest exceeding 2% on which would be paid by the state; finally, the municipal authorities were invited to contribute to payment of interest (in addition to the part paid by the state) to a maximum of 1.5%.

[13] But this unsupported by other legislation proved of little value (US Department of Labor-Bureau of Labor Statistics, 1915: 381).

[14] Decree of 14th August 1914. "The moratorium served two purposes: in the first place it prolonged expired leases for the whole of the war and suspended the effect of notice; in the second, it postponed the actual payment of rent until the end of hostilities and prevented any increase of rent until that date" (ILO 1924: 116).

[15] "By the end of the war nearly the whole of Europe was covered by some form of tenant protection" (ILO 1924: 18).

[16] "The principal aim of housing reform before the war was to improve the housing conditions of town population" (ILO 1924: 3).

REFERENCES

Ball, M. (1984) *Housing Policy and Economic Power. The Political Economy of Owner Occupation.* London and New York: Methuen.

Cardoso, A., and J.R. Short (1983) "Forms of housing production: initial formulations", *Environment and Planning A*, 15: 917–928.

Congres International des Habitations à Bon Marché (1911) *Bericht über den IX Internationalen Wohnungskongress. Wien, 30 May bis 3 Juni 1910.* Wien: Friedrich Jasper.

Conseil des Habitations à Amsterdam (1913) *L'Amélioration du Logement à Amsterdam.* Amsterdam.

Deutsche Bau- und Boden Aktiengesellschaft (1973) *1923–1973, 50 Jahre im Dienste der Bau- und Wohnungswirtschaft.* Frankfurt am Main: DBBA.

Donnison, D., and C. Ungerson (1982) *Housing Policy.* Harmondsworth: Penguin.

Duclaud-Williams, R. (1978) *The Politics of Housing in Britain and France.* London: Heinemann.

Fleischmann, J. (1036) "Financing Low-Rent Housing in Germany", pp. 120–125 in *The Journal of Land & Public Utility Economics* XII, 2.

Folin, M. (1981) "Crisis of public housing in Europe", in H. Frank, and H. Harms (eds.), *Krise der Wohungspolitik.* Hamburg: Hochschule für bildende Kunste.

ed (1982) *Esiti della politica socialdemocratica della casa in Europa.* Milano: Angeli.

(1985) "Housing Development Processes in Europe", in M. Ball et al. (eds.), *Land Rent, Housing and Urban Planning*. London: Croom Helm.

Forrest, R., and A. Murie (1986) "Marginalization and subsidized individualism: the sale of council houses in the restructuring of the British welfare state", *International Journal of Urban and Regional Research* 10:46–65.

Frank, H., and D. Schubert (Hrsg) (1983) *Lesebuch zur Wohungsfrage*. Köln: Pahl-Rugenstein.

Geist, J.F., and K. Kurvers (1980) *Das Berliner Mietschaus, 1740–1862*. München: Prestel.

Guerrand, R.H. (1966) *Les origines du logement social en France.* Paris: Editions Ouvrieres.

Harloe, M. (1980) "Current Trends in Housing Policy – Some European Comparisons", *Royal Society of Health Journal* 6.

(1981) "The recommodification of housing", pp. 17–50 in M. Harloe, and E. Lebas (eds.), *City, Class and Capital.* London: Arnold.

(1985) *Private Rented Housing in the United States and Europe.* London: Croom Helm.

Harloe, M., and M. Martens (1984) "Comparative housing research", *Journal of Social Policy* 14:255–277.

Harvey, J. (1981) *The Economics of Real Property.* London: MacMillan Press Ltd.

Headey, B. (1978) *Housing Policy in the Developed Economy.* London: Croom Helm.

Heidenheimer, A., H. Heclo., and C. Teich Adams (1975) *Comparative Public Policy: the Politics of Social Choice in Europe and America.* London: MacMillan.

ILO (1924) *European Housing Problems Since the War (Series G n^o1).* Geneva: P.S. King & Son Ltd.

(1930) *Housing Policy in Europe. Cheap Home Building (Studies and Reports Series G – Housing and Welfare – n^o3).* Geneva: P.S. King & Son Ltd.

IFHTP (1926) *International Housing and Town Planning Congress – Vienna 1926.* London: IFHTP.

Kalecki, M. (1948) "Three Ways to Full Employment", in AAVV, *The Economics of Full Employment.* Oxford: Blackwell.

Lansley, L. (1979) *Housing and Public Policy.* London: Croom Helm.

Malpass, P., and A. Murie (1982) *Housing Policy and Practice.* London: MacMillan Press Ltd.

Marcuse, P. (1982) "Determinants of State Housing Policies: West Germany and the United States", in S. and N. Fainstein (eds.), *Urban Policy under Capitalism.* Beverly Hills: Sage.

Merrett, S. (1979) *State Housing in Britain.* London: Routledge and Kegan Paul.

Miller, S.M. (1978) "The recapitalization of capitalism", *International Journal of Urban and Regional Research* 2: 202–12.

PEHW (1975) *Political Economy and the Housing Question.* London: Housing Workshop of the Conference of Socialist Economists.

(1976) *Housing and Class in Britain.* London: Housing Workshop of the Conference of Socialist Economists.

Smith, A. (1976 edn) *An inquiry into the nature and causes of the wealth of the nations.* Oxford: Clarendon.

Svensson, W. (1938) "Home Ownership in Sweden", *The Annuals of the American Academy of Political Science: Social Problems and Policies in Sweden,* 197, May.

Topalov, C. (1974) *Les promoteurs immobiliers. Contribution a l'analyse de la production capitaliste du logement en France.* Paris-La Haye: Mouton.

(1982) "Trasformazione dei sistemi di produzione della casa e politiche statali (1950–1978)", in M. Folin (ed.), *Esiti della politica socialdemocratica della casa in Europa.* Milano: Angeli.

US Department of Labor-Bureau of Labor Statistics (1915) *Government Aid To Home Owning and Housing of Working People in Foreign Countries.* Washington: Government Printing Office.

UN (1983) "Major Trends in Housing Policy", *Economic Bulletin for Europe,* 35, 1. Oxford: Pergamon Press.

UN-ECE (Industry and Materials Committee Housing Sub-Committee) (1949) *The European Housing Problem. A preliminary Revies (E/ECE/110).* Geneva: UN.

(1954) *European Housing Progress and Policies in 1953 (E/ECE/189; E/ECE/190).* Geneva: UN.

(1966) *Major Long-Term Problems of Government Housing and Related Policies I° e II° (ST/ECE/HOU/20).* New York: UN.

Wood, E.E. (1919) *The Housing of the Unskilled Wage Earner. America's Next Problem.* New York: The MacMillan Company.

(1923) *Housing Progress in Western Europe.* New York: E.P. Dutton & Co.

The Other Side of Housing: Oppression and Liberation

$232-70$

Peter Marcuse, Columbia University,
Division of Urban Planning, New York, USA

U.S.

9320 9170

INTRODUCTION

Housing is more than just housing. Housing certainly includes shelter, but it involves concepts of home and community as well. A decent, a humane, housing system must couple shelter with security, with warmth and peace and independence, with living space and space to grow for children and couples and older people, with nurturing and refuge and support, with independence and protection and recreation, with access to work and culture, with good relations with neighbors and strangers.

The housing system we see in most countries today is very different from such a humane picture. At worst, the housing system at present does not even provide shelter for many; even in the United States, where a Presidential Commission boasted just a few years ago that "Americans are the best housed people in the World[1]," the lowest estimate of the number of homeless is now 250,000, and more reliable estimates place it at 3,000,000. That figure includes many families and children, and is hardly limited to the stereotypical "Bowery bum" or mentally ill wino[2]. Over-crowding is increasing, the proportion of income most households are paying for rent is at its highest level in history, abandonment of structurally sound buildings runs on apace, displacement is accelerating, segregation is pervasive[3].

Even at its best, housing does not meet the standards that a free and prosperous people might expect. The typical suburban middle-class "home" often represents more a commercial, artificial, profit-induced, exclusionary, picture of conspicuous housing consumption sold to to its occupants as the ultimate "dream" than what those occupants would really want, if they had a choice. What they would really want, I believe, would be a humane housing system that is part of, and contributes to, a peaceful society, in which human beings relate to each other as individuals and to their neighbors and to strangers alike as an open community; in which aspirations and achievements are shared, not competitive; in which people help each other without regard to payment or profit. Housing, in such a society, can indeed be the foundation for a fulfilling personal life: certainly not the sole foundation, but an important one. Housing should provide protection, security, space, beauty, reinforcement for the special personalities and satisfaction for the special needs of its occupants. It should help bring people together, respecting each others privacy but fostering the common pursuit of their common goals.

The discord between this picture of humane housing in a humane society and what actually exists today is, I suspect, what brings most of us to our present concerns. I want to address the reasons for this discord in this paper. It is directly related to research on housing, for it is what seems to me the issue most in need of research. Yet it is such a large question, so fraught with difficulty and with controversy, that most of us tend to stay away from it as much as we can. I think research has something to offer in highlighting the discord, revealing its causes, and, hopefully, doing something to change them.

Most research that looks at housing "problems" takes one of two approaches. Either it sees the problems of housing as being the problems of those particular people that are ill-housed. I have called the approach "specialism[4]," for it assumes that housing problems are the aggregate of the special problems of particular groups within a generally well-functioning housing system. Its research focus is thus on the characteristics of the ill-housed: the elderly, the poor, large families, ethnic minorities, single-parent housholds, women. At worst, this approach blames the victim for the problem; at best, it conceals the general systemic problems of housing under a collection of separate and individual problems.

"Economism" is a term sometimes used to describe the other common approach to housing problems. It sees housing as an economic problem. Crudely, it explains the lack of adequate housing as a simple function of the distribution of income; if everyone had enough money, the "housing problem" would be solved. With greater sophistication, it concedes that there are inefficiencies within the housing market, externalities, lack of information, backward technology, etc., which also need to be addressed -- but again, as a set of separate problems, distorting a housing system that by and large functions very well. Even within Marxist circles, generally most inclined to see systemic grounds for the inequities and inadequacies of life under capitalism, the problems of housing are often seen as the by-products of the economics of housing production and distribution[5].

Such interpretations leave many aspects of actual housing patterns unexplained: the mystification of home ownership, for example, or racial segregation, or the gender bias of housing design, or the strengths and limitations of tenant organizations. I believe, in particular, that issues of oppression and liberation constitute a whole other side of housing, without which neither existing patterns nor future possibilities for change can be properly understood.

I therefore want in this paper to look at the "other side" of housing.

The Concepts of Oppression and Liberation in Housing

"Oppression" is a term not often linked to housing. Yet some forms of housing are obviously oppressive. The archetypal use of housing to oppress is of course the prison; the close relationship of the principles of discipline embodied in such institutions with other residential arrangements can be seen by comparing, e.g., Bentham's Panopticon with the housing provided by the cloisters and the prototypes of workers' housing developed in Germany and France in the mid-nineteenth century -- for which the cloisters, combined workshops-residences themselves, were often the explicit prototypes[6]. For many, particularly the poor, today, the oppressive impact of housing conditions, in terms of the necessity imposed on the resident of a run-down or abandoned neighborhood to be constantly on the defensive, to devote extraordinary efforts to basic physical self-protection, to insulate themselves from omnipresent outside threats, have destructive social and psychological impacts that exceed their physical dimensions. Moving up the income ladder, the commitments made by many working class households to homeownership as the only feasible way of obtaining decent housing in an acceptable environment is also oppressive for them in many ways. Owning a home has indeed provided economic security in their old age for many, for whom paying off a mortgage during their working years has been a form of savings; for many others, however, the constant burden of mortgage payments is a severe economic hardship, forcing them to allocate to housing far more of their income than they would wish, to work overtime and/or accept jobs at even substandard wages, to have more household members employed than wish to work, to devote more time and energy to housing maintenance (domestic work) than they wish, for lower imputed returns.

Gentrification is as oppressive, if in different ways, for those working for higher salaries, as homeownership may be for working class households. The stress of "status" housing in "status" neighborhoods is ultimately as constricting, as enchaining, as diverting from truly fulfilling activities and human concerns -- including of course social concerns -- as are cruder forms of oppression. The over-emphasis on residential consumption as a compensation for senseless and unfulfilling work operates in a vicious circle to reinforce the enslavement of such consumers to that very work.

In the U.S., Blacks and Hispanics and members of specific other minority groups, somewhat like foreign workers in most of northern Europe, and women, face particular problems of oppression in their housing. Racial segregation in housing is a continuing major problem throughout the United States[7]. Restrictive spatial residential patterns imposed on their residents against their wills and with little possibility of escape, both create and reinforce a systematic oppression under which their victims labor every day.

Women are confronted with housing patterns which reinforce sexist patterns to which they are subjected in other aspects of their lives. Housing design and locational patterns reinforce the traditional division of labor within the male-dominant family, require extensive unpaid work within the home, and restrict opportunities on the outside, both for gainful employment and for social/community life. For single women and single parent households, the conditions of life to which they are confined by existing residential patterns constrict their freedom of choice far beyond the average. For single women, the pressures to conform to the stereotype of the conventional monogamous household are reinforced by the limited alternatives available in the housing market. For single women with children, the oppressive conditions of everyday life, which could be ameliorated by the availability of forms of housing suited to their needs[8] are instead made more oppressive by a housing system in which they are treated as undesireable "problem families." Again, housing patterns both create and reinforce social and economic oppression.

Can housing serve to *undo* oppression, to counteract oppressive conditions outside of the home? Can housing, in other words, have a *liberatory* aspect? Many have certainly thought so; the concept of the "ideal community," from Fourier's Phalanstere to the religious communities of the late 19th century U.S. to Port Sunlight to Robert Owens' experiments to the alternative communes of California and elsewhere in the 1960's and 1970's, represent the conviction of at least their designers and/or participants that a liberated existence, a humane residential environment, could be created around a completely revised approach to housing and its physical context. Less utopian, yet still seeing a direct link between housing and liberation, have been those attempts to build a liberatory movement around housing issues. From the Social Democratic Party's view of cooperative housing as one of the pillars of a broad-based reform movement to the Socialist and Communist Parties' organizing efforts in working class housing sections of New York City in the 1920's to the urban social movements of the 1960's and the squatters' movements of the 1970's and 1980's, housing has been the base for efforts to reduce oppression, to move towards liberation, in a number of countries. How successful these efforts have been will be discussed further below. Housing as liberation, and housing as base for moving towards liberation, is a concept grounded in concrete experience, and, like the concept of oppression in housing, deserving of further attention.

Oppression and the Commodity Character of Housing

The oppressive character of housing co-exists with the commodity character of housing, in the developed market economies at least. To the extent that the supply and distribution of housing is determined by its profitability to the supplier[9], many of the problems of housing can be traced to its "commodification." Under "normal" circumstances, indeed, most of the acute problems of housing faced by poor people can be traced directly to the fact that housing is generally produced for profit, and only for profit; those that cannot pay enough to provide a profit for a supplier will not get decent housing, and never will as long as supplier's profit is the decisive motivation for supplying housing.

Housing differs from other commodities in a number of ways, however. Some of these are well known in the standard literature: housing is the most durable of consumer goods, it involves the largest initial costs of production, it involves land and location to an exceptional degree, it is a necessity of life, whose provision cannot be reduced below some fluctuating and socially established standard without serious social and political consequences[10]. As a sector, the fortunes of the housing industry have major effects of the prosperity of the economy as a whole, and vice versa; the credit market, in particular, is heavily influenced by what happens with housing credit[11]. Other differences between housing and other commodities are related, but not as often considered: the price of housing directly affects the cost, and the profits to be made from, other commodities, through its impact on the cost of living of those producing other commodities, and thus their necessary wages; the consumption of housing probably has the highest multiplier effect on the consumption of other commodities (refrigerators, hi-fis, furniture, etc.) of any single good; governmental action is indissolubly linked with housing production, via infrastructure provision, regulation of externalities, etc.

But housing is also differentiated from other commodities because it uniquely helps structure relationships among people, in particular those relationships of oppression and liberation that are the focus of this paper. Certainly other commodities have this "non-commodity" aspect also. Clothing or jewelry are as much a manifestation of status as protection against the elements or a tribute to conceptions of beauty; cars are status symbols as well as transportation; guns determine relations among people in too many instances, but housing pre-eminently among all commodities contributes to creating and/or reinforcing relationships among people, ultimately relationships of power. That housing is used in this way does not make it less a commodity; it simply means that housing must be considered as more than a commodity if its production, distribution and use is to be understood -- or changed.

The relationships suggested here are portrayed in Chart I.

CHART I

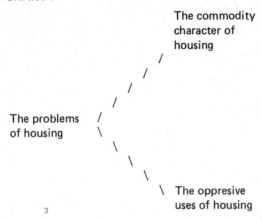

The commodity character of housing

The problems of housing

The oppresive uses of housing

The Definition of Housing

Housing is more than housing, we said at the beginning. As a formal question, what housing is is simply a matter of definition. It could simply mean shelter; more usefully, it includes the residential environment, accessibility and other characteristics of the location, the security provided by the home, its investment characteristics, the rights that come with its ownership and/or use. Legally, the ownership or rental of housing is best seen as a "bundle of rights," and those rights can be grouped, added to or diminished, defined, in an almost unlimited number of ways[12]. Public services that are residentially based: schools, parks, cultural facilities, should also be considered part of "housing" in a broad analysis.

What is and what is not included in housing is to some extent arbitrary. But it is also historically conditioned. Modern capitalist societies allocate a greater role to housing as a separate real category than did any previous society. Arguably, "housing" did not even exist as a separate category in feudal or non-capitalist agricultural societies. For the peasant or even yeoman farmer, "housing" was a part of the process of production, of making a living. It could not be separated out as belonging to a "sphere of consumption" or "reproduction," although of course it in fact was "consumed" then and necessary for "reproduction" then as now. It was simply not a *separate* thing, not part of a *separate* sphere. Thus a renter's revolt, in rural New York State in 1830, was decisively different from a tentants' strike in New York City in 1920, because the former was part of the struggle to make a decent living, to resist the exploitation of landlords claiming too great a share of the direct product of the farmer's labor, not simply part of a struggle to reduce the commercial profit made by a landlord in the sale (rental) of a commodity to its user. Rights to housing in earlier times were part of what we would today call "work-place" or "sphere of production" struggles; today they are more generally separated out from those struggles (although see the discussion below) as "residential" or "sphere of reproduction" conflicts. The line between individual and social, private and public, is also historically conditioned, and directly affects housing. The changes within evolving capitalism have been as striking as the differences between capitalism and former periods. In a few cases, formerly private functions have been socialized: education, for example, used to be undertaken in the home, today it is overwhelmingly outside. More recently, the movement has been in the opposite direction, from public to private, at least for higher-income groups. Laundry is done separately in each residential unit, not socially in public facilities or private laundromats. Recreation is provided in back yards, not public parks.

The higher the income, the greater the privatization -- except where the state so completely dominates the local scene that the distinction between public and private disappears. Where it remains, private residential communities provide their own security, are surrounded by their own walls, do their own street maintenance, own their own golf courses. The private/public/social line is blurred also: the maintenance of individual landscaping is done at the same time as the street and public area landscaping. In the condominum residential community, the broad concept of housing as the total residential environment is the legal reality. With private ownership of the house goes private ownership of the streets, the public spaces, the community center, the park, the club.

The pattern varies both by class and by historical period. For the majority of the population and the majority of the world's history, the private aspect of housing was shelter. The attendant uses of the private home were all public: originally even the plumbing facilities were in common in the cities, and certainly recreation, socializing, laundry, food storage, entertainment, reading, were all done in public areas or collectively.

Privatization is not some autonomous "trend," however, reflecting changing tastes that can be described but not explained, or an inevitable adjustment to new technological potentials. Rather, privatization in residential life relates directly both to economic needs and to cultural/ideological paradigms. Economically, advanced industrial private market societies depend centrally on the maintenance of consumption (and are thus distinguished from real existing socialist societies). Fordism is well served by the increasing privatization of residential life; what used to be provided as one item collectively now is sold in plural copies to multiple individual households. Not one laundry center, but a washing machine and dryer in every basement; not one movie, but a television set in every living room; not a concert hall, but an hi-fi built in to every new house. And not efficient brick multi-story apartment buildings, but free-standing individual houses, using more materials, more labor, more land, more maintenance, more heating, more financing.

The economic contribution of current housing patterns is thus historically determined and specific. High levels of consumption are essential to the life of the economic (and political) system. Housing contributes substantially to consumption. Today the home *is* the sphere of consumption, literally as well as figuratively, in large part. The enlargement of that sphere is part of the historical process of which we are a part. Hence, the issues of housing will predictably occupy an increasingly central place in most of the private market economies of the world.

OPPRESSION FOR WHAT, OF WHOM, BY WHOM

Oppression can be defined both by what it is not and by what it is. It is *not* simply the result of the system of private provision of housing for a profit. That system does indeed result in bad housing -- even oppressively bad housing -- for many, and particularly and inevitably, for the poor. The problems of housing for many is thus a direct result of the way housing is provided: what one gets is what one pays for, and if the poor can pay for less, they get less. In this sense the poor are clearly, and quintessentially, ill-housed. Such ill-housing, however, is the result of the normal functioning of the housing market. No concept of "oppression" needs to be brought in to explain it.

Oppression refers to a different source and a different consequence of housing, not simply explicable by the interests of a private housing industry concerned to maximize its profits. Oppression in housing refers to that aspect of housing that circumscribes opportunities, that dictates roles, that inhibits protest, that subtly produces conformity and acceptance, that undermines resistance, that integrates into a system, makes tolerable a system, in which the quality of housing is in fact inadequate. It is not the provision of inadequate housing that is necessarily oppressive, but the form in which it is provided, the logic by which it is imposed and accepted. Home ownership, as an example, can be oppressive, regardless of the quality of housing that is involved: it can impede mobility, it can force individuals into stereotyped roles, it can set neighbor against neighbor, it can create a fear of loss which inhibits protest, it can produce a vicious cycle of behaviour in which ever increasing consumption leads to an ever-increasing need to work harder and avoid risks that might jeopardize what has already been acquired. These are consequences of the housing system that are not explained by the interest of housing suppliers in their own profit -- or they might be considered unintended by-products of that system.

Yet I suggest that oppression is an integral part of the housing system in most countries of the world today, one that runs deeper than the direct economics of the housing supply system would dictate. Public housing can be as oppressive as private; socialist societies create as oppressive housing estates as capitalist ones. Is the oppressive aspect of housing then a "non-economic" characteristic of housing, to be explained without reference to the economic system in which it is embedded or by which it is produced? *Why* is there oppression in housing? What purpose does it serve, who exactly is it that is oppressed, and who is doing the oppressing?

Oppression for What?

The key concepts between which I want to differentiate to explain the existence of oppression in housing are exploitation and repression. Both terms are unfortunately often jargon, and I would welcome suggestions for better words. Their central meaning is sharply defined, however, even if there is substantial over-lap and a critical internal relationship between them. They parallel the distinction between the economic and the political. Exploitation is, in a sense, the economic aspect of oppression, repression its political/social/cultural aspect. The concept is illustrated in Chart II.

CHART II

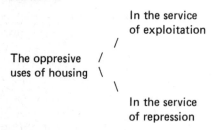

To make the concepts clearer: business profits depend on costs; costs include labor as a major -- Marxists would say the only $\frac{1}{M}$-surplus-value-producing factor; raising labor costs, all other things being equal, will lower profits, and vice versa. If exploitation is used to describe the extraction of profit from others' labor, then the level of exploitation will depend on the amounts paid for labor. It the costs of living are high, including the costs of housing -- if the social costs of the reproduction of labor power are high -- there will be an upward pressure on wages, a downward trend in levels of exploitation[13]. Hence it is directly in the interests of employers, in order to maximize exploitation, to hold housing costs down. In part this may bring them into direct conflict with the housing supply industry. In part, it will lead them to favor a reduction in the standards of housing (the amount of housing included in the "socially necessary costs of reproduction of labor"). These tendencies are widely recognized in many discussions of the housing problem.

But housing can also be used to oppress workers into accepting lower wages. (I use the word worker generically here, to cover anyone working for another; Wall Street law firms have the same interests vis-a-vis their younger lawyer members as General Motors does vis-a-vis an assembly-line worker, even if the techniques of oppression -- see the discussion of gentrification below -- may be quite different.) The threat of eviction from a house in a company town is the classic example; more are provided below.

Repression refers to systematic efforts to enhance political stability, cultural integration, and acceptance of ideological legitimacy of the prevailing system generally. Repression, again, is not the ideal term; it implies an active putting down of opposition, whereas it is here taken to include (as with housing) a process of cooptation that may seem quite pleasant from the short-term experience of those affected. Home ownership is of course the classic example. Praise of home ownership as contributing to social harmony and political stability can be found in innumerable contexts over the last two hundred years at least. From the crude limitation of the vote to property owners to the income tax preferences given to home owner-occupants, the political undercurrent of home ownership is strong and omnipresent[14].

Oppressive housing may reinforce exploitation and repression at once; indeed, in general the two are closely linked. Home ownership, for example, reinforces exploitation in the same ways it reinforces oppression: the willingness to go on strike is undermined by the large loss that might result from mortgage delinquency, the status confered by homeownership may block united political action with those of lower status, and so forth. In Section III below, we will discuss some direct examples of the use of housing to buttress exploitation (III A), then to buttress repression (III B). In most cases, however, the two uses of oppression are so closely linked that it is better to consider the issues by the particular oppressive aspect of housing involved, rather than by whether it supports either exploitation or repression. The more general discussion by aspect of housing is thus presented in Section IV.

The structure of the concepts suggested thus far may be summarized by Chart III.

CHART III

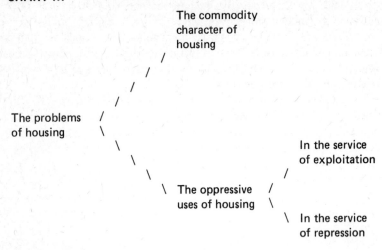

Before turning to the forms of oppression in housing, two other substantive questions need to be answered.

Oppression of Whom?

People are not uniformly oppressed by their housing. The well housed, at first blush, might seem to be free of oppression in their housing: the single-family homeowner in the exclusive suburb, the inner city condominium owner with private doorman and indoor swimming pool, the young professional couple with elegant small apartment in town, do not seem to suffer in their housing. But their housing may seriously restrict even the well-housed in what they can and cannot do, sometimes directly, sometimes insiduously, as in the classic yuppie gentrification scene. Specifics will be discussed later; the point here is that it is not only the poor and the ill-housed that suffer oppression in their housing.

But some groups are more clearly oppressed than others. The poor, first and foremost. Women, in general, are clearly limited as a group in the opportunities available to them because of their housing. The oppression of blacks and members of particular minority ethnic, religious, and cultural groups is a pervasive feature of American life, with parallels in most countries of the world. Non-conformists, the elderly, large families, all face particular problems.

General Oppression. The oppression of each of these groups differs in kind, and general distinctions can be made among them. The source of the oppression of the poor is economic. That is to say, the poor are defined along economic lines: poverty is a question of money. That basis for oppression is here considered "general;" other bases for oppression are called "special." Calling economic oppression general derives from the view that the underlying structure of society lies in its economic relationships. There are alternate theories, which would lead to alternate definitions of what is general and what is special. The distinctions between general and special drawn here would hold even with alternate views; the lines between the two would simply be drawn elsewhere.

General oppression in housing, then, as that term is used here, is that set of oppressive characteristics that confront the poor through the mechanism of the market, that are imposed on the poor because of their poverty[15]. In addition to this general oppression, particular groups face a special form of oppression: oppression imposed regardless of income, or independent of it.

Special Oppression. The two clearest and most prevalent forms of special oppression are racism and sexism. In both cases special oppression operates to increase general oppression; blacks earn less because they are discriminated against. Thus they are doubly oppressed. The housing problems of women, blacks, Hispanics, illegal immigrants (to single out only the largest groups) are indeed in part traceable to their inadequate incomes, but that inadequate income is in turn traceable to special exploitation which holds those incomes below the average for the type of work in question. (The term "special exploitation" comes from the concept that all workers for wages are, to one extent or another, exploited; some however are exploited over and above the "normal," through the techniques here described.) Blacks and Hispanics are discriminated against in the level of their wages, divided from their peers through prejudice, separated from them by residential segregation, denied opportunities for education, for advancement, for investment. Many women are confined to unpaid labor in the home, discriminated against in rates of pay, divided from their peers, by sexism. For illegal immigrants, or those concerned about their residency status, the insecurity created by their status is used to pay them substandard wages in sweatshops or for homework. The restricted possibilities available to Native Americans on reservations, and the prejudice they encounter elsewhere results in substandard compensation for their work also.

Housing patterns contribute to these forms of special exploitation. Blacks and Hispanics are confined to ghettoes, limited in where they can live, excluded from major areas of most metropolitan regions. They are thus restricted in their choice of jobs by the restricted accessibility their housing provides -- many jobs in the suburbs, for instance, are not realistically available for them. They are charged more than whites for comparable housing, and given less than comparable public services, transportation, education, recreation. They are less secure in their every-day lives, more dependent on fragile linkages to make the day go smoothly, more subject to disruption in the pursuit of the day's necessities. They are thus less well situated to climb the ladder of success -- to improve their incomes, to resist exploitation.

Many women are restricted to jobs they can reach from suburban locations with limited public transport, or to unpaid work within the household, or to jobs in locations not of their choosing but chosen by men on whom they are dependent. Their locational choices are restricted by discrimination in the housing market, in the granting of mortgages or the preferences (and prejudices) of landlords. The lack of child care connected with or near their housing restricts the job choices of many severely. For immigrants worried about their legal status, the vulnerability to the whims and the over-charges of landlords or sellers is extreme, and the insecurity of their housing reinforces their vulnerability to exploitation in jobs and homework.

Oppression by Whom?

Who benefits from oppression is a deceptively simple question: the "oppressors," of course. But there is no such simple category. In terms of exploitation and repression, it is possible to say, at one level, that particular individuals and groups benefit directly from the exploitation of others: their profits increase. And certain individuals and groups benefit from the repression of others: they maintain their power. Yet oppression in housing hurts some of those who benefit also, because profits and power do not define all of life. In critical ways, those who are benefited directly by the oppressive housing conditions of others are also harmed by those conditions. Their residential environment is impoverished, major parts of cities become off-limits to them, their range of contacts and experiences is diminished, their self-perception is distorted. The oppressors are also oppressed.

"Residential" life plays a greater role for members of developed industrial societies, one may speculate, than it did for the majority of people in any previous society[16]. The extent to which productive labor permits a full expression of the human potential, always severely restricted, is perhaps more flagrant today than ever before, because the levels of education and skill required for much work today are so high, the call for a limited and narrowly directed creativity so strong. The frustration thus engendered is sought to be eliminated by consumption, by ways of life elevating the residential environment and what happens in it to a major place in the fulfillment of human aspirations. That process becomes self-defeating. Consumption is not production, hobbies are not creative work, passive participation is not artistic effort. The residential riches made available to the "oppressors" by their separation from the residential lives of the "oppressed" are ultimately shallow and unsatisfying.

The evidence for these statements is not plain -- indeed, the entire system is geared to conceal it. The media exaltation of the "yuppie," and of the parallel in housing, gentrification, is overwhelming. But the gentrifiers are themselves oppressed also, even though the housing problems they cause others are much sharper and more evident. The point is discussed further below; all that is suggested here is that the separation of the spheres of production and consumption in the lives of those benefiting from the oppressive housing conditions of others is not problem-free, and the liberation of some from their housing problems may be liberating even to those whose actions cause those problems.

DIRECT FORMS OF OPPRESSION IN HOUSING

Exploitation and repression are intimately related to each other, and any form of housing that contributes to or undermines one contributes to or undermines the other as well. But there are a few classic situations in which the oppressive purposes of housing are so clear and well defined that exploitation and repression may be considered separately. We start, in this Section III, with these clear cases.

Exploitation

Employer-owned housing is perhaps the classic case in which employment and housing are directly and obviously connected. It is not the earliest; certainly the discipline of the slave quarter combined the two[17], and the cloister and the prison have already been referred to as elementary unities between patterns of control at work and in housing.

The company towns of the early years of the English, American, and German industrial revolution reflect the desire to control all aspects of workers' lives, in the interests of enhanced productivity and profits. The settlements in the Ruhr are among the most interesting examples, for the record is explicit as to the hopes of the large mining and smelting magnates.

> The pervasive oversight which the distrustful and efficiency-oriented (Alfred Krupp) put into operation, otherwise only to be found in military barracks, reached even to the point where every nose blown in the worker's house was known, and even to the point where whether a worker read a social democratic newspaper or leaflet could be spotted.[18]

Even beyond such direct control, the company town founders hoped a controlled residential environment would contribute to a "settled and happy" workforce. Worker's colonies (so called by their owners) were to promote the "productivity and dedication to work" of their inhabitants. A "healthy, satisfied, settled and loyal breed of workers" was the intended product of these sometimes quite attractive settlements.[19]

Company-owned housing enhanced the benefits of the employment relationship for employers in more ways than one, of course. The journey to work was shortened, making longer hours more feasible. Providing small garden plots permitted workers to grow some of their own food, lowering the costs of feeding a family and thus the pressures on wages[20]. But garden plots had a more directly social function as well, in the eyes of employers. As Alfred Krupp said in 1884,

> I believe it is both economically and morally very useful to win over the worker and his family to the cultivation of gardens. The men will forget about the tavern, and women and children also will get pleasure both from the harvest and from their own productivity.[21]

The physical form of housing, whether it be rental or single-family plot with garden, can reinforce exploitation in these ways. Tenure relations can also undermine resistance to exploitation. For company towns, the simple threat of eviction operates to dissuade militant protest and strikes[22]. Even today, at such institutions as Columbia University, the availability of University-owned housing is a significant inducement to both clerical and professional employees to be reasonable in their demands for compensation, and makes losing a Columbia job that much more to be feared.

Even the location of working-class housing can be dictated by concerns about discipline at the work place. David Gordon cites testimony supporting the locational dispersion of working class areas on the grounds that workers passing by a particular factory having protest activities under way might be corrupted thereby; better to separate workers from such influences. The overlap with the political, repressive, aspects of slum clearance, discussed below, is large.

Women's housework is rarely paid; exploitation is certainly an appropriate term for what happens to most women who work within the house. The precise analysis of the benefits of that exploitation has been the subject of extended discussion. In particular, the question is whether the benefit runs to the male "head of the household" in what was once the typical family, or whether it is in fact seized by his employer in the form of lower wages, made possible because the woman's work does not have to be paid for out of wages. To some extent no doubt both happens. Jeanne Boydston argues, as to the pre-Civil War northeastern U.S.:

Employers were enabled by the presence of this sizeable but un-counted labor in the home to pay both men and women wages which were, in fact, below the level of subsistence... housework added several hundred dollars a year to the value of working-class subsis-tence -- several hundred dollars which the employer did not have to pay as a part of the wage packet. Had the labor of housework been counted, wages would have soared to roughly twice their present levels[23].

She calculates, for this period, that the wife's labor time as landlord/cook to boarders was by itself worth $130 a year, almost half the minimum subsistence pay for a single adult male[24].

In any event, housing is so structured as to make optimum use of such unpaid labor. If the type of work women do in the home had to be paid, it would be provided otherwise, collectively and/or socially; the prolifer-ation of day care centers and fast food restaurants as the proportion of women in the paid work force rises is dramatic evidence. For the woman forced to work at home, her housing is also her work-place, and its archi-tecture and its location confine and oppress her in such a manner as to keep her at her work whether she wishes or not; she simply has no alter-natives.

Racial segregation is used directly to enforce industrial discipline. The most flagrant example today are the "homelands" in South Africa; com-bined with the notorious pass system, they harken back to the use of concentration camps by the Nazis as sources of slave labor, labor that was seen in long-range planning terms as being used to build housing for the "free" population. Thus, ironically, housing some in concentration camps was seen as the basis for solving the housing problems of those on the out-side[25].

As the horror of the South African homelands is less than the horror of some of the concentration camps during the Second World War, so the horror of some of the segregated ghettoes of the U.S. is less than that of South Africa, but the relationships to the prevailing economic system are the same. Thus the metaphor of the "city as sandbox[26]," suggesting that the surplus population, predominantly minority, can be left there to "play" while the economic life of the society goes on elsewhere, to be re-called when and if needed by a particular emergency, is used in respectable circles in the U.S. The housing of foreign workers (or workers from abroad, in the case of colonial powers) in many European countries is similar: Turkish areas in German cities, Algerian areas in France, Indonesian areas in the Netherlands, West Indian areas in England, all play the same role, as segregated "camps" of marginal workers, where the living costs are held down and public investment minimized.

Repression

The prison, and its ultimate extension in the concentration camp, are the archetype of housing used repressively. Foucault finds the model of discipline in the evolution of the prison system, in which the architecture of living quarters plays a prominent role[27]. The segregation of minority populations in major cities throughout the world today is in a sense an extension of that concept: group the under-privileged together, and they can more easily be controlled, be kept from doing harm outside of their own quarters.

For those on whose labor the system depends, however, dispersion may be as desirable a method of political control as concentration. The strength of working-class quarters as seats of revolt was proverbial in Paris from the days of the French Revolution onwards. The streets Hausman bulldozed through had as an explicit purpose reducing the defensibility of working class quarters as seats of resistance to the central authority.

Slum clearance in the United States has a similar over-lay, although the revolt sought to be controlled has been more individualistic than collective. From the times of the Committee for Decongestion of the Population in New York City[28] down through the slum clearance schemes of the 1930's on the Lower East Side to the "integration" policies of the Federal government after the ghetto riots of the mid-1960's, state action has been in part a response to fear of the political evils that the slums might breed. Remove, disperse, isolate their residents, the theory has gone, and they will be less dangerous. Even their voting power will be thus reduced. Both their legal and their extra-legal capacity to resist will thus be weakened.

Good housing can be used just as directly as a reward for good behaviour as prisons can be a punishment for bad. Evidence suggests that the assignment of housing based on Party membership is a prevalent pattern in Eastern Europe and the Soviet Union. It was certainly an allegation leveled against the Viennese Social Democrats in the 1920's[29]. Public housing authorities in the U.S. have been faced with the same charges, and the distribution of information and contacts about housing was an integral part of the machine politics of earlier years in many American cities.

Access to housing, and particularly to ownership, was of course very directly the basis for the entire system of choosing rulers in the early years both of the English and the American electoral system. The property qualification for voting, although it has feudal antecedents, was long maintained as an integral part of democracy; property owning, in the form of home ownership, was a simple way of separating the citizenry from the rabble, and seen as a directly political device of government by many of the Founding Fathers in the U.S. A more direct link between the form of housing and the power to govern can hardly be expected.

THE INDIRECT FORMS OF OPPRESSION IN HOUSING

A few aspects of housing can be easily classified by their exploitative or repressive functions: company towns, prisons, assignment of housing based on party loyalty. Others are more complex. We look as some here: home ownership, conformism, commodification, ghettoization, social status, gentrification, consumerism. Other aspects could as easily have been selected; hopefully further research will illuminate these and others as well.

Home Ownership

The negative aspects of home ownership for the individual and the contribution it makes to the preservation of the established economic and social order have been much discussed, and Jim Kemeny's recent work summarizes and extends much of it. Tenure relations of course make a critical difference in the economics of housing[30]. The political and social implications are also fairly well known[31].

The linkage between the economic/legal (the "real") aspects of home ownership and the social/political (the "perceived") aspects is however not completely clear. There is nothing in the reality of home ownership that justifies the almost mystical reverence in which it is held in most developed private market economies. Its tax advantages, in many countries, are substantial. But they are a creature of the state, and can easily be extended or contracted; they are not inherent in the tenure. In periods of inflation, owning a home may be a good investment; so may many other things be, and a house may be an even better investment if it is rented out or held for sale than if it is owner-occupied.

Why is home ownership such a powerful idea, then, and given such substantial support by all kinds of established authorities -- Ray Forrest and Alan Murie go so far as to call it "state subsidized individualism[33]"? Certainly the allegiance to homeownership is not justified by any economic or legal advantages it has as a form of tenure, apart from arbitrary tax benefits; Kemeny goes so far as to speak of the myth of homeownership, and others have pointed out how easily it can be a losing, as well as a winning, proposition for homeowners, particularly working class and lower income[33]. Even apart from its investment aspect, it has other deleterious consequences; Edel, Solar and Luria speak of "social entrapment" restricting occupational mobility, for instance.

I suggest home ownership is so widely favored because, at a quite deep psychological level, it is a means by which individuals seek to overcome a sense of alienation in their lives as a whole. The growth of capitalism has been accompanied by a deepening conversion of labor power to a commodity, of the productive and creative energies of women and men into things to be bought and sold on the market place. Productive work no longer joins individuals to each other, establishes a place for people in society by virtue of its social contribution, provides personal or social satisfaction as an activity in itself. Work is a means to the end of pay. And what pay can buy is itself more and more measured in money, not the deeper satisfaction of free use and enjoyment.

The home, in this context, is seen as an exception to this commodified world. It is a place of retreat, a refuge, a shelter for human life in a cold world. But renting puts that shelter at some one else's mercy, someone whom the earlier history of the transition to capitalism has painted as an unproductive scoundrel, living off the unearned rents derived from the basic needs of others -- the landlord. Home ownership is the escape from the arbitrary power of the landlord, and symbollically from the arbitrary power of the society as a whole[34].

Home ownership serves the interests of the prevailing system in many other ways; its oppressive characteristics are not limited to this symbolic sense. Home ownership serves both exploitation and repression; it increases both the economic profitability and the political stability of the system. It divides the working class and inhibits its potential for opposition by giving it a "stake in the system"[35]. Particularly in countries like the United States, Canada, or Australia, where rates of home ownership are the highest, its stabilizing role can hardly be exaggerated. Roosevelt's immediate action in the United States in imposing a moratorium on mortgage foreclosure when the Depression threatened the integrity of home ownership suggests the awareness of government of the dangers when it is threatened.

The interpretation offered here does not dispute any of these points, but suggests that something further is needed to understand why such a system-supporting mechanism should be so readily and fundamentally accepted by those whose exploitation and repression it in reality serves to further. The answer suggested here lies not so much in the real nature of the tenure, but its social and psychological meaning[36]. One of the important questions open for housing research is why this mechanism of social integration is less needed in countries with lower rates of home ownership, such as Sweden. It may be suspected that where the implicit social compact begins with a higher role for government, the importance of home ownership as essentially a private social compact between the individual and "the market" (in the perception of the individual) is less needed, since the compact runs more between the individual and government.

Housing to Mold Character

Housing conditions have been seen as a decisive influence on character from the earliest days of the housing reform movement. Housing reformers

very explicitly wanted to change conditions in the slums so that their inhabitants would become better, more reliable workers. The border line
between reinforcing exploitation on the one hand and repression on the
other is fluid; at the same time that work discipline is to be strengthened,
the reformers also believed that social order would be better maintained
by good housing. The history of the housing reform movement in England[37], France, Germany[38], and the United States[39], is shot through
with references to the contributions improved housing could make to
social stability and work discipline.

The family is a critical element in the chain of causation that is supposed to lead from better housing to regular work habits and good citizen-
ship. Alfred Krupp told his workers, more than 100 years ago:

> Enjoy that which you have coming to you. After your work is done,
> stay in the circle of your loved ones, with your parents, with your
> wife and children, and care about your household and its education.
> Let that be your politics; thus will you have many happy hours.[40]

Nor is the relationship between housing and family life a thing only of a
by-gone era: in 1985, a leading U.S. cardinal pointed out:

> Housing is essentially a "family" issue. It is about people, parents,
> children, neighborhoods and whole communities. In their 1975 state-
> ment, "The Right to a Decent Home," the U.S. Catholic bishops said:
> 'Our concern is not simply for houses or programs, fit for the people
> who inhabit these dwellings or are affected by these programs. These
> include families whose attempt to create a stable and wholesome
> family life are inhabited (sic) by inadequate living conditions; people
> and parish communities in neighborhoods without the housing ser-
> vices or community life which foster love and Christian service;...
> and countless young families who lack the resources to acquire
> decent housing[41].'

Women and men are both molded into specific roles, given little choice but
to conform to specific stereotypes, by the structure of housing provision.
The special oppression of women by the predominant forms of housing
available to them has already been pointed out. Men are similarly constrained, although in different directions. For both, there is an economic
as well as a political/social element. In simple money terms, the privatiz-
ation/individualization of housing forces its occupants to devote substantial
labor-time of their own to its maintenance and repair. That time is unpaid;
it serves to reduce their cash housing costs, and thus to reduce the pressures
on their wages. At the same time, it restricts their opportunities, and even
their desires, to engage in other activities, including collective activities
that might involve in political or social issues. It leads to a privatization and internalization of problems, housing and other; if something

goes wrong, the individual, not any more general circumstances, are to blame. If housing is bad, it is the individual's own fault; the remedy is individual, not collective, action. The lesson supports the status quo both economically and socially. The forms of housing reinforce the lesson. It seems to me such a result may fairly be called oppressive.

The mold into which housing casts its residents is overwhelmingly that of the nuclear family. The housing industry's profit has much to do with it; the nuclear family is (even today) still the largest household configuration among those with economically effective demand for housing, and its proportion rises as income (and the ability to pay for housing) rise. Normal marketing principles would further lead to most suppliers aiming for the center of their market, not its fringes.

But the shortage of housing for non-conforming household types cannot, it seems to me, be explained solely by housing economics. Good money can after all be made by building for single-parent families, for unrelated single individuals living together or alone, for those who would like to cook with others or not at all -- yet the range of housing choices available to such households is far short of their demand, even where the demand would justify greater production. The slowness with which ideas such as those of Jackie Leavitt and Troy West for combined residential/ work developments are taken up is evidence for the existence of some barrier other than pure rational economics.

In the non-market oriented sector, indeed, the same patterns exist. Sophie Watson has documented in detail the extent to which Council housing in England has treated as marginal the non-family household[42]. In the United States, public housing from the outset sought out nuclear families[43], and only admitted single-parent families and single elderly because of the unexpected pressures of demographic change and urban renewal dislocation.

The social role of the nuclear family, and in particular its contribution to maintaining work and social discipline (exploitation and repression), perhaps account for the discrepancy between latent market demand and actual supply. Just how the usefulness of the family as a socializing institution is translated into the profit-motivated reactions of housing suppliers, to some extent against their own interests, will be discussed at the end of this paper. The existence of the pattern seems clear.

This molding of character to which housing contributes may be seen in a more general context: the pressure for conformity in general, the dissuasion of non-conformity[44]. Zoning laws are perhaps the classic example of the pressure exerted by housing patterns to conform to the prevailing mode. Not only the separation of work from residential life, or commercial activities from both, the control over architecture and design and the potentials for self-expression in housing, the segregation of tenures, but even the personal characteristics and family relationships of members of a household may be regulated by zoning laws[45]. Thus conformity to socially accepted behavior is reinforced in large as well as small ways by the legal, economic, and design characteristics of housing.

The Social Role of Commodification and Consumerism

The treatment of housing as a commodity -- its production, financing, management, occupancy, and sale for profit, rather than for use or based on need -- has been commented on extensively in the literature[46].

But there is another aspect to the commodification of housing: the need to convert *all* values to commodities, in order to make their users, human beings, fully "economically rational." It is a characteristic of modern capitalism that its hegemony is supported by its ability to convert all potentially dangerous conflicts, all questioning of its basic values, into market issues. Capitalism fundamentally seeks to induce those working under it to answer all problems by going out and earning money: if you don't have something you want or need, go earn the money and buy it. The current president of the United States adopts this approach intuitively, and has applied it to the area of housing policy among many others. Such an approach of course does not address the fundamental questions of human growth and happiness, of relationships among people free of power or coercion, which can only be achieved in a non-commodified, unreified fashion.

So the human demand for a humane living environment, for free and democratic and un-power-constrained, unreified relationships among people in their everyday lives, is converted into a "market" for housing, in which "consumers" express their preferences through "economically effective demand." The rules of the game are implemented through the exchange of money for goods and for labor. Anything that cannot be bought for money is a threat to those rules, a potential threat to the legitimacy of that society.

And of course there is resistance to those rules that precisely arises in dangerous form when the denial of human needs is seen not as a problem of money but a problem of dealing with needs only through money. In other words, when the market is totally rejected as the means for meeting needs, as the rules of the game. Social movements pose precisely this threat; this is why they are potentially so dangerous. As John Mollenkopf says,

> Within any society... there are always people who want to place community life before economic growth... The more economic actors try to negate 'economically irrational' communal responses, the more they run the danger of triggering political conflict.[47]

'Economically irrational' conduct is not just dangerous because it is political, but because it rejects the economic as the appropriate mechanism for making decisions. That is a fundamental threat to the legitimacy of the system.

The enslavement to consumerism may be seen as a further consequence of the commodification of housing. The house or apartment is probably the largest consumption item in most people's budget. As such, the supply of land for it, its construction, its financing, its sale, sometimes its management, are a source of tremendous profit for land speculators, developers, builders, banks and lending institutions, real estate firms, management agents, investors. What is sold is what will produce the highest profit for them, not what will best meet aspirations for home and community. But beyond the direct profit to be made by promoting the consumption of housing, the house itself becomes a dynamic engine of further consumption. Its purpose becomes the creation of needs, not their satisfaction. In good times, at least, housing is a carrot to induce full-scale absorption into the merry-go-round of capitalism. Housing thus promotes acquiesence, both in the economic and the political order. The oppressive effect is sugar-coated, but all the more effective.

The Ghettoization of Minorities

"Internal colonialism" is a striking metaphor suggesting both the exploitative and repressive character of ghettoization. Black slaves in the American South before the civil war, black and Hispanic ghettos in the contemporary U.S., Turkish quarters in West Germany, Algerian quarters in Paris are not so far removed from their economic counterparts overseas[48]. Detailed discussion is hardly necessary here.

Ethnic segregation can itself be seen as a subcategory of what Don Parsons has called the creation of "reserve space,"

> ... the way in which particular 'space' has a reserve function as in general a locale of the reserve army of labour. Spatially oriented (sic) policies e.g. in regional development and urban renewal can be seen as state mechanisms for facilitating the underdevelopment of the 'space' and its present and potential human contents.[49]

Thus ghettoization can be seen generally as supportive of economic activity and political rule; it is in addition specially oppressive of those particular groups specially subjected to it.

Housing as Status

The private single-family house, the prevalent commercially-sold "dream" of many Americans, represents status earned. Status is comparative, and to have value, it cannot be had by all. Bigger picture windows, more garage space for more cars, greener lawns, "better" neighbors -- not as values in themselves, but to show, and to reinforce, the difference between one person and another -- these are socially conditioned aspects of the dream. City apartments are similarly built to be shown off, to protect their residents from the hurly-burly of their environment with doormen and security systems, to provide within their walls the safety, the facilities, the appeal, that are so threatened in the ouside world -- by shutting their occupants off from the intrusions of that outside world.

The association of housing with status reinforces the divisive impact of the privatization of housing. Even in local political terms, it engenders parochialism, exclusiveness, as communities become self-segregated along status lines, and then organize to preserve their status against all comers.

Further, the rewards not to be found in the work place, whether in wages or in the satisfactions of creation and production, are compensated for by the rewards of status. If life is unsatisfying, at least it appears even less satisfying for others; that is some source of satisfaction in itself. The current uses of housing promote such false satisfactions. Economic aspects of the dream are also inconsistent with its human meaning.

Gentrification

Gentrification is clearly oppressive to those that are displaced by it. The economic causes of gentrification and displacement have been extensively discussed recently, and their roots traced to the restructuring of space in the city as a whole[50]. The role of gentrification in the oppression of the gentrifiers has been less frequently examined. To the extent that gentrification "originates in processes much broader than the operation of the land and housing markets," however, in Damaris Rose's words, the "production of gentrifiers" as well as the production of gentrified buildings, needs to be explored[51].

Gentrification produces a form of housing oppressive to gentrifiers as well as displacees. For a limited section of the professional/managerial/administrative group, gentrification is permitting housing to play a qualitatively new role. The replacement of one population group by another in particular areas of a city is not of course new. What is new is the social/cultural as well as, ultimately, economic role of gentrification. To understand it requires looking at who the gentrifiers are and what their role in society is.

Economic (industrial) restructuring has, in the post-war period, created the need for an expanded technically competent and motivated work force. But the traditional mechanisms for obtaining the acquiescence and support of this group, largely drawn from families already in the upper class, no longer function. They are no longer pulled by the lure of entrepreneurship, power and riches, nor pushed by the fear of penury and hardship, including the technique of gentrification of people. The stratum in question involves neither the idle rich nor the decisive powerful, but the well-paid adminstrative, managerial, technical, cultural, professional, often with inherited as well as current income[52]. Gentrification can be seen, I believe, as one way of dealing with this problem: a way of getting the gentrifiers to acquiesce in their own exploitation and repression.

The gentrification of people through the evolution of a sophisticated consumerism, not only as to goods but of culture, the environment, and crucially of residential space, is thus a mechanism to provide a motivation for and satisfaction with continued integration into essentially unproductive and humanly meaningless jobs, where quality of performance is important but usefulness of result is not. Earlier mechanisms to these ends no longer suffice, as the technical potentials for production and plenty expand. (Many of those reading this paper, as well as its author, are directly affected by these developments.) The gentrification of space is both a by-product of, and contributes further to, this process.

The enslavement to consumerism represented by gentrification is thus only a conspicuous and current example of a fundamental oppressive aspect of society, to which housing patterns contribute significantly.

LIBERATION, OR THE RESISTANCE TO OPPRESSION

Housing patterns are not imposed by all-powerful forces on passive and helpless victims. In relationships among people or groups or classes, no result is ever determined solely by the interests of one side or the other. In most cases victories are only partial, and will reflect some accomodation, some compromise. Even where victory seems most complete, its form and meaning will have been shaped by conflict, by the need of the victorious to take into account the dynamics of the opposition. Housing is no exception. If it is oppressive to some, and if that oppression serves the interests of others, the activities of the oppressed themselves are also felt, the service to the intersts of the oppressors is never complete.

Does or can housing, then, serve or reflect resistance to oppression?

How Deeply Can Housing-based Resistance Go?

The most bitter struggles in society tend to be around issues of wealth and power. They involve efforts to change or consolidate economic and political patterns. Residential issues, as a subset of issues involving consumption rather than production or power, are thus often seen as secondary issues. The theoretical argument is that residential conflicts, from the point of view of those oppressed by housing, can at best produce minor and reformist victories, and at worst divert or absorb energies that should go into other arenas of struggle. Only to the extent that struggles around housing are linked to work-place struggles, goes the argument, particularly among some Marxists, can they have real significance. Thus "neighborhood" organization is bound to be short-lived and ineffective unless it is linked to outside issues, such as organizing in mining communities in Wales during the recent British miners' strike. Even on issues such as the rent strikes in Glasgow in 1915, opinion is divided whether the issues were really "housing" issues or "production-based" issues[53].

Discussions in the sociological literature about whether or not there are "housing classes," in John Rex' term, reflects much of the same disagreement on the theoretical role and depth of housing conflicts[54]. The disagreement is also reflected in the distinctions often drawn between the "sphere of everyday life" and the "sphere of production"[55].

While fundamental issues are involved in these distinctions, they are not a useful basis for research about housing issues. Individuals, after all, are unities, and their everyday lives include consumption and production both. They are the same people with the same complex of interests whether they are viewed as belonging to a "working class" or a "tenant class." The distinction between the various places people spend their lives, the kinds of activities they engage in during working hours and what they do outside of work, is an artificial distinction, one which itself has a negative impact both on the quality of people's lives and their abilities to change them. Whether one can better deal with the conditions that oppress through activities "in production" or in the neighborhood, at work or at home, is a decision that must be made based on the particular circumstances. General rules are not likely to be helpful, absent the historical context; it is a point Manuel Castells has frequently made.

In any event, research as to how people deal with oppression in housing should not be shut off by the a priori conclusion that, whatever they do, it is unimportant in the larger picture.

Housing and the Resistance to Oppression

Resistance to oppression may relate to housing in three ways: 1) as resistance directly addressed to the oppressive aspects of housing; 2) resistance more generally to oppressive social conditions, using housing as a base for organizing collective resistance; and 3) individual resistance relying on the home as a base of strength to resist. The ultimate step, using housing to try to establish a non-oppressive society -- in other words, housing offensively used as a base for initiatives for change, rather than defensively as a reaction to oppression, is discussed in section C. below.

Resistance to Oppression in Housing. The tenant rent strike is a classic form of resistance to oppression in housing[56]. Rent strikes and anti-eviction organization is probably the most wide-spread of all collective forms of resistance to housing oppression. There have been "mortgage strikes" also; in England, for instance, some 3,000 people took part, led by the Coney Hall Association, which also played a leading role in organizing the Federation of Tenants' and Residents' Associations[57]. Similarly, there was wide-spread resistance to mortgage foreclosure in the mid-western U.S. during periods of agricultural crisis, and during the early Depression. That is why the Roosevelt Administration was so quick to declare a bank holiday and then consolidate mortgage repayments through the Home Owners Loan Corporation[58]. But neither rent nor mortgage protests resulted in large or long-lasting organization, nor did they broaden out to other issues. The strongest of the apparent housing-related movements in the U.S., the Renters' Revolts in New York State in the 1820's and the midwestern rural organizations, were more a protection of farms and the ability to make a livelihood from the land than a protection of residential housing.

The high points of tenant activity are illuminating. In New York City, before the first World War, the level of tenant militancy was high. Both then and in the post-World War I period, it was led by convinced political radicals, largely women, and had strong ties with the labor movement. After World War II, during and to some extent after the ghetto riots of the 1960's, tenant unions were again wide-spread, but shorter-lived. They connected with the civil rights movement and the struggles of black communities, but much less with directly politically radical movements (which indeed barely existed) and almost not at all with labor. Housing was perhaps accepted as a central issue by establishment groups concerned with assuaging the discontent that threatened to spread and deepen politically in both periods, perhaps because housing could be a visible and relatively cheap and non-threating reform to institute. Separated from explicitly political content, neither tenant nor mortgage resistance spread much beyond housing, and even within housing it remained defensive and short-term[59].

Some neighborhood actions around housing, particularly in working-class and, in the U.S., white ethnic communities, have very different components. Such forms of defense of housing can indeed be politically reactionary, that is, what is seen as resistance to oppression in housing tends objectively to reinforce oppression in other areas, and in housing for other people. The racially exclusionary aspects of many militant home-owners and neighborhood association protests against zone changes are an example. Neither militancy nor level of organization by themselves say much about the extent to which resistance is effective to limit oppression in housing.

Why do some instances of resident activity seem to be narrow and short-term, others broader and of more general effect? Two answers may be hazarded, although neither one can really be substantiated at the present state of knowledge.

The first explanation is that resistance to oppression in housing will be effective in direct relation to the extent to which it goes beyond housing issues and engages questions of more general power relationships, or workplace as well as residential issues[60]. It is an explanation that fits comfortably with the theoretical presuppositions of Marxist analysis. There is evidence to support it: the support of some Labor Party constituencies for council housing in England, in Liverpool for instance; the activity of the New Jersey Tenants Organization in the electoral arena; the links between rent strikes and radical organizing referred to above in New York City.

But it may be a dangerously circular argument: resistance is judged "effective" if it goes beyond housing issues, and then housing protest is examined to see why some is effective. The result is predictable: because it goes beyond housing issues. Definition becomes explanation. The linkage between depth and breadth of resistance may be real; a satisfactory review of the evidence remains to be undertaken.

A different explanation might look to the *nature* of the housing issue involved. We divided housing issues into two "sides," at the beginning of this paper: the economistic, and the "other" side of housing, its oppressive/liberatory aspect. Many conflicts about housing involve purely economic issues -- economic in the narrow sense of the bargaining between supplier and user of housing as to the payment to be made for it. The amount of rent to be paid is of course the central issue in most rent strikes, and in much tenant organizing. It gives rise to acute conflicts, and sharply heightened levels of organization and militancy during the period of bargaining. But when it is over, it is over; residents go back about their other business, organization disappears, the conflicts around housing seem to vanish until, perhaps, the next round of bargaining.

In some situations, however, what is in dispute is more than simply the amount of the rent: the whole issue of control of the housing unit, the residential environment, becomes involved. In the massive rent strikes in public housing in St. Louis in 1968, for instance, the issue was not only whether and how much rent should be paid; it was also who would run the projects and how they would be run, what services would be provided, what rules would be followed -- who was in charge. More generally, the National Tenant Organization, whose mainstay was and is public housing tenants[61], has spent as much time and energy on issues of tenants' rights as on issues of the rent. Developing a model lease setting forth when and how the landlord had the right to enter an apartment to inspect it; who established regulations on noise, pets, visitors, uses; what rights existed to due process on evictions, and what the causes of eviction should be; these were the issues that moved tenants, and have continued to move them.

In private housing, security may well have been, historically, an even sharper issue than the level of rents. Anti-eviction activities have certainly been, in cities like Chicago and New York, as spontaneous, as militant, as effective, as empowering, as any organizing around housing issues has produced. Neighborhood anti-displacement activities today are probably the central collective activity engaging the attention of residents and housing organizers[62]. It also involves more than just money; it involves security, the protection of that integrity of the individual and the household which is central to the concept of home.

Thus resistance to oppression, rather than simply to the economic burdens of housing, may be central to the most militant and deep-going of collective action by residents around housing.

Housing as the Basis for Resistance to Broader Oppression

Collective Resistance. Housing is not only the instrument of certain forms of oppression, and the subject-matter of resistance to those forms. It is also the base within which broader social conflicts take place, the camp, in a sense, from which particular segments of society venture forth for battle around non-housing issues. Superficially the use of neighborhoods as the basis of organization is common-place for political parties throughout the world. Particular neighborhoods then become the power bases of particular parties or groups. The more cohesive those neighborhoods, the more other forms of collective action support a collective spirit and enthusiasm, the stronger the party. The use of housing to promote such collective action thus becomes explicitly political, supporting organization around non-housing as well as housing.

The great housing estates of Red Vienna are a pure model of such a use of housing. Karl Marx Hof was seen both by its residents and by their enemies as a "fortress of Social Democracy." It formed the physical as well as social structure around which the working class of Vienna conducted its activities, held itself together, identified itself. Very little of what happened there actually involved the Hof or its management directly; qua housing, it was quite conventionally run. But as a base for a political effort to resist oppression from the outside in general, to build a new society within Vienna from the ground up, it was exceptional[63].

Other examples are plentiful, if not as extreme. Ghettoes, negative and imposed by definition, can also be sources of strength, bastions of resistance. They were in the U.S. in the 1960's; Frances Piven has made the argument that their advantages in this regard may outweigh their disadvantages from a narrow housing standpoint[64]. Working class neighborhoods were certainly viewed by established powers as dangerous breeding grounds of discontent (read: resistance), and Hausman's political concerns in Paris were not that different from the concerns of some of the slum reformers of London or New York. The Social Democratic Party's support of the cooperative movement in housing in several countries reflects a similar sense of the relationship of collective housing to collective action. The mutual support networks found in working class communities have supported militancy in factories, mills, and mines; recent French research has showed just how strong and important those residential networks were for workers' lives.

Resistance to other forms of oppression (as well as to housing oppression) may thus also be found among residents of housing, centered on their housing.

Individual Resistance. When it comes to the impact of his or her housing on the individual's feelings about oppression, the situation is more complicated -- or at least more ambiguous. On the one hand the home as refuge, as castle, as shelter, is central to most people's ability to survive, and thus also to their ability to fight back. On the other hand, the conception that the home actually offers a refuge and a shelter from the outside world supports a withdrawal from outside struggles, a separation of spheres of activity, a reduced willingness to take on oppression outside since it can be avoided by retreating inside. There is an unavoidable two-edged quality to the home as a base for individual resistance to oppression.

The whole debate about home ownership faces this ambiguity as a central issue, although it is rarely confronted. In an earlier time, the essentially homeless model of "the organizer[65]," of which the Bolshevik and the Wobbly are prime examples, would have been put out of business if he or she had to worry about a "home." That model hardly appears relevant today; Che Guevera may have been the last notable example of the breed. Today, organizers are more likely to see a secure home as helping create the space for risk-taking abroad, for maintaining a measure of personal security while going from one insecure outside confrontation to another. And if this is so, would it not be all the more true for the less fully committed, the average participant in the struggles around oppression and liberation in the society?

The answer to the question of whether secure housing is a support for, or a dissuasion from, action in resistance to oppression is a difficult one. Possibly it lies in the degree: some security is essential, "too much" is detrimental, to outside activity. Possibly it depends on the times: in the absence of outside threats, the tendency is to use the home as retreat; in the presence of outside threats, unemployment, turmoil, war, the home is a base for engagement.

Good Housing as Liberation?

Considering housing as a basis for resistance, or even for organization for more radical social change, is one thing; can housing in fact provide for the nucleus of a more humane society within this society?

Such a utopian potential for housing has been prominent in discussions for centuries. From Fourier to California communes, from religious orders to the squatters of Berlin and Amsterdam, the concept that a small band of people can together forge a more satisfying life for themselves around a residential community, a collective and ideal form of housing, has been a recurrent theme.

Nor has the hope been limited to small group actions, essentially escapes from broader efforts at change. Much of the most progressive housing literature of the 1920's sees modern housing as serving to produce "modern man (sic)," to create new character and new aspirations and new relationships. The language differs in essentials from the somewhat similar language of the philanthropic housing reformers of the 19th century. The philanthropists wanted to conform the poor to the prevailing mores and customs. The radicals of the 20's wanted to reform people as a step towards reforming society.

Most would probably concede that such dreams are today utopian, in the bad if also in the good sense of that term. It is not possible to insulate any small group from what goes on in the society as a whole; non-oppressive relations in a small group are bound to be impacted by oppressive relationships in the society to which the members of the group willy-nilly belong, in which they must live much if not all of the time. Yet housing *can* support non-oppressive relations. Much of feminist work on housing suggests patterns of living which at least provide a model of what a non-oppressive environment -- and a non-oppressive society -- might look like[66]. The development of limited equity coops, forms of social ownership, democratic governance within a housing estate, can all contribute to the rejection of more oppressive ways of housing, and of living, by those that participate in them or observe them.

While the hope that the construction of small and insulated non-oppressive environments will ultimately lead, if often enough duplicated, to the rejection of oppression in the society at large, seems to me a futile and indeed dangerous proposal, the value of example and experiment to make concrete what a better, less oppressive life might be like, seems to me an entirely different story, one with an important potential to support moves in the direction of a more liberatory system of housing and life.

The potential of utopian images of housing is not lost on those concerned to maintain the status quo. From the Club Med to walled-in retirement communities in California and Florida to the luxury condominiums of Manhattan, real estate firms and politicians and employers hold out the promise of a utopia right around the corner, a reward for hard work and good behavior. But islands of happiness for the rich must ultimately be as humanely unsatisfying as their more modest counterparts for the poor. Human relationships cannot be confined or played out only within the boundaries of a housing estate, however small or large. Neither a better world, nor the good of this world without its evil, can be secured within any particular configuration of isolated housing today, although in both cases something indeed can be gained (from different points of view) for some by moving in such directions.

SOME REMAINING PROBLEMS AND DIRECTIONS FOR RESEARCH

All of the above discussion is clearly very tentative and exploratory. It mixes conjecture with fact, leaps to hypotheses if not conclusions, and undoubtedly masks value preferences as summaries of fact. It is based largely on the U.S. experience, e.g. the discussion of homeownership, is a typical example. Even recognizing the pervasive need for more work on much of what has been said, however, there are certain large questions that even at the present level of exploration are wide open. Let me here only outline two.

Oppression and Liberation at the Same Time: How?

Housing can be both oppressive and liberating at the same time. The literature is full of formulations recognizing this fact. For instance:

> The home is... a key symbol of stereotyped womanhood, the root of so much of women's oppression... and the source of great strength and dignity according to others.[67]

Or look at different interpretations of the implications of ethnic divisions (of which residential divisions are a major part):

> ... a culturally divided workforce that is encouraged to celebrate its differences has political implications; ethnic boundaries are strengthened at the expense of working class solidarity and industrial militancy.[68]

Yet precisely the opposite point has also been made: that ethnic solidarity can be a major supportive structure for class resistance and working class solidarity[69]. At a larger scale, the relationship between movements of national liberation and the international class struggle is close indeed. Ethnic and cultural solidarity can be divisive and solidarity-building at the same time.

Similar ambiguities have cropped up constantly in this paper. Home ownership is at the same time oppressive and the substance of liberation. Utopian architectural schemes can be both inspiring to change and diversionary and thus system-maintaining. And examples can be multiplied.

At one level of abstraction, it is simply true that in each case there is a potential in each of two different directions. Differences can co-exist; contradictions abound in reality, but that abstract statement is not very useful for housing policy. Under what circumstances will one potential emerge, under what circumstances the other? How can the liklihood of one be minimized, the other maximized? Can conflicting potentials be separated, or is their inter-relationship inevitable?

Most research, unfortunately, has examined these various aspects of housing and tried to show that housing either "is" or "is not" one thing or another: home ownership is or is not system-supporting, design can or cannot influence behavior, housing issues are or are not major arenas of political conflict. What is needed first is a recognition of the contradictions inherent in many of these concepts. After that, the work that needs to be undertaken is the specification of the precise nature of the opposing aspects, and of the concrete circumstances under which the one or the other will emerge. The challenge is a difficult one, but it seems to me both inescapable and important.

Avoiding the "Hidden Hand" in the Determination of Housing Policy

The "hidden hand" issue is well known in the discussion around the links between the economic and the political, the by-now-stale base-superstructures argument[70]. The "hidden hand" problem remains not dealt with in the discussion in this paper.

Most simply put: I contend that there is an important oppressive aspect to housing, that residents resist such oppression, and that there are liberatory potentials in housing also. The oppression undergirds, I argue, both exploitation and repression. Those that exploit and those whose power is supported by repression thus benefit from the oppressive aspects of housing. But I further argue that the oppressive aspects of housing are apart from its real estate aspects, exist outside of and sometimes in contradiction to the supplying of housing for the economic benefit of the suppliers. But then who brings about the oppression? Why do those that supply housing for their own gain also shape it so as to support the profits and power of others than themselves? Must one rely on a "hidden hand" somehow automatically producing what is good for "the system," or is there some more human and more concrete agency at work?

There are of course answers to the question. To look at the same problem in a slightly different context: John Mollenkopf has a perceptive discussion in a recent article on the relationship between the development of "community" and the changing needs of accumulation in the evolution of the U.S. city[71]. In the course of it, he says (correctly, in my opinion):

> Over the long term, economic actors have attempted to transcend the industrial city's generic problems by breaking the historic link between production and urbanization. *By creating* 'factories in the fields' on the one hand and a new central-city community of cosmopolitan professionals on the other, *economic elites mostly succeeded.* p. 331 (underlining added).

He deals at length with the analytic problems involved with translating the desires of "economic elites" into the public institutional structures needed to effectuate those desires. But the analytic problem involved with the translation of the desires of the economic elite into changes in land use patterns -- and housing patterns -- which run largely through the real estate market and the shaping of demand and supply in housing is not addressed.

To hazard a guess at the answer: the translation takes place in at least the following forms: 1) political conflicts within the economic elites themselves, between the broader interests of the business community in the general level of accumulation and the narrower interests of the housing industry, in which governmental land use policies are shaped; 2) market mechanisms, functioning imperfectly, that translate economic interests into prices and allocate land use by price; 3) alliances, sometimes explicit and formal but more often arising though independent but parallel action, between the housing industry and various groups of residential users, ranging from environmentalists fighting disamenities threatening to their residential lives to low-income community residents fighting displacement. In their interactions, the interests of those benefiting from exploitation and repression manifest themselves and in general dominate.

Other mechanisms for the translation of the interests of those benefiting from oppression into actual housing patterns and policies can also be identified. Racial prejudice is one such. Prejudice has clear economic roles and uses, increasing the levels of exploitation; economic uses are reinforced (made possible) by social and individal psychological stereotypes; those stereotypes in turn affect public actions; those public actions in turn shape economic results. Thus if economically "rational" real estate agents anticipate social (non-economic) racial prejudice, they will act in a fashion that is indistinguishable from prejudice in their conduct within the economic housing market. The social and economic are mutually reinforcing[92].

The "hidden hand," in other words, is not necessary as an explanation for the patterns described in this paper. But much work remains to be done to define just how, by whom, when, under what circumstances, these patterns have been produced. And that work is crucial if the hypotheses set forth in this paper have any validity. If oppression does not come about by magic, by some hidden hand, then it must come about concretely, by real people taking real actions on specific subjects in particular ways. If these people, actions, subjects, ways, are known, then something can be done about them.

By exposing the details of the process by which oppression in housing comes about, the people and interests that bring it about, the sources of resistance to it, the liberating potential that lies in it, research can make a significant contribution to helping end such oppression. That, it seems to me, is a worthwhile purpose for research.

NOTES

1) President's Commission on Housing, *Report*, Washington, D.C., 1982, p. 5.

2) See Marcuse, "Why Is There So Much Talk About Homelessness?" Columbia University Papers in Planning, 1986.

3) For an overview of the current situation in the United States, see Chester Hartman, ed., *America's Housing Crisis*, Boston, Routledge & Kegan, Paul, 1983.

4) See "The Pitfalls of Specialism," In Hartman and Rosenberry, eds., forthcoming.

5) Shoukry Roweis, for instance, criticizes what he calls the "economism of politics," in a recent review of Ball, Michael, et al., *Land Rent, Housing and Urban Planning. A European Perspective*, London, Croom Helm, 1985. (A trifle unfairly, because some of authors are in fact much aware of the issue.) IJURR, 1986, 10:1, p. 123.

6) See Michel Foucault, *Discipline and Punish*, and Hubert Treiber and Heinz Steinert, *Die Fabrikation des Zuverlässigen Menschen: Über die 'Wahlverwandschaft' von Kloster- und Fabriksdisziplin*, Münich, Heinz Moos Verlag, 1980.

7) The recent events in Philadelphia, in which bottles and stones were hurled through the windows of a home purchased by a black couple in a white neighborhood, and where an inter-racial couple was threatened with violence if they did not move out three blocks away, are a reminder of just how blatant racism is today even in the City of Brotherly Love.

8) See, for instance, the work of Dolores Hayden and Jacqueline Leavitt.

9) This definition is not synonomous with the Marxist definition of a commodity, but the distinctions are not, at this stage of the discussion, relevant. Ultimately, a number of difficult issues need to be clarified: the relationship between profit (or the production of surplus value) in the production of housing, as opposed to its distribution; the particular characteristics of land as a "not-produced" commodity, at least in part; the sources of profit (only in part surplus value) in the ownership and management of housing; etc. See Achtenberg and Marcuse, "Towards the Decommodification of Housing," in Hartman, ed. *America's Housing Crisis*, supra; Michael Harloe's several discussions of the subject, focusing on the historically changing role of tenure; Jill Hamburg's contribution to Bratt, Hartman, and Meyerson, eds., *Critical Perspectives on Housing* Temple University Press, 1986, suggesting the "partial" commodification of housing in Cuba today; Alan Hooper's explorations of the commodity character of land, in the Bartlett School's summer institute sessions; the two volumes on the economic analysis of housing by Helmut Brede and his collaborators in Germany; and other work.

10) For a typical discussion, see Wallace Smith, *Housing: The Social and Economic Elements*, Berkeley, the University of California Press, 1970.

11) See Michael Stone's work, in Bratt et al., *supra*, and elsewhere.

12) See the discussion in Marcuse and Clark, *Ownership and Rental Forms of Housing Tenure*, Washington, D.C., The Urban Institute, 1974, for a discussion of how closely rental and ownership tenures can be brought to each other simply by varying the legal provisions incorporated in the underlying documents relating to occupancy.

13) The moral concept of exploitation does not mesh neatly with the economic usage in the text; a worker can work just as hard, and end up with exactly as much money in his or her pocket at the end of a week after paying necessary bills, with quite different levels of exploitation, as the term is here used. If the higher costs of housing are coupled with correspondingly higher wages, the worker will be as well off either way, the employer will however have less exploitative profits.

14) See Jim Kemeny, *The Myth of Home Ownership*, London, Routledge and Kegan, Paul, 1981, and Edel, Sclar, et al., *Shaky Palaces*, New York, Columbia University Press, 1986.

15) It does *not* follow that providing income for the poor would eliminate general oppression in

housing, unless indeed income were provided and equalized to such an extent as to eliminate the societal division into classes. General oppression exists because some benefit from the work of others (called exploitation above), and need a social structure legitimizing and, where necessary, enforcing the right to so benefit (called repression above). It is the relationship between those who benefit and those from whose work the benefit is derived that gives rise to oppression, not the absolute level of income available to those at the bottom. Thus the present argument is *not* an argument for housing allowances or demand-side subsidies. On this point, see the criticisms of housing allowances by Chester Hartman, and the international comparative studies being edited in honor of Helmut Brede in Frankfurt.

[16] Slave-holders, the aristocracy, the elite in other societies might also be spoken of as leading lives overwhelmingly concentrated in the residential sphere, the sphere of consumption, to the extent they were not immediately engaged in rule; but the separation of classes, and the sources of power and wealth, were so separated by class that the problems of one group related much less to those of another than they do today. The distinctions deserve further exploration.

[17] See Chapter Three of Gwendolyn Wright's *Building the Dream,* New York, Pantheon Books, 1981, for an illuminating discussion of how even the architectural style of the houses in the slave quarters of the American South reflected the tension between domination and resistance.

[18] Quoted in Weisser, below, p. 48. My translation.

[19] See quotations in Michael Weisser, "Arbeiterkolonien--über die Motive zum Bau von Arbeitersiedlunger durch industrielle Unternehmen im 19. und frühen 20. Jahrhundert in Deutschland," in Joachim Petsch, hrsg., *Architektur und Staedtebau im 20. Jahrhundert,* vol. 2, West Berlin, VSA, 1975, esp. pp. 22, 23, 36; Renate Kastorff-Viehmann, *Wohnungsbau für Arbeiter: Das Beispiel Ruhrgebiet bis 1914,* Aachen, Klenkes, 1981, and the work of Drs. Franciska Bollery and Kristiana Hartman. Gwen Wright provides an overview of the comparable American company towns in Chapter 10 of her book, supra. In the United States, as

in Europe, employer housing was provided not only in pure "company towns," but also in smaller or larger housing developments built and owned by individual companies and rented –sometimes sold–to their employees only, in the midst of more conventional neighborhoods of private housing.

[20] As Engels pointed out at the time: "What the family can grow on its own garden and fields competition enables the capitalist to offset against the wages he pays." *The Housing Question,* 2nd ed.

[21] Quoted in Weisser, *supra,* p. 43.

[22] Although it can work in the opposite direction also, as many concluded after the long Pullman strike in the 1890's.

[23] Jeanne Boydston, "To Earn Her Daily Bread: Housework and Antebellum Working-Class Subsistence," in *Radical History Review,* L 35, April 1986, p. 7–25, at 21–22.

[24] Op. cit., p. 18, 19.

[25] See the recent, and fascinating, work of Gerhard Fenl on Nazi housing policy, and the related work of Hartmut Frank.

[26] After the title of an article by George Sternlieb in *The Public Interest,* Fall, 1971.

[27] See *Discipline and Punish.*

[28] See Roy Lubove, *The Progressives and the Slums,* Pittsburg, The University of Pittsburg Press, 1962.

[29] See Marcuse, "Red Vienna in the 1920's," in Bratt et al., eds., *Critical Perspectives on Housing,* Philadelphia, Temple University Press, 1986.

[30] Recent work by Michael Harloe, Michael Ball, Steve Merritt, and others associated with the Conference of Socialist Economists in England have shed much light on the economic issues.

[31] Damaris Rose's contributions are particularly sensitive to the social-psychological aspects.

[32] IJURR, 10:1.

[33] See Edel, Sclar, and Luria, *Shaky Palaces*, New York, Columbia University Press, 1985, and Marcuse, "Home Ownership for Lower Income Households," *Land Economics*, 1975.

[34] For a very preliminary version of the argument, see Marcuse, "Residential Alienation," in *Journal of Sociology and Social Problems*, 1973.

[35] See Peter Saunders, "Domestic Property and Social Class," IJURR, vol. 2, 1978, pp. 233–51, and Matthew Edel, "Home Ownership and Working Class Unity," IJURR, vol. 6, 1982, pp. 205–222. See also the sources cited earlier, particularly Kemeny and Edel, Sclar, and Luria, for reviews of these and other arguments.

[36] Damaris Rose' discussion, in the third volume of the Conference of Socialist Economists' Housing series, makes, I believe, essentially the same point.

[37] See, for instance, Enid Gualdie, *Cruel Habitations, A History of Working-class Housing, 1780–1918*, London, Harper and Row, 1974.

[38] See Nicholas Bullock et al., *Housing Reform in Germany and France*, Cambridge University Press, 1984.

[39] See Roy Lubove, op. cit.

[40] Quoted in Weisser, p. cit., p. 37.

[41] Campaign for Human Development of the United State Catholic conference, *Housing: The Third Human Right*, Introduction by Cardinal John J. O'Connor, Washington, The Conference, 1985, p. 7.

[42] "Housing and the Family: the Marginalization of Non-family Households in Britain," *IJURR*, vol. 10, no. 1, March 1986, pp. 8 ff.

[43] Marcuse, "The Beginnings of Public Housing," *Journal of Urban History*, forthcoming.

[44] See the more extended discussion in Marcuse, "The Pitfalls of Specialism," op. cit.

[45] For the U.S., for instance, see Village of Belle Terre vs. Boraas, 416 U.S. 1, 94 S. Ct. 1536, 39 L. Ed. 2d 797 (1974); but see also Moore v. City of East Cleveland, 431 U.S. 494, 97 S. Ct. 1932, 52 L. Ed. 2d 531, for some limitations of this use of the zoning power under the U.S. Constitution.

[46] See, for instance, Achtenberg and Marcuse, Harloe, and Kemeny, all supra.

[47] Supra, at p. 321.

[48] See S. Castles and G. Kosack, *Immigrant Workers and Class Struggle in Western Europe*, London, Oxford University Press, 1973, and Philip Sarre, "Choice and constraint in Ethnic Minority Housing," *Housing Affairs*, vol. 1, no. 2, p. 71.

[49] As summarized by David Byrne, "Dublin-A Case Study of Housing and the Residual Working Class," IJURR, vol. 8, no. 3, September 1984, p. 403. See David Byrne and David Parsons, "The State and the Reserve Army – The Management of Class Relations in Space," in J. Anderson et al., eds, *Redundant Spaces?* London, Academic Press, 1984.

[50] See Neil Smith and Peter Williams, eds. *Gentrification*, London, 1986, and Marcuse, "Gentrification, Abandonment, and Displacement: Their Relationships in New York City," *Washington University Journal of Urban and Contemporary Law*, 1986.

[51] Damaris Rose, "Rethinking Gentrification: Beyond the Uneven Development of Marxist Urban Theory," in *Environment and Space D: Society and Space*, 1984, vol. 2, pp. 47–74.

[52] Rose finds it useful to distinguish among the gentrifiers, the "pioneers," of whom she speaks as often "educated young people... find(ing) creative ways to respond to new conditions of paid and unpaid work and worsening economic conditions." p. 64. Her comment reinforces the interpretation here.

[53] See contributions of Peter Dickens and Sean Dammer in the collections of the Conference of Socialist Economists in England.

[54] The discussion was initiated around John Rex and Robert Moore's *Race, Community, and Conflict*, London, Oxford University Press, 1967, but has been widespread since.

[55] See discussion by Damaris Rose, *op. cit.*, p. 68, with citations.

56) See the various studies by Ronald Lawson, Alan Heskin, Stephen Barton, Michael Lipsky, Gary Delgado, Frances Piven, and Marcuse, examining specific conflicts and forms of organization around housing in the United States.

57) See Peter Craig, "The House that Jerry Built? Building Societies, the State and the Politics of Owner-Occupation," in *Housing Studies*, vol. 1, no. 2, April 1986, 87, at 98, and N. Branson and M. Heinemann, *Britain in the 1930's*, London: Wiedenfeld and Nicholson, at 189.

58) See Gertrude Fish, *The Story of Housing*, New York, Macmillan, 1971, p. 186.

59) See Atlas and Dreier, in Hartman, *op. cit.*, for a somewhat different view of the potential of tenant organization in the U.S. today.

60) Manuel Castells' early work, including *The Urban Question*, suggest this explanation.

61) See Marcuse, "The Rise of Tenant Organizations," in Pynoos, et al., eds. *Housing Urban America*, Chicago, Aldine, 1973.

62) See Hartman and Legates, *Displacement and How to Fight It*, Berkeley, 198.

63) See Marcuse, "The Housing Policy of Social Democracy: Determinants and Consequences," in Anson Rabinbach, ed., *The Austrian Socialist Experiment: Social Democracy and Austromarxism, 1918–1934*, Boulder, Westview Press, 1985.

64) See "The Case Against Urban Desegregation," in *The Politics of Turmoil*, New York, Pantheon Books, 1972.

65) The Italian film of that name is a striking illustration of the apparent irrelevance of housing to "the struggle:" the Organizer essentially has the shirt on his back and a satchel in his hand as his "home."

66) The suggestions of Jackie Leavitt and Dolores Hayden have been referrred to above.

67) City Limits, vol. x, no. 4, April 1985, p. 2.

68) de Lepervanche, M., "Immigrants and Ethnic Groups, in S. Encel and L. Bryson, eds. *Australiam Society: Sociological Essays,* 4th ed., Melbourne: Longman-Cheshire, as quoted in Michael Berry, "Housing Provision and Class Relations Under Capitalism," *Housing Studies*, vol. 1., no. 2, p. 112. The theme is extensively and subtly addressed in Ira Katznelson, *City Trenches.*

69) See, for instance, Jeremy Brecher's work on Brass Valley.

70) Among the more provocative of newer approaches to some of these issues, see the recent work of Anthony Giddens in England and Christian Topalov in France. See also D. Hardy and Colin Ward, ARCADIA FOR ALL; THE LEGACY OF A MAKESHIFT LANDSCAPE, London, Mansell, 1984, which Fred Gray in a review in IJURR 10:1 p. 140 says avoids the hidden hand generator.

71) "Community and accumulation," in Michael Dear and Allen J. Scott, eds., *Urbanization & Urban Planning in Capitalist Society,* London, Methuen, 1981.

72) The complex reciprocal relationship between economic and social factors are discussed in Philip Sarre's recent article, *supra*, p. 81, which deals with the process by which estate agents discovered that there was profit in selling to immigrants, overcoming their internalization of the social conditioning that had economic uses for others in the same situation.

Dilemmas of Reducing Direct State Control: Recent Tendencies in Hungarian Housing Policy

2'71- 91

Iván Tosics, Institute for Building Economy and Organization, Department of Housing Market and Housing Policy, Budapest, Hungary

Hungary
9320

RAISING THE PROBLEM. RELATIONSHIP BETWEEN THE MARKET AND STATE INTERVENTION

From the mid-1960s onwards, intensive attention has been given from both Western and Eastern block countries to a range of experiments which aimed to transform the Hungarian economic system. This major focus of attention can be derived from the fact that in Hungary relatively wide-spread debate was directed towards *evaluating the relationship between central control and the market,* or, at any rate, defining more clearly the recent models of this relationship.

The practical measures taken to promote the role of market processes in the Socialist economy are considered as *"reform"* by the Hungarian public. The extensive use of market mechanisms indicates progressive change in the former concept of the functions and development of alternatives to the Socialist economy. This change has not been limited to the strict economic planning mechanism but has spread over other sectors of the economy as well.

In our study we will investigate results and problems in the area of *housing policy* which arise during the transformation of the basically state-controlled sector into a more "market sensitive" sector. This analysis links to the discussions in the present Western literature, which study the "reprivatization" process experienced in some capitalist countries. Our hypothesis in connection with this is that the housing market has a different meaning in Hungary and in the Western housing policies, and the state intervention differs too; therefore the strengthening of the market orientation of the housing policies can't have the same meaning.

The *main statements* of our paper can be summed up as follows: The most spectacular results of Hungarian building activity were achieved in the 70's, when Hungary came to the forefront of the European countries, as regards the number of newly built homes related to the number of the population.[1] The considerable quantitative results of new building activity were connected with the strengthening of direct state intervention into the housing market.

At the beginning of the 80's, as a consequence of the worsening of the economic situation, essential changes also took place in housing policy. The preceding direct forms of state intervention, the volume of state building, and it's share of the budget couldn't be retained any more because of the economic difficulties and the problems of the state budget. In 1983 it came to the initiation of a new housing policy: the volume and the share of housing forms receiving the most state subsidies was diminished; moreover, some of these forms ceased entirely. In other words, state control over the housing market processes became more indirect and housing policy became more market-oriented.

Enough time has passed since the initiation of the 1983 Housing Reform to form an opinion not only of the results, but also of the problems. In our opinion, the main problem is that the effective demand has remained limited for the bulk of the families, in addition to the fact that the possibility of getting a new house has shifted towards the (more costly) market forms. One visible sign of the growing tensions in the housing market is the fact that the costs of new homes exceed the financial possibilities of increasingly large parts of the society.

One possible theoretical solution to the problem outlined above could be the *total separation of the role of the state and the market*. This would mean the creation of a "true market situation" in the building sector (leading to price competition between the contractors), at the same time as the creation of a "truly independent" social policy. Until the conditions develop for this separation of roles, however, it seems to be necessary to look for temporary solutions to ease the tensions arising from seemingly contradictory aims (to raise the quality standard of new housing and solve the social housing problem). Our proposal to *connect the "filtrational logic" to direct state distribution* could be a contribution to such a temporary solution. Our concept corresponds to a broader standpoint; namely that market-elements — inspite of their problems — should be used in the course of the development of housing policy. The strengthening of the market orientation of the development, however, should be connected to new methods to ease social tensions.

THE TRANSFORMATION OF THE HUNGARIAN HOUSING POLICY: FROM THE DOMINANCE OF STATE INTERVENTION TOWARDS MARKET

Period Up to the End of the 1960s

Following the Second World War and up to the beginning of the 1960s, Hungarian housing policy was clearly characterized by the *dominance of central state control* (see, e.g. Hegedüs–Tosics, 1983a). Even if private building predominated in this period (the share of it was about 2/3), according to official formulation, the provision of dwellings was considered a state task. In these years housing policy didn't bother much about the construction of single family houses and about construction in villages. The gradual forging ahead of market mechanisms and of promoting private building activity from the end of the 1950s was seen as secondary.

Direct state intervention provided roughly one third of the newly built housing, and state subsidies were concentrated upon these forms (eg. council flats, cooperative flats, houses built for the workers of state enterprises) whereas the state supported to a much lesser extent the other forms of housing (eg. single family housing). Following Burns–Grebler (1978), this housing support system can be called one of *"deep subvention"*. This means a particular strategy of distribution of state subsidies (the subsidies are distributed very unevenly between the housing forms, settlement types and social strata). It is general, that in housing policies of a deep subvention character great inequalities develop among the various strata of the population.[2] In obtaining a dwelling with low rent supported mostly by the state, the position of the family head in the distribution of labour, ie "merit" played a great (greater than intended) role.

In one of their latest work – to be cited frequently later[3] – Manchin and Szelenyi concluded theoretically from their empirical studies made in the 1960s that during this period the extensive state intervention underpinned the inequalities in housing. In their opinion, this was a much more significant effect of state intervention than that of solving social problems.

Housing Policy in the 1970s

The *new economic system,* introduced in 1968 brought an essential change in the relationship between state control and the market. This had the effect of increasing the role of market relations in regulating the economic processes. The turning of the economy to a new path was followed also by a housing reform in 1971. (In reality the new, more market oriented housing policy lasted only for 2–3 years.)

The "reform character" of the 1971 housing regulations is shown by the more even redistribution of state subventions and the reductions of inequalities between the housing forms by increasing the financial burdens of rented dwellings. Nevertheless, the 70s can be described also with tendencies of a different character, mainly in the building and construction sectors. From the middle of the 1960s, the growth of the factories producing prefabricated, systems-built units produced a concentration in the design, investment and contractor networks. As a result, by the beginning of the 1970s, a very centralized building industry had developed with a monopoly in largescale state and NSB[4] housing contruction.

The changes in the housing policy can be illustrated well by the development of the housing construction by *subvention categories*[5] (Table 1).

Table 1. The Share of the Different Subvention Categories within New Construction and Resale, 1966–1984. (5/a) (in percents)

	1966–70	1971–75	1976–80	1981–82	1983–85
Deep subventioned	29	36	46	39	18
Medium subventioned	14	14	13	19	28
Low subventioned	57	50	41	41	54
Total	100	100	100	100	100
The average number of newly built and resold flats in one year	68.000	90.100	92.500	82.600	81.400

The influence of the 1971 housing reform in supporting the market-based low subvention forms lasted for too short a time for the proportion of these forms to increase. The reversal of the housing reform, however, can be seen in the housing statistics: the deep subventioned housing forms reached a maximum rate of production in the second half of the 1970s.[6] Along with this, *the inequalities in the bearing of burdens were reproduced on a higher level* again. From Table 2 it can be seen that in the 1970s the cash burden of the deeply subvented housing forms increased less than that of the other housing forms, where – due to the relative containment of

Table 2. The Amount of Cash Money to be Paid by Families in the Different Subvention Categories (thousand Forints).

	1966–70	1971–75	1976–80	1981–82	1983–85
Deep subventioned	7	17	22	37	52
Medium subventioned	80	76	128	177	214
Low subventioned	127	178	263	314	(343)
Average	87	105	135	178	255

state subsidies and the influence of inflation – the cash down payment to obtain a dwelling increased considerably.

This analysis suggests that the original concept of the 1971 reform prevailed only for a short time, *the 70's can rather be interpreted as a return to state dominated housing policy*. However, there was an important change during the 1970s in contrast with the former period: access to the deeply subventioned forms of housing became associated with demographic factors, particularly family size, rather than with the preferential treatment of certain job categories. This change can be verified from the vacancy chain study done by Hegedus and Tosics (1983b)[7] and from a number of other empirical studies (Daniel, 1984).[8] We can state, therefore, that parallel with the growing state intervention in the seventies, the "sociological" inequalities of housing decreased.

Although the reduction of inequalities was small during this period, it can be important from a theoretical point of view. The identification of the changes complements the typology developed in the study of Manchin– Szelenyi (1984). According to Manchin and Szelenyi, the primary redistribution mechanism strengthened inequalities, whereas the secondary market mechanism – at least in the beginning – was seen as reducing inequalities. During the 1960s this statement can be verified by processes in the housing market. But on the basis of housing policy during the 1970s (which has not been analyzed in sufficient depth by Manchin and Szelenyi), this theoretical model has to be supplemented with a situation in which the primary redistributive processes are themselves able to moderate the inequalities. To achieve this, of course, several external conditions had to develop properly. In Hungary during the greater part of the 1970s, conditions were favourable to improving central distribution: investment in housing was increasing, financial conditions were reasonably healthy and housing construction achieved record levels. This decade can be considered as the "golden age" of public housing.[9] Not so the next decade, when these external conditions went through essential changes.

Hungarian Housing Policy During the 1980s

In continuing the economic reform process the development of the economic crisis played, in a paradoxical manner, an essential role. The "first", 1968 economic reform was brought to a sudden halt[10] about 1972 by the reassertion of dominant central economic interests. These interests remained powerful in the 1980s, but at the beginning of this decade very significant steps were taken to recognise formally and even encourage market processes. Why should this now be the case? The reason is that, concerning the reform of the 80s, there were much greater economic pressures which favoured the strengthening of the economic-reformist line, than there were at the end of the 60s. In our opinion the main reason for the reduction of state intervention was not the moderation of the economic contradictions but the need to reduce the pressure on the state budget (and raise it's efficiency). This statement is true also in the case of the housing sector, where the new reform period was expressed by the initiation of the 1983 Housing Reform.

Hence in practice, the development of the new housing policy was dominated – due to economic pressure – by the effort to reduce state intervention. As a "natural" consequence of the withdrawal of central regulation, the *financial (bearing the burdens) inequalities* are automatically reduced. From the data of Table 2 it can clearly be seen that the great inequalities characteristic for the 1970s changed dramatically to the 80s. Between 1976–80 in the two great spheres of the housing market (the deeply subventioned institutional distribution and the low subventioned "market" spheres) there was twelve times the difference in the sum of cash necessary for obtaining a dwelling.[11] This is greatly reduced by the middle of the 1980s: most people obtaining a dwelling are concentrated in the medium subventioned category where there are only two to three times the cash differencies in obtaining a dwelling. The contradictions from the economic point of view of financing housing are therefore lessened.

The reduction in inequalities of burdens and the transformation of the structure of housing construction means that the changes in housing policy at the beginning of the 1980s represents a step toward a *more reasonable regulation* of housing sector as compared to the deep subventioned system of the former period. Instead of the principles of distribution, construction and settlement policy being determined centrally, market mechanism are gaining ground. The cost of obtaining a dwelling depend more and more on the size of the dwelling, on the financial form and on the size of the settlement (particularly that in Budapest costs are higher than in the provinces). The deeply subventioned housing forms have retreated, and it is now characteristic for the greater part of the housing sector that obtaining dwellings of a certain size or quality depends only on the solvency (or working capacity partly replacing it) of the family[11a] Table 1 clearly indicates that by the middle of the 1980s, the ratio of highly state-subsidized and state-distributed deeply subventioned dwellings fell to 16 per cent from the former 38–42 per cent. And by the same token, the ratio of privately constructed dwellings increased by over 50 per cent. It can be stated *that housing policy has become more market-oriented.*

So the reform wich took place in 1983 had similar objectives to that of 1971. Between the two periods of housing reforms, however, there were important differences the most important of which is in the increase of economic growth and in the expectations of its further development. At the beginning of the 1970s it was theoretically possible – under the conditions of expanding housing investment – to extend the market mechanisms and at the same time not to reduce the absolute numbers of "social" dwellings provided by the state. During the 1980s it was already not possible to expand the building programme and so the move towards the market caused also a reduction of the numbers of social dwellings. This had serious consequences for the inequalities in the housing situation of the social groups.[12] From Table 2 it can be seen that between 1976–80 almost half the people obtaining a dwelling did go at a low price, at a fraction of it's value (in the deeply subventioned sphere the average cash paid was equal to five months' earnings of a worker). In the middle of the 80s, however, obtaining a "cheap" dwelling already required ten to twelve months' earnings and only one sixth of the people obtaining new dwellings could get such a dwelling. As a result of this data we can state that *the inequalities in dwelling consumption have not diminished*. Ultimately, the reason for this is the impact of worsening economic conditions, and of the withdrawal (regrouping to other sectors) of one part of the state capital. The financial burdens being borne by the people became more proportionate than previously, but this equalising took place on a higher level of cash money burdens for the families. The real income (i.e. income related to the price level) stagnated in the eighties, whereas the prices of new flats (and also real estate properties) went up considerably.

Manchin and Szelenyi state that the market mechanisms create contradictions not only in the Western market system, but in the socialist housing system as well. In this manner, it could be considered as a natural consequence of the changes in housing policy that in the first half of the 1980s inequalities in dwelling consumption increased (or at least did not decrease) in Hungary. The increase of these "sociological" inequalities, however, is not in accordance with the socialist goals of the distribution of goods, and this problem is highlighted in the Hungarian housing literature with growing emphasis.

It seems from the above that the development of market processes in Hungary has had the same effect as in western countries. In the next section, however, we will show that the Hungarian housing system has several specific features which give a peculiar character to the housing market processes in Hungary.

SPECIFIC FEATURES OF THE HUNGARIAN HOUSING SYSTEM AND THEIR DEVELOPMENT DURING THE DECREASE IN THE STATE INTERVENTION

Specific Features of the Hungarian Housing System

Limitation of housing demand. The main way in which housing demands are limited results from the fact that *housing costs are not built into income structure.* Socialist income policy has not been able to break definitively, even today, with the principle that the basic social services, housing, education and health are provided free of charge by the state. The radical change of this principle, the adapting of these primary economic sectors to real life would need a far-reaching reform of prices, wages and taxes. But present economic circumstances do not seem suitable to carry out a reform of this kind. The development of market processes in housing policy, therefore, took place without the transformation of income policy. The gap between income and expenditure necessary to obtain a dwelling is being widened by the fact that, in line with the tendencies experienced in most countries, the price of construction and building materials is increasing faster than income. Attempts are made to balance these "inflation scissors" by increasing state subsidies and credits. But because of the economic reality, non-repayable state subsidies and credits with low interest (though they are periodically modified) cannot balance the increasing burden on the population. Under such circumstances, the limitation of housing demand means that large groups of the population become immobile and are unable to improve their housing situation.

The low proportion of people going up the housing market is shown by our vacancy chain investigations[12a]. The average length of the chains and the proportion of vacancies is small compared to other housing systems[12b]. This is not only a problem of the inefficiency of housing policy[13] but is also a social problem. The problem of families stuck in dwellings smaller than they want is nowadays nearly as great as that of families without a dwelling.

Specific features of housing supply. Under this heading we mean that the possibility of moving up the housing hierarchy is not continuously regulated according to the material situation; rather, it depends on satisfying special criteria. Obtaining a better, larger dwelling (upward mobility) can be achieved:

– by official help, by means of organized exchanges – but for this, families must be of the "right" size and structure with the required number of children prescribed by the housing policy regulations;

— by private market exchange; but for this, a suitable material background is needed since Hungarian housing policy has never supported buying and selling in the real estate market to any great extent;

— by building private dwellings; for which sufficient cash is needed or the ability of a family to build a house using its own energy and exchanging work with other private-builders.

In Hungary, the reality is that in most cases practically, the only alternative to living in an average dwelling built on a housing estate is to build a private dwelling. Official exchanges to a much larger flat within the public sector are almost impossible because, in most areas, suitably sized dwellings are not available.

Building a family house generally takes place in the framework of a family/neighbour collaboration ("kalaka"). There is no alternative to this because building small house "key-ready" is not undertaken by the construction organizations and tradesmen can be paid only by the most wealthy. Not all families wishing to build a family house have, however, the capacity to organise such a "kalaka". It can be verified empirically, that this ability is a special distrinctive factor, which is relatively independent from the income or wealth, but it causes also the development of inequalitites in the chances of getting a better home.

It can also be argued that because of the "duality" of the housing market (ie. the dominance of two, extremely different building forms, flats in high rise estates and single family houses), the housing demand is not continuous; that is to say, there are limited options available — public or savings bank housing, or private self-made construction. The majority of families who want have a better home do not satisfy either of the mobility critera so they are forced into long periods of "waiting". Our empirical experience suggest that in this situation many people opt for the line of least resistance by accepting a certain minimum rather than an uncertain maximum. This minimalist position generally means the purchase of a dwelling of private (savings bank) type on a housing estate which is very expensive, but the cheapest state credit can be acquired with this type of housing. For some buyers, such a dwelling is far from their preferences so here a forced replacing takes place.

Structural distortion of the housing market. In spite of the rent increases at the beginning of the 1970s and 1980s, the tenants of rented dwellings can solve with less expenditure the maintenance and reconstruction of their dwellings than residents of privately owned dwellings. The state assistance of tenants is not limited by any restrictions on security of tenure depending on the level of wealth or income. This means, having obtained a cheap rented dwelling, the tenant is entitled to live in it until the end of his life.[14] A similar inequality is observable within the privately owned dwellings: families obtaining a dwelling during recent years bear more financial costs than families obtaining a dwelling some years ago. These inequalities, called the "structural distortion" of the housing market, and the contradictions within them, differ from the problems discussed in the previous two paragraphs in that they can be seen in the housing systems of other countries, they are not a special feature only of the Hungarian housing system. It can be stated, however, that in Hungary relatively less effort has been made to manage these structural stresses than in some other countries[15]. (This is an indirect consequence of the fact, that in Hungarian housing policy the main concern has been directed towards new housing, and much less towards the problems of the existing housing stock.)

The Effects of Market Process on Housing
(Recent Tendencies in the Housing Market)

Having reviewed briefly the special features and contradictions of the Hungarian housing system, we will now consider the reform of 1983, the strengthening of market elements of regulation, and what effect this had. As a consequence of the transformation of the subvention system and the much more even distribution of state subsidies than previously changes considered to be very positive took place in the *structure of housing supply.* Within the new regulations, in principle, there is no difference in the extent of the state subsidy whether a flat is built within the public building sector or by individuals or group self-builders. So the selection and distribution of the population between the alternative housing forms is "freed" and becomes much more the expression of individual preferences. (Before this, the selection was influenced much more by the inbuilt differences of subsidy between the housing forms.) In areas where the housing shortage is not critical, the demand for dwellings built by the public building sector — mostly housing estates of ten-storey buildings — has declined.[16]

As a result of these changes in market conditions, some public building enterprises reacted by shutting down their housing factories (practically, this means reorganising them for another task).

The *structural inequalities* of the housing market have been influenced by these changes to a lesser extent. It can be considered positive that the gap between the maintenance and reconstruction costs of rented and privately owned dwellings is being continuously reduced as a consequence of the rise in rent. Because of inflation, however, the difference between the burdens of the new and old dwellings is not being reduced, and is even increasing.

The market orientation of housing policy in 1983 undoubtedly creates most problems in connection with the *limitation of housing demand*. This problem consists partly of the fact that not every social group can join the "second economy"[17], facilitating an increase in income related to extra work effort, and partly because of the imperfections of tax policy – the state and local authorities cannot easily or accurately determine family income in relation to housing need. This means, that an increasing proportion of households become unable to improve it's housing situation, while another part of society is induced (urged) to spend on housing an appropriate (required) share of its savings. So the state subventions distributed directly cannot perform their role in the desired manner even if their real value were kept. Essential changes considering this problem are only expectable with the initiating of the new personal tax system.

The review of the special features of the Hungarian housing system has convinced us that the consequences of the decreasing state control, or, the "market-orientation" of housing policy differs (and should differ) from those which arise in Western countries. Therefore, the methods, which have been introduced in the West can't be surely sufficient for managing the developing stresses of the new housing policy in Hungary.

MODES OF REACTION TO THE TENSIONS OF THE HOUSING MARKET AND THEORETICAL ATTEMPTS TO TACKLE THE PROBLEM

Contradictory Measures in Practical Housing Policy

On the basis of the former chronological review, it is clear that important social forces can be aligned against one another in these alternative strategies of housing policy, as can the interested institutions and the researchers studying the problems. In the absence of a new and extensive conception of change, many contradictory measures, conceptions develop. The strengthening of the market tendencies of housing policy is shown eg. by the fact that the selling of rented dwellings as private property was made considerably easier over the past few years[18]. This measure can momentarily alleviate the stresses of public maintenance of dwelling houses, but it contradicts the efforts aimed at increasing the proportion of rented dwellings within new housing. It is clear that none of the measures, mentioned can be considered as the comprehensive solution of the problem.

A similar "confusion" can be experienced in the local housing policy of most settlements. A case in point is the distribution of building plots provided by local councils, where the social-political criteria (distribution according to need) clashes with "market" considerations aiming to mobilise the housing stock. By the middle of the 1980s, central control of local housing policy was essentially limited (it is not, for example, "centrally" prescribed any more how many social dwellings should be built).[19]. In this situation some councils themselves build up their own redistribution systems imitating the former central distribution system (for example, in some councils they give building lots to homeless families), while in other areas, more indirect ways of securing public intervention are practised.

In our opinion, the meditating on the dilemma chosen as the subject of our study could contribute to the conceptual development of present Hungarian housing policy. In practical policy, forced by daily decision-making, the problem of harmonizing the market and social principles cannot be solved except by flexible "balancing" of one type of measures with the other type. It seems that in this situation we should turn to approaches of a *theoretical character* and policy guidance should be directed by them leading to the solution of the daily problems.

Experimental Answers of a Theoretical Character to the Dichotomy of Market and Social Distribution

In the latest Hungarian literature, discussions are primarily connected with developing further the economic mechanism and/or with the potential role of social policy, including arguments in the market/social distribution dichotomy. The two extreme positions which seem to have crystallized press their own claims, one of them underlining the further increase of the role of the market, whereas the other concentrates upon the consequences of worsening the social problems. On the basis of our study, there seems to be some truth in both standpoints (there is no question that policy should be oriented towards the market in order to improve the quality of housing stock and to reduce the inequalities of financial and distributive burdens, but at the same time it is equally true that a further increase of inequalities in housing consumption and the increasing tendency for some social groups to lag behind should not be tolerated either).

The key problem of the present situation, therefore, is to relate the two extremes to each other, ie the solution of the dilemma of market and social distribution. In the following section, we describe first the theoretical solution found by Manchin and Szelenyi briefly and then present another approach which is less theoretically rooted but seems to be closer to the present Hungarian practice, to the real processes in the housing market.

The Conception of Independent "Welfare Distribution". Manchin and Szelenyi state that in Socialist societies, the "economic" redistribution playing the dominant role increases social inequalities against its declared intentions. They base this position on empirical studies of several branches of the economy. The "market-oriented" process commenced more than one and a half decade ago and developed intensively. This so called "secondary mechanism", they argue, produces its own "secondary inequalities". On the basis of data analysis, studies and interviews, the authors prove that these two systems of inequalities strengthen rather than weaken each other. They do not consider another solution, of balancing the social inequalities so as to establish a "third mechanism" which in its type was similar to the "primary/redistributive" mechanism, but was entirely independent from it, as to the institutional and material conditions as well. This independent mechanism in its institutional and budgetary respects might well be called "wellfare redistribution" and may reduce the gap between the ideas of the economic and social trends, giving realistic possibilities for the unity of "economic and social reform" against the alternative of the entire "lack of reform".

In our study individual parts of the study by Manchin and Szelenyi are mentioned several times. In some respects, our remarks and supplements touch upon the theoretical model, for example, raising the idea that under favourable economic circumstances the "primary" redistribution is also capable of moderating social inequalities. All this, however, does not mean that the idea of "welfare redistribution" is considered as totally unacceptable. Theoretically, this idea seems suitable for ameliorating the dilemma of the market process and social stress. Nevertheless, we consider the concept insufficient, in that it is a theoretical construction and, as such, is far from the present Hungarian realities. The authors themselves also remark that the basic conditions for realising their idea is the "minimal institutional and budgetary separation of the economic and political state" and, in addition, the development of a general personal taxation system. Because of the differences in the theoretical and practical dimensions, it is important to think of other – maybe only temporary – solutions. In the following section, we make a proposal for such a solution on the basis of our own theoretical investigations and of the empirical experience gained from Hungarian housing market processes.

The Conception of "Controlled Filtration". When reviewing the professional literature on filtration theory, it is clear that the popularity of this theory in Western countries collapsed during the 1970s. In the first place, this was a consequence of the fact that the filtration processes brought positive changes mainly at the top of the housing hierarchy (in the case of the best housing classes), and it is not at all clear whether any positive consequences for the base of the housing system and social groups in real need are generated. So filtration theory does not answer (or it gives at least an uncertain answer) to the dilemma of market and social supply. In other words, it is a conception which adopts itself to the requirement system of the market rather, than to the social housing supply. This is exactly the reason that persons acting for the protection of the welfare state and for the reduction of social inequalities abandoned the idea of filtration enlarging greatly its negative consequences (see eg. Boddy–Gray, 1979).

During our studies on vacancy chains, it was clear to us that the filtration idea could not be applied in an unaltered form to the Hungarian housing system. We know this to be the case not only because of the uncertainty of the social consequences of filtration, but, also because "market" means something different in Hungary than in the West; this is one of the central points of this paper. But why cannot the direct housing distribution which has failed in many respects be exchanged for a distribution system in which the idea of filtration is also used?

The Hungarian housing system has several problems (the relative backwardness of the structure of the housing stock, the lack of housing of good quality, and the as yet unsolved more efficient involvement of the population's savings) which could be eased by the help of filtration and market mechanisms.

It seems that the question raised (to use filtration, but not exclusively) could be answered by the idea of "controlled filtration". This means that the public authority in a given local housing market would have a novel policy strategy. Until now the main goal of public intervention has been the improvement of the situation of those in the population considered to be socially in need (i.e. redistributive interventions). In the proposed new situation, the public authority *has to combine the redistributive elements with explicitly market methods.* The housing market activity of the public authority has to be separated into two parts, managed separately from each other. It should participate in local housing market processes (it should regulate by indirect means the operation of the local market and should encourage the better off strata of the population to become more interested in mobility). On the other hand, it should retain its direct housing distribution function, as a social function, not mostly over the new stock, but over the dwellings which have became vacant during the mobility process as a consequence of new construction. The combination of redistributive and market elements must not mean the mixing of the two principles. Social support should be applied only in the second stage. The "market phase" can also, of course, be supported but here the logic must differ (it has to promote the launching of market processes and at the same time balance the distortions of the market).

Experience has shown that there are a great many possiblities in applying the market and redistributive elements simultaneously. A good example of this is the "key-money" paid officially when the council and the tenant agree on a price for which the tenant gives back his dwelling to the council. The previous tenant can solve his housing problem with this money plus his own savings. In this way, the authority could stimulate the building up of a good quality new dwelling, and at the same time it would obtain a vacated flat, which could be distributed according to the criteria of need.

Controlled filtration has, of course, several problems. The experience gained by the local authorities up to the present time shows the "venturesome councils" are not common. Controlled filtration differs from the traditional distribution mechanism in that the intervention strategy available to the council will be different in each area. It is clear that the special features of the housing market of each area must be a primary consideration when developing a filtration strategy. The development of such a strategy is not an easy task but it is our belief that it can be an important means through which local councils can develop a desirable independence (increasing the local autonomy is nowadays a political accepted and stressed goal).

CONCLUDING REMARKS

The starting point of our paper was the observation that, in a socialist country at the beginning of the 1980s, a centrally directed development took place to increase the role of the market in housing policy. In our paper, we have attempted to find the answer to the question as to whether the step towards the market (the reducing of direct state control) can be consistent with the socialistic aims emphasizing the importance of social factors and of decreasing the inequalities of housing consumption. Another issue, that we refer to, concerns the comparison of the Hungarian market-orientation to that of the Western countries: what are the reasons for this seemingly common change of policy, its actual contents and its consequences?

In our analysis we argue that although there are similarities in the market tendencies and their characteristics, the *Hungarian experience differs from that of the Western states in several key respects.*

In the first place, there are differences in the intitial conditions (the Hungarian housing stock is more backward, both in its quantitative and qualitative aspects, the Hungarian housing market has special features on both the demand and supply sides), but at the same time there is an important difference in the reasons behind the new market oritentation. In Hungary the primary reason for the changes in the policy developed at the economic level due to the impossibility of further increases in or maintenance of the financial support of the deep subventional system. In the West commodification has also an important ideological character in the context of attacks on the need for and efficiency of public intervention.

Housing market processes and the market systems are different in essential features in Hungary from those in Western countries. The arguments of Western critical sociology against a market-orientation in housing, therefore, cannot be similarly applied to the Hungarian housing system. Furthermore, we can state that *in the present situation in Hungary, there are many positive features of the market-orientation of housing policy,* because it opens up the possibility of key changes in previous housing policy, strongly implying an improvement in its economic and social effectiveness.

The nature of the Hungarian "market-oriented" reform has been influenced by the fact that the motivation for changes came from mainly economic challenge. The three years following the introduction of the reform has revealed a number of contradictory tendencies (which are, of course, not intended effects):

– although the greater part of the institutional system accepted the change and would do so without an economic pressure some of the measures of the market-orientation are often judged differently among local political-social organisations. The general political acceptance of the housing reform has not yet been established;

– some of the other sectors of the economy can be considered less market-oriented, then the housing sector (especially important here is the problem of the limitations of income policy influencing effective demand in the housing market);

– the market orientation has not been followed by well-considered measures alleviating social problems and so the reform could involve the actual deterioration of the housing situation among certain layers of the population[20].

According to our standpoint, in spite of the criticism of the Western market-orientation and of the domestic contradictions, *the market oriented reform should be pursued.* During the increasing role of the market, however, *the main arguments of the "social point of view" and the experiences of market process in the West should be taken into account.*

We see the primary meaning of the Hungarian market-oriented housing reform, in making possible the break up of the former housing policy. This created – through the system of deep subventions – great financial (bearing the burdens) inequalities, and wasn't even fully successful in fulfilling its intended social principles. The change in the economic situation also makes it obvious that a significant part of the population has to make greater sacrifices for improvement in the housing situation. The increase in the role of market mechanisms – in our opinion – is the precondition of elaborating a more socially just and also more effective housing policy.

Our standpoint differs from that of the Manchin—Szelenyi's study in that before transforming the social policy and taking it onto new bases, it is necessary to deepen the market conditions. Furthermore, we do not consider it sufficient to establish new social — political mechanisms until the effects of market-orientation have reached the rental sector, which is now declared to be more or less "social housing", but performs in reality more or less a different role.

The main task of Hungarian housing policy in the future could be the elaboration of such social-political principles and mechanisms as could remain in accordance with the — in our opinion inevitable — market-orientation. The idea of "welfare redistribution" and of "controlled filtration" seems to be a good basis for future investigations into the relationship between the market and social policy. Continuing the research is also important because of the fact, that the next total revision of housing policy is to be undertaken at the end of the 80s. This means, that politics promotes research in connection with the housing problem, for the sake of elaborating a new policy, a better "coexistence" of market and social principles.

ACKNOWLEDGEMENTS

This paper involves the theoretical and empirical research, which was carried out in the last three years together with József Hegedüs. Grateful thanks are given to Dezsö Ekler, Stuart Lowe and János Zsebedits for their valuable remarks on the previous version of this paper.

NOTES

[1] In the first half of the seventies, Hungary was, with 8.4 flats/1000 heads, in the middle in the hierarchy of European countries; in the second half of the decade, however, the same achievement brought Hungary to fifth place.

[2] More exactly at least two forms of inequalities can be distinguished. One of these are the "sociological inequalitites", (inequalities in housing comsumption) which arise in the housing situation of the different social strata, the other is inequalities in the bearing of burdens. If a flat belongs administratively to the deep subventioned sector, the family living in it has much less to pay for it, then for the same flat not deep subventioned.

[3] Manchin and Szelenyi's paper can be read for the time being only in manuscript (it will be published in the course of 1986 in the book "Comparative Social Policy", edited by Sharpe). For this reason we will quote the more important statements we deal with.

[4] NSB stands for National Saving Bank, which performs one significant part of new building activity from the savings of the population. Houses built by NSB hardly differ in physical terms from those built by the state, nor is there essential variance in the allocation process (the majority of new NSB flats is sold to applicants on counsil housing waiting lists). The difference is mainly in the financial conditions under which these flats are sold (NSB flats are much more expensive for families than those built and distributed by the state).

5) The subvention categories were established as follows:
– "deeply subventioned" are those housing forms where effective demand is minimal, whereas state subvention (financial allowance from the price of a dwelling not to be paid back) is greater than credit to be paid back (examples of this forms are council housing, cooperative flats and houses built for manual workers in state factories);
– "Medium subvention" refers to those housing forms where there is state subvention, which is less than cash paid. The latter, however, is exceeded by credits (examples are: NSB flats distributed through the council, flats built privately in detached houses with 4–12 dwellings);
– "low subventioned" are those housing forms where state subvention is minimal (or there is none at all), and cash demand also exceeds credits (examples are: NSB flats sold by auction, self built single family houses).
See Hegedus–Tosics, (1981), for a further description, while the operationalization of these terms. The calculation based on official housing statistics were made by Szekely, (1984).

6) Manchin and Szelenyi (1984) wrongly date the growth of market housing forms to the beginning of the 1970s. Our data show that the ratio of market housing forms in fact increased only in the 1980s. We should note that in the Hungarian housing statistics there are several dwelling forms which are officially called "not public" or "private"; in fact, however, they enjoy almost the same extent of state subsidy as rented dwellings. In our analysis these housing forms appear in the "deep subventioned" category according to their acutal meaning. In their study, Manchin and Szelenyi investigated only the rate of rented dwellings though in fact the deeply subvented housing forms extended over a much wider range.

6a) The data contain all forms of new construction, and also most forms of resale by local authorities and NSB are included. After the 1983 Housing Reform, the subsidies and long term loans for new single family houses were increased, so that this form is now *between* the medium and low subventioned speres.

7) In the course of empirical research of the housing policy of the 70s, it could be proved (Hegedus–Tosics, 1983b) that the mobility process is mostly influenced by demographic factors. New flats are mainly distributed for (or sold for or built by) families with two or more children, and in about 2/3 of all cases the vacated flats are given to families which have fewer children. This "infiltrational effect' is much weaker in the case of the variable social status (only 43% of the families getting the vacated flats are of lower social status group, than the previous family of the flat, but 20% have higher status!), and nearly disappear in the case of the income (45% lower, 34% higher income).

8) Zs. Dániel (1984) could prove on a household-sample, that the variance of a complex variable (showing the number of rooms and the convenience of the flat) diminished in the course of the 70s. This means, that the inequalities decreased to a certain extent.

9) According to the opinions of several researchers (eg. the architect Dezso Ekler), the increase in the ratio of dwellings built as a result of the decisions of central organisations took place – though in different periods – in every other European country as well. The "building of housing estates" or as it is called elsewhere: "social, public housing" is therefore an historical fact and it is to be investigated with such an approach (see, eg Dunleavy, 1983) and not from the aspect of market redistribution or of the development of inequalities.

10) This "sudden halt" of the reform could be described in the housing policy with the recent increase in direct state distribution. At the time of the economic boom of the 70s housing policy was less efficient in mobilizing the increasing income of the population than in mobilizing the investment funds of the state budget.

11) From the statistical investigations made during the 1970s, it is known that there was a 4–5 times difference in the income of the population between the upper and lower deciles with an explicitly decreasing tendency (Székely, 1984).

11a) Subsidized long-term state loans are given practically with the same conditions for all forms of new owner-occupied housing, depending above all on the size of the family, and to a much lesser extent on the income-level (repay capacity) of the family.

12) In the light of our findings, one of the statements of Manchin–Szelenyi's paper has to be modified, They argue that "... the reduction of rules for the housing market and the diminishing presence of the government in the housing sector... had a favourable influence upon the situation of the poor". This conclusion is true in the case of the reform of 1971 but it does not hold water for the changes in 1983, since in the latter case the reduction of state intervention means mostly the lessening of socially aimed redistribution.

12a) The method of vacancy chains, which elaborated for testing the filtrational hypotheses, has an extensive literature, see for example Kristof (1965), Lansing–Clifton–Morgan (1969), Watson (1974), Sharpe (1978) and Clark (1981).

12b) According to our three vacancy-chain studies (in medium sized Hungarian cities) the average chain length is above 1.4, and there is no difference in the chain length of the local authority distribution and the "market forms" of new housing. Dates of other countries show great variety from 1.5 to 3.5; two fresh examples are that of Sweden average chain length 3.4, see Clark, 1984) and that of Nowway (1.9, see Bysween–Knutsen, 1984). The results shouldn't be compared automatically, but they suggest, that the mobility level is low in Hungary.

13) The larger the investment necessary for moving to a "better" dwelling, the greater the proportion of those persons who cannot make this jump. Their savings are therefore not used in the housing sector.

14) It should be noted here that in the Hungarian housing system the regulation of rented dwellings is far more liberal than it is in the West. The circulation of dwellings is not limited and tenants control their dwellings almost as thought they were the owners. In addition, rented dwellings have an officially recognised value (which can be realised in the free market by eluding some minor administrative restrictions).

15) In our opinion, the developing of the personal income tax system (which is planned to come into force by the end of the 80s) is needed to tackle the structural problems of the housing market.

16) There are more cases – which were unprecedented during the past four decades – of new dwellings on housing estates remaining vacant for several months because families assigned to purchase them withdraw in favour of some alternative.

17) About the exciting problems of the Hungarian second economy (which was initiated partly in the framework of the economic reform) see eg. Galasi–Szirdczky (1985).

18) During recent years selling rented dwellings has been regulated many times. First, in 1983, the restriction which limited the sale of rented dwellings to those buildings which contain maximum 12 flats was abolished. From the beginning of 1986, the cash sum to be paid for the purchase of a rented dwelling was reduced.

19) Recently there is a new by-law, regulating in a manner through the financial interest the decisions on local housing policy.

20) There are new by-laws accepted in 1985–86 to increase the possibilities of local counsils to work out their own social policy. The effects of these new measures, however, cannot be judged now.

REFERENCES

Bauer, P. (1982) "A második gazdasági reform és a tulajdonviszonyok" (The Second Economic Reform and the Propietorship), *Mozgó Világ* 11/1982.

Boddy, M., and F. Gray (1979) "Filtering Theory, Housing Policy and the Legitimation of Inequality", *Policy and Politics* 7: 39–54.

Burns, L.S., and L. Grebler, (1977) *The Housing of Nations*. London and Basingstoke: The Macmillan Press.

Bysveen, T., and S. Knutsen (1984) *Housing demand and vacancy chains*. Oslo: Norwegian Institute for Urban and Regional Research, NIBR-Report 1984:9.

Clark, E. (1981) *Housing Residential Mobility and Studies of Chains of Moves*. Stockholm: Departments Reprocentral.

(1984) "Housing Policies and New Construction. A Study of Chains of Moves in Southwest Skåne", *Scandinavian Housing and Planning Research* 1: 3–14.

Daniel, Sz. (1984) "Még egyszer az igazságos lakáselosztásról az adatok tükrében" (Once more about the fair housing distribution), *Gazdasag* 4: 22–44.

Donnison, D., and C. Urgerson (1982) *Housing Policy.* --------: Penguin Books.

Dunleavy, P. (1981) *The Politics of Mass Housing in Britain, 1945–1975*. Oxford: Clarendon Press.

Galasi, P., and Gy. Sziratzki (eds.) (1985) *Market and Second Economy in Hungary*. Frankfurt: Campus Verlag.

Hegedus, J., and I. Tosics (1981) "Lakáspolitika és lakáspiac" (Housing Policy and Housing Market), *Valóság* 7: 76–90.

(1983a) "Housing Classes and Housing Policy: Some Changes in the Budapest Housing Market", *International Journal of Urban and Regional Research* 7: 467–495.

(1983b) *Helyi lakáspiacok vizsgálata, Somogy megye*. (Local Housing Market Survey, County Somogy.) Budapest: EGSZI–EMPIRIA GM, manuscript.

Kemeny, J. (1983) "Towards 'Unfair' Public Rents in Britain", pp. 39–48 in *Current Trends in British Housing*. Gävle: The National Swedish Institute of Building Research, Bulletin M83:17.

Kristof, F. (1965) Housing Policy Goals and the Turnover of Housing, *Journal of the American Intitute of Planners* 31: 232–245.

Lansing, J.B., C.W. Clifton, and J. Morgan (1969) *New Homes and Poor People.* Ann Arbor: Michigan.

Lundquist, L.J. (1983) *How Potent is the Welfare State? An Examination of Housing Policy Effects in Sweden.* Gävle: The National Swedish Institute of Building Research.

Manchin, R., and I. Szelenyi (1984) *Social Policy under State Socialism* (The role of redistribution and market in the formation of social inequalities.) Madison—Wisconsin, to be published in Comparative Social Policy, Sharpe, 1986.

Sharpe, C.A. (1978) "New Construction and Housing Turnover: Vacancy Chains in Toronto", *Canadian Geographer* XXII. 2.

Szekely, I. (1985) *"A lakáspolitika és a lakásgazdálkodás pénzugyi feltételrendszerenek tovabbfejlesztese".* (The Improvement of the Financial Conditions of Housing Policy and Housing Economy.) Budapest, manuscript.

Szelenyi, I., and Gy. Konrad (1969) *Az ui lakótelepek szociológiai problémái.* (The Sociological Problems of New Housing Estates.) Budapest: Akadémia.

Watson, C.J. (1974) "Vacancy Chains, Filtering and the Public Sector", *AIP Journal* 40.

About the Authors

About the Authors

HOUSING AND ECONOMIC RESEARCH

William Clark, University of California, Los Angeles (UCIA), USA

Professor of geography. Recently associate director of the Institute for Social Science Research at UCIA and visiting professor at the Free University, Amsterdam. His research interests in recent years have focused on general questions of urban structure and – within the general area of migration and mobility – on the nature of residential search and the way in which information influences search behaviour and search processes.

Duncan Maclennan, University of Glasgow, Scotland

Professor and director of the Housing Research Centre at the university. His recent research focuses on housing investment and urban economic regeneration, and also tenure choice and the growth of owner occupation. He is also a housing economy consultant for OECD.

John M Quigley, University of California, Berkely, USA

Professor of economics and public policy. He has previously taught at Yale, Harvard, and Gothenburg Universities. He studied economics at Stockholm as a Fulbright scholar (M Sc 1965) and served as a visiting researcher at the Swedish Industrial Investigation Institute in 1971–1972. He has written extensively on the economics of housing and urban labour markets, on local public finance and other topics in microeconomics. He serves as a consultant to a wide variety of public and private agencies and is a member of the Committee on National Urban Policy of the US National Academy of Sciences.

Raymond J Struyk, Urban Institute, Washington DC, USA

Director of the International Activities Center and senior research associate at the Center for Housing and Community Development Research. He has worked on such problems as the economic determinants of home-ownership, development of an urban housing market simulation model, analysis of the investment behaviour of landlords and owner-occupiers, and economic aspects of the housing of elderly households. In recent years, he has concentrated his work in countries outside of the United States, working in the Philippines for the World Bank, with Korean five-year economic plans, in Sri Lanka and Barbados with a micro-computer model for doing housing needs assessments, etc.

RESEARCH ON HOUSING POLITICS AND HOUSING POLICY

David Donnison, University of Glasgow, Scotland

Head of the Department of Town and Regional Planning. Formerly lecturer and research fellow at Toronto University, School of Social Work, and professor of social administration at London School of Economics. Former chairman of the Supplementary Benefits Commission. He has served on several government – and other – committees for education and housing.

Ulf Torgersen, University of Oslo, Norway

Professor of political science, formerly research coordinator at the Institute for Social Research. He has been attached, temporarily, to the Planning Department of the Norwegian government and to the Institute for Applied Social Research, where he has also been chairman of the board. Research activities mainly in the following fields: the study of party organisation, the organisation and function of the academic professions, and the housing market and related government efforts.

Carolyn Teich Adams, Temple University, Philadelphia, Pennsylvania, USA

Associate professor of urban studies. Having spent several years as dean of the College of Arts and Sciences at Temple University, she has now returned to teaching and research in urban public policy. Her research focuses on the relationships of infrastructure to urban growth and post-industrial development. One of her books won an award for the best book on national policy published in 1975. She is active in policy studies and consulting for local government bodies in Philadelphia, where she has participated on the Mayor's Task Force on Economic Development, and she chairs a committee of the Community Services Planning Council of Southeastern Pennsylvania, which is working to consolidate into a single regional data bank the information that is collected by planning and social service agencies throughout the metropolitan region.

Nathan H Schwartz, University of Louisville, Kentucky, USA

Assistant professor of political science. He has taught at Oakland University and the University of Kentucky. His research interests in public policy have focused on housing policy, starting with work on race and housing in the United States that he did while working for the US Commission on Civil Rights in the early 1970's. His doctoral dissertation examined race and the allocation of public housing in Great Britain. His published work includes work on race and housing in Great Britain, as well as general work on trends in housing policy in the United States and Great Britain. In the coming year he will be conducting research on housing policy in France.

HOUSING AND SOCIAL RESEARCH

Michael Harloe, University of Essex, England

MA, Ph D, senior lecturer at the Department of Sociology and director of the Institute for Urban Studies. Formerly principal scientific officer, Centre for Environmental Studies, London, and senior research Officer, London School of Economics and Political Science. Former member of the Labour Party National Executive Committee, Housing Sub-Committee. Former advisor to House of Commons Environment Committee, OECD Environment Directorate and Secretary of State for the Environment (UK). Current research concerns recent developments in housing markets and policies in Western Europe and the USA and also the local impact of economic restructuring in the UK.

Maarjte Martens, Department of Sociology, University of Essex, England

Maartje Martens studied Architecture & Planning at the Technical University of Eindhoven (the Netherlands). Appointed as senior research officer at the University of Essex since 1981, Ms Martens has been the principle researcher on a number of comparative research projects involving Western Europe and the USA such as the provision of social rented and owner occupied housing, recent changes in mortgage finance markets and their impact for housing consumers, and on recent innovatory developments in lower income housing provision.

Marino Folin, University of Architecture, Venice, Italy

Architect, professor of urban system analysis and head of the Department of Economic and Social Analysis of the Environment at the University of Architecture of Venice. He has worked on the form and nature of town planning and is now doing research on housing policy in Western European countries.

Peter Marcuse, Columbia University, New York, USA

Professor of urban planning. Former chair of an anti-poverty agency in Connecticut and president of the City Planning Commission in Los Angeles. Now chair of the housing committee of a community board in Manhattan. He has both privately practiced real estate corporate tax and labour law and has taught housing and city planning. He has done comparative work, principally between Germany, France and the US, and he is interested in the relationship between long-term political conflicts and public housing and planning policies.

Ivdn Tosics, EGSZI (Institute for Building Economy and Organisation),
Budapest, Hungary

Mathematician and sociologist. Formerly working at the town-planning
institute of the city council of Budapest. Now investigating local housing
market processes in medium-sized Hungarian towns. The aim is to give
up-to-date information to the local housing managers about the state and
tendencies of their housing market, and also to give them some new ideas
of how to connect state intervention with market processes.